KU-052-622

GOLDEN YEARS OF
RAIL TRAVEL

Published by Times Books
An imprint of HarperCollins Publishers
Westerhill Road
Bishopbriggs
Glasgow G64 2QT
www.harpercollins.co.uk

First edition 2019
© HarperCollins Publishers 2019
Text © Julian Holland

The Times® is a registered trademark of Times Newspapers Ltd

All rights reserved. No part of this publication may be reproduced, stored in a retrieval system,
or transmitted, in any form or by any means, electronic, mechanical, photocopying, recording
or otherwise without the prior permission in writing of the publisher and copyright owners.

The contents of this publication are believed correct at the time of printing.
Nevertheless the publisher can accept no responsibility for errors or omissions,
changes in the detail given or for any expense or loss thereby caused.

HarperCollins does not warrant that any website mentioned in this title will be provided
uninterrupted, that any website will be error free, that defects will be corrected,
or that the website or the server that makes it available are free of viruses or bugs.
For full terms and conditions please refer to the site terms provided on the website.

A catalogue record for this book is available from the British Library

ISBN 978-0-00-832375-2

10 9 8 7 6 5 4 3 2 1

Printed in China by RR Donnelley APS Co Ltd

If you would like to comment on any aspect of this book,
please contact us at the above address or online.
e-mail: times.books@harpercollins.co.uk

www.timesbooks.co.uk

MIX
Paper from
responsible sources
FSC
www.fsc.org
FSC™ C007454

This book is produced from independently certified FSC™ paper
to ensure responsible forest management.

For more information visit: www.harpercollins.co.uk/green

THE ✦ TIMES
GOLDEN YEARS OF
RAIL TRAVEL

JULIAN HOLLAND

THE OLDEST NAMED TRAIN IN THE WORLD

BY
THE IRISH MAIL
TO
DUBLIN (WESTLAND ROW)

· 1848 · 1948 ·

Contents

Observation Coach Train at Lochy Viaduct near Fort William

THE WEST HIGHLAND LINE

 SEE BRITAIN BY TRAIN

LEFT: *Early 20th century Midland Railway poster promoting the tourist resorts of the Peak District in Derbyshire, featuring Monsal Dale, Peveril Castle, Peak Cavern, Eyam and Hathersage.*

ABOVE: *Poster produced by British Railways in 1959 promoting the West Highland Line in Scotland, featuring a beaver tail observation coach on the rear of a train crossing Lochy Viaduct near Fort William. Original artwork by Jack Merriott.*

Introduction

For most of the 19th century passengers on Britain's railways suffered uncomfortable and slow journeys to reach their destination. However, by the beginning of the 20th century the introduction of Pullman cars, interconnected corridor coaches and dining and sleeping cars on Britain's railways, along with the development of more powerful and faster steam locomotives, had transformed rail travel across the country. The Great Western Railway, always to the fore, introduced the 'Cornish Riviera Limited' between Paddington and Cornwall as early as 1904, while other railway companies introduced, as yet un-named, restaurant car expresses between London and Wales, the North of England and Scotland – this was the beginning of a golden age in rail travel for the travelling public that lasted nearly 100 years, albeit interrupted by two world wars.

By the 1930s British railway companies were competing for the title of the 'World's Fastest Train'. At the forefront was the Great Western Railway, which in 1932 claimed this title with its record breaking 'Cheltenham Flyer'. Not to be outdone, the London & North Eastern Railway first introduced its non-stop 'The Silver Jubilee' between King's Cross and Newcastle in 1935. This high-speed train was hauled by Nigel Gresley's new streamlined 'A4' Pacific locomotives, one of which, *Mallard*, still holds the world speed record for a steam locomotive of 126 mph, set in 1938. The 1930s were heady days for these trains but the streamlined high-speed era was brought to an abrupt end by the onset of the Second World War in 1939.

Austerity and Nationalization of Britain's railways in 1948 first saw a very slow return of these named express trains on the country's run-down railways. However, the publicity departments of the new British Railways were

soon hard at work, glamorizing rail travel again by bringing back a plethora of named trains, not only reintroducing many of the pre-war named trains but also a host of new trains. Ornate headboards, publicity material, luggage labels, restaurant car menus and fold-out route guides were designed to lend an air of romanticism to these journeys that criss-cossed Britain through the 1950s and into the 1960s. Sadly this golden age of rail travel was soon to end with the demise of the steam locomotive. In their early years the new diesels still carried the all-important train headboards but these were soon quietly forgotten as the railways entered a new age of uniformity followed by the unmitigated disaster of modern privatization. You don't know what you've got till it's gone.

King's Cross shed's Class 'A4' 4-6-2 No 60025 Falcon departs from Leeds Central station with the last steam-hauled 'The White Rose' express to King's Cross on 22 June 1963. On the left is 'Deltic' diesel D9004 (later named Queen's Own Highlander) at the head of the down 'The Queen of Scots' Pullman train to Glasgow Queen Street.

Late 19th century to 1922

The late 19th and early 20th centuries witnessed the zenith of Britain's railways and by 1914 there were over 20,000 route miles of track controlled by 120 competing operating companies. Apart from a few remote areas, the travelling public could travel from virtually anywhere-to-anywhere in Britain by train. By 1892 the troublesome problem of different rail gauges had at last been laid to rest when the Great Western Railway finally converted all of its broad-gauge (7 ft 0¼ in.) track to the standard-gauge (4 ft 8½ in.) used by other railway companies.

Coupled with the speeding up of services, great strides had also been made during this period to improve passenger comfort. The old and uncomfortable four- and six-wheel compartment coaches were being replaced by bogie corridor coaches with the principal trains also conveying restaurant cars – a Pullman car with catering facilities was first introduced by the Great Northern Railway in 1879. Slip coaches, attached to the rear of a train, were detached from a moving train and brought to a halt in a station by an onboard brakeman. Slip coaches were first introduced by the London, Brighton & South Coast Railway as early as 1858, and they allowed stations to be served by trains without the need for them to stop – by 1914 nearly 100 coaches were being slipped each day. Sleeping cars, first introduced by the North British Railway (for the East Coast route) and the Caledonian Railway (for the West Coast route) in 1873, allowed passengers to sleep the night away while travelling between England and Scotland. For those travellers wishing to pay a premium for luxury travel, Pullman cars, first introduced by the Midland Railway in 1874, proved to be very popular, especially on the London, Brighton & South Coast Railway, which introduced Britain's first

all-Pullman train in 1881 – this mode of opulent travel was soon taken up by other companies. Of course, Britain was still a deeply class-ridden society and to this end 1st Class travel was reserved for the upper classes while the working classes had to put up with a less comfortable and crowded environment in 3rd Class coaches. There was also an intermediary 2nd Class but most companies had abolished this by the end of the 19th century, although the Great Western Railway waited until 1910 before it followed suit.

Coupled with great strides in printing large colour posters, by the early 20th century all of the major railway companies were going to great lengths to lure the travelling public to use their services. Poster artists were in great demand at this time, none more so than Norman Wilkinson who produced many iconic images for the London & North Western Railway – he continued in this vein for the London, Midland & Scottish Railway and the Southern Railway in the 1920s and 1930s.

This period also saw great strides in the design of more powerful steam locomotives that were capable of hauling heavier trains at greater speeds. Some of the locomotive designers have stood the test of time and have since gone down in the annals of British railway history – George Jackson Churchward of the Great Western Railway, Nigel Gresley of the Great Northern Railway, Henry Fowler of the Midland Railway and Richard Maunsell of the South Eastern & Chatham Railway, to name but a few. Apart from the latter, their powerful locomotives were all fitted with water scoops enabling them to collect water at speed via water troughs laid between the rails, thus cutting journey times.

Although electrification of railways was still in its infancy, the North Eastern Railway, the Lancashire & Yorkshire Railway, the London & North Western Railway and the London, Brighton & South Coast Railway had all embarked on major electrification schemes for busy commuter routes by the outbreak of the First World War.

While the majority of Britain's extensive rail network had been completed by the end of the 19th century there were some new additions. Notable among these was the Great Central Railway's mainline between Sheffield and Marylebone, completed in 1899, and new Great Western Railway routes, notably the Badminton route to South Wales, the Castle Cary cut-off, the Tyseley to Cheltenham route, the Birmingham Direct Line and the Swansea District Lines, all completed by 1913.

While railway companies were often in direct competition with each other, there were also many inter-company trains. The London & North Western and the Caledonian railways jointly operated Anglo-Scottish trains along the West Coast route, while the North British, North Eastern and Great Northern railways jointly operated trains on the rival East Coast route. The Midland Railway had similar arrangements with the Glasgow & South Western and the North British railways. Some unusual bedfellows were also involved in operating the 'Sunny South Express' (London & North Western Railway/London, Brighton & South Coast Railway), which was introduced in 1904 between Liverpool, Manchester and South Coast resorts, and the 'Ports-to-Ports Express' (North Eastern Railway/Great Central Railway/Great Western Railway), which was introduced in 1906 between Newcastle and Barry.

LEFT: *20 May 1892 – the last broad-gauge train from Paddington to Penzance on the Great Western Railway passes through Uffington Cutting behind 'Rover' Class 4-2-2 Great Western.*

BELOW: *Dating from 1901 this poster depicts the delights of the Callander & Oban Railway. Completed in 1880, this scenic Scottish railway was worked from opening by the Caledonian Railway.*

In addition to providing rail services many of the railway companies also owned docks and harbours and operated large fleets of steamships to carry passengers, mail and cargoes to Northern European and Irish ports – by 1913 the Lancashire & Yorkshire Railway owned 26 steamers, the largest fleet of ships of any British railway company at that time. This was closely followed by the Great Central Railway which exported coal from its docks at Immingham, which opened in 1912.

With such a multiplicity of railway operating companies, keeping track of the through bookings of passengers and through workings of freight and livestock between different companies was a logistical nightmare. The Railway Clearing House (RCH, founded in 1842) managed this by dividing passenger receipts based on mileage, with each company receiving its allotted share. Classification of goods traffic was also organized by the RCH with a standardized rate on each of these paid per mile. By 1914 the RCH had a staff of 3,000 employed in these painstaking tasks, each movement of passengers and freight being recorded by hand on sheets of paper.

All of this progress for Britain's railways soon came to a grinding halt on the outbreak of the First World War in 1914. During this tumultuous period Britain's vitally strategic railways came under Government control, a situation which lasted until 1921. By then the country's worn out rail network was in pretty bad shape, both physically and financially and so, after calls for Nationalization were rejected, the 120 railway companies were grouped into four larger regional companies – the era of the 'Big Four' began on 1 January 1923 (see pages 62–63).

BELOW: *The 'Scotch Express' departs from Euston behind one of the London & North Western Railway's 4-6-0 locomotives, c.1909. The train travelled down the West Coast Main Line to Carlisle where a Caledonian Railway locomotive would have taken over for the rest of the journey to Glasgow Central.*

Caledonian Railway

The Caledonian Railway (CR) was incorporated in 1845 and four years later opened its mainline up the Clyde Valley from Glasgow and Edinburgh to Carlisle, for the first time providing a through service between London and Scotland via the West Coast Main Line (see pages 60–61) – albeit a journey of 12 hours. By a series of amalgamations and takeovers the 'Caley', as it was affectionately known, went on to control a sprawling network of railways stretching from Wemyss Bay in the west to Aberdeen in the east, the latter reached via Perth and Forfar. Along the south and north banks of the Clyde commuter lines served Gourock and Dumbarton respectively while another route reached Ardrossan on the Ayrshire coast. In the industrial Central Belt the Caley's tentacles stretched across the Lanarkshire coalfields to reach its Edinburgh Princes Street terminus via Shotts. Here, deep in North British Railway territory, the company opened branches to docks at Leith and Granton.

Notable Caley stations included Glasgow Central, Glasgow Buchanan Street, Edinburgh Princes Street and Perth. The CR opened Glasgow Central station in 1879, at the same time rebuilding its former terminus at Bridge Street into a through station. The cramped confines of Central station were much enlarged by 1906 and its one and only signal box was brought into use in 1908 with points and signals being operated by electro-magnetic and electro-pneumatic equipment – at that time it was largest signal box of its type in the world.

The Caley's route to Stirling and Perth also provided access to its route to Oban on the west coast. Branching off at Dunblane the CR-controlled Callander & Oban Railway had opened throughout in 1880 reaching Oban via a highly scenic route through Callander, Glen Ogle, Crianlarich and the Pass of Brander. A short branch line was built from Killin Junction to Killin and Loch Tay in 1886. On the opening of the Ballachulish branch in 1903 road vehicles were carried across Connel Bridge from Connel Ferry station to North Connel on a specially adapted goods wagon until 1914, when the bridge was then resurfaced to accommodate both road and rail traffic.

Perth was an important junction for the railway with lines radiating out to Glasgow, Dundee, Crieff and Balquhidder via the Almond Valley, and Aberdeen via Stanley Junction, Forfar and Kinnaber Junction – the latter was the finishing line for the famous Railway Race

to the North (see page 15). Branching off the Caley mainline in Angus were several branch lines to small towns such as Kirriemuir, Edzell and Brechin.

In the early 20th century the Caledonian Railway operated a series of luxurious trains between Glasgow Buchanan Street and Aberdeen via Perth and Forfar. Known as 'The Grampian Corridor' (after the new 12-wheeled corridor stock used for the trains) and 'The Granite City' (see page 76), the trains were discontinued on the outbreak of the First World War. They resumed after the war but were no longer named. In 1922 the 7.15 a.m. departure from Glasgow (which included a

BELOW: *Dating from the early 20th century, this poster shows the railway network of the Caledonian Railway and its connections.*

Pullman breakfast car) arrived at Aberdeen at 11.50 a.m. The service was continued by the London Midland & Scottish Railway from 1923 (see page 73).

The CR also had running rights over the Glasgow & South Western Railway's line between Dumfries and Castle Douglas and thence westwards to Stranraer Harbour over the jointly-owned Portpatrick & Wigtownshire Joint Railway. Dumfries was reached on a CR-owned branchline from Lockerbie, on its Clyde Valley route, allowing the company to run its own Irish boat trains.

The Caley's locomotive works at St Rollox in Glasgow was established in 1856 and spawned several eminent Chief Mechanical Engineers including Dugald Drummond, J. F.

McIntosh and William Pickersgill. McIntosh's 'Dunalastair' Class 4-4-0s and 'Cardean' 4-6-0s were considered to be some of the finest steam locomotives made at that time. The company also owned the Caledonian Steam Packet Company, which started operating ferry services on the Clyde in 1889. With its 1,114-route-mile network the Caley became a constituent company of the newly-formed London Midland & Scottish Railway (LMS) in 1923.

BELOW: *This up West Coast Express to Euston makes a fine sight double-headed by Caledonian Railway locomotives, a Conner 2-4-0 and a McIntosh 4-4-0, near Eglinton station, Glasgow, in the early 20th century.*

Cheshire Lines Committee

The Cheshire Lines Committee (CLC) operated 143 route miles, making it the second longest joint railway in Britain. Owned jointly by the Great Northern Railway, the Great Central Railway and the Midland Railway (MR) it operated routes in Cheshire and Lancashire in competition with the London & North Western Railway. The CLC's main routes were Manchester Central – opened jointly with the MR in 1880 – to Liverpool Central, Manchester Central to Chester Northgate, and Liverpool Central to Southport Lord Street. Designed by Sir John Fowler, Manchester Central station was built for the CLC and opened in 1880. It closed in 1969 and is now an exhibition and conference centre. After the 'Big Four Grouping' of 1923, the CLC continued to be jointly owned with a two-thirds share going to the LNER and a one-third share going to the LMS. It was nationalized in 1948.

BELOW: Dating from the early 1920s, this poster promotes rail services operated by the Cheshire Lines Committee on its principal route between Liverpool and Manchester.

East Coast Route

As a through route the East Coast Main Line (ECML) between King's Cross and Edinburgh Waverley was completed in 1850 by three separate railway companies: King's Cross to Shaftholme, north of Doncaster, by the Great Northern Railway (GNR); Shaftholme to Berwick-upon-Tweed by the North Eastern Railway (NER); Berwick-upon-Tweed to Edinburgh Waverley by the North British Railway (NBR). However, through services between the two capitals were hindered by the lack of standard passenger coaches and in 1860 the three companies formed the East Coast Joint Stock (ECJS) to remedy this situation. Initially through services along the ECML were operated by the

three companies along each of their own stretches of track. However, in 1869 the NER started running its own locomotives through to Edinburgh, receiving payment from the NBR for this at a rate of 1 shilling (5p) per mile.

By 1862 new ECJS carriages for the first 'Special Scotch Express' were ready and the train became a regular feature departing simultaneously each day at 10 a.m. from King's Cross and Edinburgh Waverley stations. At that time the train took a leisurely 10½ hours to complete the 393 miles including a stop at York where the passengers disembarked for lunch. This leisurely pace did not last long and when Patrick Stirling, the GNR's

Chief Mechanical Engineer, designed his famous Stirling 'Single' locomotives in 1870 the East Coast route soon saw a rapid acceleration of schedules with a whole 2 hours soon being lopped off the King's Cross to Edinburgh journey. Restaurant cars were introduced by the GNR in 1879 and were soon introduced on this train, thus cutting out the mandatory lunch stop at York and saving even more time. The 'Special Scotch Express' was the forerunner of the 'Flying Scotsman' introduced by the London & North Eastern Railway in 1924 (see pages 96–98).

The final section of the ECML between Edinburgh and Aberdeen was completed following the opening of the Forth Bridge in 1890 – the ill-fated Tay Bridge which collapsed in 1878 had already been replaced by the second structure completed in 1887. Now trains could run between London and Aberdeen along the ECML and the three railway companies lost no time in trumpeting this achievement. The King's Cross to Aberdeen overnight sleeper train had its origin in the famous East Coast express of 1895 that raced its West Coast rival (see page 61) for the fastest overnight service from London to Aberdeen. In the end the West Coast route won but not until some fast high jinks by the two rivals to the finishing post at Kinnaber Junction north of Montrose – north of here the rival trains took the same route. Operated by the Great Northern Railway, the North Eastern Railway and the North British Railway the lightly loaded East Coast train (weighing only 105 tons) managed to cover the 523.7 miles in 8 hrs 40 min on the night of 21/22 August and deposited its passengers at Aberdeen Joint station at the unearthly hour of 4.40 a.m. The rivalry continued until 1896 when an Anglo-Scottish express, operated by the London & North Western Railway, was derailed at Preston – safety limits had been flouted and a speed limit was imposed on the two rivals which stayed in place until 1932. Over the following years the evening departure from King's Cross of the Aberdeen sleeper became heavier and longer with the inclusion of additional sleeping cars to Perth, Inverness and Fort William. The train continued to be run by the London & North Eastern Railway from 1923 (see page 90).

The beginning of the 20th century brought major improvements to the 'Special Scotch Express' with modern corridor carriages and dining cars. The heavier and longer trains were now headed by Ivatt's new 'Atlantics' as far as York but timings remained the same due to the 1896 speed restriction. The arrival of Nigel Gresley as Locomotive

Engineer of the Great Northern Railway in 1911 led to the building of a series of groundbreaking 'Pacific' locomotive types. Two of his Class 'A1' 4-6-2s were built at Doncaster in 1922 and 10 more had been ordered just before the 'Big Four Grouping' of 1923. The 'Special Scotch Express' continued to be operated until that year when its operations were taken over by the newly-formed London & North Eastern Railway (see page 96).

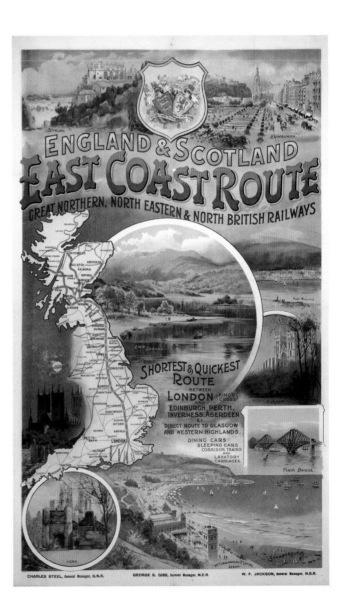

ABOVE: *The East Coast Route between King's Cross and Aberdeen was operated jointly by the Great Northern Railway, the North Eastern Railway and the North British Railway.*

LEFT: *The plush interior of an East Coast Joint Stock 1st Class dining car introduced in the early 20th century.*

Furness Railway

By the beginning of the 20th century the Furness Railway (formed 1844) owned a network of lines in south and west Cumbria. Centred on Barrow-in-Furness, the network radiated out eastwards to Carnforth (on the West Coast Main Line) from where a joint line with the Midland Railway headed east to Wennington, and northwards along the Cumbrian coast to Whitehaven. Branches also served Hincaster Junction (on the WCML), Windermere Lake Side and Coniston Water. Although the company's prosperity initially came from exporting locally mined haematite ore via Barrow Docks, it had also started to promote tourist traffic to the Lake District by the 1890s. The latter venture was so successful that by the early 20th century passenger revenue had increased considerably – no doubt helped by improved coaching stock and the company-owned steamers operating on Coniston Water and Lake Windermere as well as between Barrow and Fleetwood. With its 158-route-mile network, the Furness Railway became one of the constituent companies of the newly formed London Midland & Scottish Railway in 1923.

RIGHT: *Featuring Lake Windermere, this front cover of a Furness Railway timetable dates from 1 October 1915.*

BELOW: *A steam rail motor on the Coniston branch of the Furness Railway, 1910.*

Glasgow & South Western Railway

The Glasgow & South Western Railway (G&SWR) was formed in 1850 by the amalgamation of the Glasgow, Paisley, Kilmarnock & Ayr Railway and the Glasgow, Dumfries & Carlisle Railway. The railway opened its locomotive works at Kilmarnock in 1856 where Patrick Stirling was Locomotive Superintendent until 1866 before he took on the same job at Doncaster for the Great Northern Railway (see pages 24–25).

While a shortage of funds prevented the G&SWR from expanding its own network, it financially supported many new schemes with arrangements for working them until funds later became available to take them over. Notable among these were the Ayr & Dalmellington Railway, the Ayr & Maybole Junction Railway, Maybole & Girvan Railway, Ardrossan Railway and the Castle Douglas &

Dumfries Railway. Replacing its overcrowded Bridge Street station, the G&SWR opened a grand new terminal at St Enoch in Glasgow in 1876. With the opening of the Settle–Carlisle Line (see page 46) in the same year the Midland Railway came to an agreement with the G&SWR to operate through trains between St Pancras and St Enoch. Although in direct competition with the West Coast Main Line, so successful was this venture that the G&SWR opened a grand hotel in 1879 adjacent to the new terminus which itself required expansion in the early 20th century.

While the south bank of the Clyde was traditionally Caledonian Railway territory the G&SWR was able to drive deep into it by supporting the Greenock & Ayrshire Railway (G&AR), which opened to Albert Harbour in

Greenock in 1869. The G&AR was absorbed by the G&SWR in 1872 and a price war broke out for the rival Clyde steamer services and competing lines to Glasgow. Facilities were much improved at Greenock in 1875 when the G&SWR opened its Princes Pier station.

Attempts by the G&SWR to reach the harbour at Stranraer – jumping-off point for Northern Ireland – took many years to come to fruition. Having already reached Girvan in 1860 it took several attempts before the G&SWR-backed Ayrshire & Wigtownshire Railway opened between Girvan and Challoch Junction in 1887 – the company was absorbed by the G&SWR in 1892. From Challoch Junction G&SWR trains used the Portpatrick & Wigtownshire Joint Railway (P&WJR) to reach Stranraer. The P&WJR had been jointly operated by the G&SWR and its arch-rival the Caledonian Railway since 1885.

Serving many harbours on the Ayrshire coast and also Greenock on the south bank of the Clyde, the G&SWR naturally operated a large fleet of ferries serving the islands of Arran, Greater Cumbrae and Bute. During the summer months vast numbers of daytrippers escaping from industrial Glasgow were carried on G&SWR trains and ferries to the Ayrshire coastal resorts and Clyde Estuary islands.

With its magnificent terminus at St Enoch and mainline connections to England the G&SWR also had a virtual monopoly transporting coal from the Ayrshire coalfields as well as serving the harbours, towns and resorts along the Firth of Clyde coastline. In complete contrast it also served the remote settlements of Galloway and the Northern Ireland ferry port of Stranraer. At its peak it operated 498-route-miles of railway, becoming an important constituent company of the newly-formed London Midland & Scottish Railway in the 'Big Four Grouping' of 1923.

PREVIOUS PAGE: *Glasgow & South Western Railway 4-6-0 No 500 makes a fine sight as it hauls an express from Glasgow St Enoch.*

RIGHT: *A bookmark produced by the Glasgow & South Western Railway in 1911 publicises golfing resorts, such as Turnberry, which could be reached by the company's lines. It features Sandy Herd who won the British Open golf championship in 1902.*

FAR RIGHT: *Dating from 13 July 1914, this Great Central Railway poster promotes the 'Sea to Sea Expresses' between Liverpool, gateway for North America, and Hull, gateway for Northern Europe.*

"Far & Sure."

GOLFING RESORTS

ON   THE

A. HERD.

Glasgow & South Western Railway.

DAVID COOPER, General Manager.

Great Central Railway

Until the opening of the 67-mile Channel Tunnel Link, or HS1, between Folkestone and St Pancras in 2007 the Great Central Railway (GCR) of 1899 was the last mainline to be built into London. The GCR had its roots in a smaller company, the Manchester, Sheffield & Lincolnshire Railway (MS&LR) which had existed since 1847 and had built the trans-Pennine route between Manchester and Sheffield via the Woodhead Tunnel. The MS&LR was formed by the amalgamation of four existing railway companies and the Grimsby Docks Company in order to improve communications across the Pennines between the important northern industrial centres of Manchester and Sheffield, the coalfields of south Yorkshire and the fast-growing port of Grimsby. Under its ambitious

General Manager, and, later, Chairman, Edward Watkin the MS&LR soon flourished and expanded its territory through takeovers and the arrangement of joint running rights with other railways in the region. Up to that point, despite intense competition from its larger rivals, the MS&LR, a major coal carrier, was a thriving concern. However, Edward Watkin had a dream of building a railway tunnel under the English Channel and to this end planned further expansion southwards to London.

The new 92-mile railway, from Annesley in Nottinghamshire to a new London terminus at Marylebone, would transform his company from a regional player into a major north-south strategic route that would compete head on with giants such as the

Midland Railway and the Great Northern Railway. One section of the line, southward from Quainton Road in Buckinghamshire to Harrow, was to be jointly run with the Metropolitan Railway, of which Edward Watkin was also Chairman – the Metropolitan had already started operating suburban services on this route in 1892.

The MS&LR obtained Parliamentary approval for the 'London Extension' in 1893 and four years later Watkin changed the name of his company to the Great Central Railway (GCR). Work started on the construction of the new 92-mile line in 1895 and it was opened for passenger traffic on 9 March 1899. The line was designed from the outset for fast traffic with a continental loading gauge and no level crossings. Despite the mainline reaching London, the most important part of the new Great Central was the 'branch' between Culworth Junction, south of Woodford & Hinton (renamed Woodford Halse in 1948), and Banbury which carried enormous quantities of freight and coal traffic and also inter-regional cross-country passenger trains, such as the unofficially named 'Ports-to-Ports Express' (see page 9). Major towns and cities that were served by the new Great Central route included Nottingham, Loughborough, Leicester and Rugby, all of which were already well served by other major railway companies and the company soon ran into trouble as the actual cost of building the new line far exceeded the original estimate of £6 million.

Before the new mainline had been completed there was a major falling out between the GCR and the Metropolitan Railway and so an 'Alternative Route' was built from Grendon Underwood Junction on the GCR mainline and Ashendon Junction on the GWR's line from Birmingham and Banbury. From Ashendon Juncton to Northolt Junction the line was jointly owned by the GCR and Great Western Railway. The 'Alternative Route' was opened in 1906 by which time the GCR and the Metropolitan had patched up their differences, making the new route rather superfluous.

In addition to operating passenger services across the Pennines between Manchester, Sheffield and Grimsby, the GCR heavily promoted its new route to London in the face of competition from existing railway companies. Its answer was the slogan 'Rapid Travel in Luxury' which it applied to all its long distance trains, equipping them with luxurious accommodation and refreshment cars.

Serving both Grimsby Docks ('the largest fishing port in the world') and Immingham Dock (completed in 1912 for the export of coal) the GCR naturally operated a large fleet of ships for the lucrative North Sea trade to Northern Europe – between 1872 and 1914 the company had built no less than 31 steamers, many of which were sunk in the First World War.

Despite all the slogans and hype, passenger traffic on the 'London Extension' never lived up to expectations but the railway did achieve much success as a freight carrier, especially in the moving of coal, in which it excelled. Founded near Manchester by the MS&LR in 1848, Gorton Locomotive Works went on to build over 900 steam locomotives for that company and the GCR by the time of the 'Big Four Grouping' in 1923. From then the Great Central became part of the newly formed London & North Eastern Railway (see page 89) and, on Nationalization, in 1948, was allocated to the Eastern Region of British Railways (see pages 127–128).

ABOVE: *Great Central Railway leaflet announcing the ceremony of the opening of the London extension to Marylebone station on 9 March 1899.*

Great Eastern Railway

Formed in 1862, the Great Eastern Railway (GER) was an amalgamation of many railway companies in East Anglia of which the Eastern Counties Railway (ECR) was by far the largest constituent. By future takeovers of more companies the GER eventually operated 1,200 route miles throughout Norfolk, Suffolk, Cambridgeshire and Essex giving it a virtual monopoly of railway services in this region. The monopoly ended with the formation of the Midland & Great Northern Joint Railway (M&GNJR) in 1893 which allowed that company access to Norfolk's important fishing ports and seaside resorts (see page 43).

In London the GER used the former ECR's terminus at Bishopsgate until its new Liverpool Street station was opened in 1874. The 10-platform overall-roofed station was designed by GER engineer Edward Wilson but within 10 years of opening it was working to capacity. The company's Great Eastern Hotel was opened in 1884 and an extension to the station including eight new platforms was added in the early 1890s.

While much of its network served scattered rural communities the GER also operated one of the busiest commuter operations in the world. Intensive suburban services operating in and out of Liverpool Street station during the morning and early evening rush-hour periods later became known as the 'Jazz' – so named after the yellow and blue stripes on carriages denoting first and third class respectively.

The company's main workshops at Stratford had already been established in the 1840s by its predecessor the ECR. Although locomotive building commenced here in 1850 the GER greatly expanded the site in the 1870s with just under 1,000 locomotives being built by the end

of the century. The adjoining engine shed at Stratford was one of the biggest in Britain which at its peak just after the First World War housed over 500 locomotives. From 1882 all GER passenger locomotives were finished in a smart blue livery which, when seen at the head of a train of varnished teak carriages, must have been a stirring sight.

For nearly three decades two GER routes vied for the fastest mainline services between Liverpool Street and Norwich but by the 1890s the route via Ipswich had won against the alternative via Cambridge. During summer months the GER's lines to the Norfolk seaside resorts became very busy with overflowing trains carrying holidaying Londoners to the delights of Hunstanton, Sheringham, Cromer, Mundesley and Yarmouth.

The GER installed water troughs on their mainline between Liverpool Street and Norwich in the late 19th century. This enabled the company to start operating non-stop expresses on the route and the most famous of these was the 'Norfolk Coast Express', which was introduced in 1907. Operating only from July to September, the restaurant car express ran non-stop between Liverpool Street and North Walsham, via the Norwich Thorpe avoiding line, a total distance of 130 miles. At North Walsham the train divided with several coaches being taken to Mundesley-on-Sea and Overstrand. The rest of the train continued to Cromer where it divided again with two coaches being forwarded to Sheringham. These heavy trains, sometimes loading up to 15 coaches, were hauled by newly-introduced 'Claud Hamilton' 4-4-0s that had been built at the GER's works at Stratford in East London. The train was discontinued on the outbreak of the First World War.

Starting in 1863 the company also operated a large number of passenger ferries for North Sea services from the port of Harwich to Rotterdam and Antwerp while a service from Parkeston Quay to Hook of Holland commenced in 1904. To connect with these the GER introduced fast and luxurious boat trains in 1882 running between Liverpool Street and Harwich and later Parkeston Quay. By the early 20th century the ferry port of Parkeston Quay was being served by luxurious Great Eastern Railway trains from Liverpool Street which connected with the company's steamers to and from the Hook of Holland. The port assumed even greater importance after the First World War when a new service to and from Zeebrugge in Belgium was introduced. With the addition of Pullman cars after the war the Hook of Holland train was one of the heaviest to be operated by the Great Eastern Railway and was entrusted to the powerful Holden '1500' Class 4-6-0s from Parkeston Quay shed. This service continued to be operated by the London & North Eastern Railway from 1923 (see page 101).

The Great Eastern Railway was one of the major constituent companies that formed the London & North Eastern Railway in the 'Big Four Grouping' of 1923 (see page 89).

PREVIOUS PAGE: *Poster produced by the Great Eastern Railway in 1890 for continental customers, promoting its hotels in London, Harwich and Parkeston Quay.*

BELOW: *This Great Eastern Railway poster of 1910 promotes the new Harlow Garden Village to commuters. It certainly was a safe investment!*

Great North of Scotland Railway

The Great North of Scotland Railway (GNoSR) was incorporated in 1846 but it took another eight years to open its first line, from Aberdeen Kittybrewster to Huntly. The line was extended southwards to Aberdeen Waterloo and northwards from Huntly to Keith in 1856. Doing away with its rather temporary structure at Waterloo the GNoSR started using the new joint station in Aberdeen in 1867.

Meanwhile, in 1866, the GNoSR had absorbed the Formartine & Buchan Railway with its lines from Dyce to Fraserburgh and Peterhead. Also in the same year it absorbed the Alford Valley Railway, the Inverury & Old Meldrum Junction Railway, the Banff, Macduff & Turriff Railway, the Keith & Dufftown Railway and the Strathspey Railway. Other railways absorbed were the Banffshire Railway in 1867, the Deeside and Deeside Extension railways in 1875, the Aboyne & Braemar Railway in 1876 and the Morayshire Railway in 1881. The GNoSR now owned a network of railways throughout Aberdeenshire, Banffshire and Morayshire, serving the important fishing ports of Peterhead, Fraserburgh and Macduff, the all-important whisky industry in the Spey Valley and running an intensive commuter service on the Deeside line.

The all-important Morayshire coastal route was finally extended from Portsoy to Elgin with viaducts and high embankments at Cullen and the viaduct and bridge over the River Spey at Garmouth, all finally completed in 1886. The opening of this new route cut journey times for GNoSR trains travelling between Aberdeen and Elgin – the alternative route via Keith and Craigellachie was much slower.

At the very end of the century the GNoSR opened a hotel and golf course at Cruden Bay, connecting it to Ellon on the Fraserburgh branch with a new 15½-mile branch line. The line up Deeside to Ballater saw frequent visits by royalty on their way to Balmoral with the first official Royal Train arriving in 1866. The company's locomotive works was originally based at Kittybrewster in Aberdeen until 1903 when a new site for construction and repair was opened at Inverurie alongside the mainline to Keith. In the early years of the 20th century the GNoSR also pioneered motor omnibus services acting as feeders to many of its branch lines – the first from Ballater to Braemar started operating in 1904.

At its peak the GNoSR operated 333½ route miles and in the 'Big Four Grouping' of 1923 became one of the constituent companies of the newly-formed London & North Eastern Railway (see page 89).

BELOW: *Designed by William Pickersgill in the late 1890s, 4-4-0 locomotive No 115 hauled express passenger trains on the Great North of Scotland Railway's mainline between Aberdeen and Keith.*

Great Northern Railway

The Great Northern Railway's (GNR) mainline between King's Cross and Shaftholme Junction, north of Doncaster, was completed in 1852. This route formed the southern part of the East Coast Main Line to Edinburgh, which was worked by the GNR, the North Eastern Railway and the North British Railway.

Traffic on the GNR out of King's Cross was initially slow to develop but by 1860 the railway was enjoying a massive surge in both freight and passenger traffic along its mainline. By then, through trains were being run from King's Cross to Edinburgh and the three companies involved developed special rolling stock for this service known as East Coast Joint Stock (see page 14). Introduced in 1862, the 10 a.m. 'Special Scotch Express' departure

from King's Cross to Edinburgh was the forerunner of the London & North Eastern Railway's 'Flying Scotsman' (see pages 96–98 and 140–141). Dining cars were first introduced in Britain in 1879 by the GNR on services between King's Cross and Leeds – at that time a Pullman dining car was added to the train to provide the service which proved to very popular with the travelling public.

In addition to its London to Doncaster mainline, by the end of the 19th century the GNR's empire had expanded to reach Leicester, Burton-on-Trent and Stafford in the west, Lincoln, Skegness and Grimsby in the east and Leeds, Bradford and Halifax in the north. The company shared joint lines with many of its neighbours, notable among them being the 183-mile

Midland & Great Northern Joint Railway (the longest joint railway in Britain – see page 43), the 123-mile Great Northern & Great Eastern Joint Railway, the Great Northern & London & North Western Joint Railway and the 20-mile South Yorkshire Joint Railway. The company also had a one-third share in the 143-mile Cheshire Lines Committee (see page 13), the second longest joint railway in Britain. All in all, the Great Northern certainly spread its tentacles wide.

The GNR's locomotive, carriage and wagon works was established at Doncaster in 1853 and under successive chief mechanical engineers, Patrick Stirling, Henry Ivatt and Nigel Gresley, produced some of the finest steam locomotives in the world, all of which were the mainstay of motive power on the GNR's expresses. Notable among them were the 53 Stirling 'Single' 4-2-2s built between 1870 and 1895, the 94 Ivatt large boiler 'Atlantic' 4-4-2s built between 1903 and 1910 and the two Gresley 'A1' Class 4-6-2s that were built in 1922 – so successful were these latter locomotives that the London & North Eastern Railway, the successor to the GNR from 1923, went on to build another 50, finally rebuilding 51 along with 27 new locomotives as Class 'A3' 4-6-2s between 1923 and 1935.

From 1 January 1923 the Great Northern Railway ceased to exist, being one of the largest constituent railway companies of the newly-formed London & North Eastern Railway.

LEFT: *With artwork by Frank Henry Mason, this Great Northern Railway poster of 1910 promoted rail travel to the Yorkshire coast and the company's booklet* Alice in Holidayland.

BELOW: *Taken from* The Book of Trains, *this illustration features the 'Flying Scotchman', being hauled by one of Henry Ivatt's 'Klondyke' 4-4-2 locomotives, in the early 20th century.*

This is the "Flying Scotchman", Great Northern Railway.

Great Western Railway

Without doubt the Great Western Railway (GWR) was unique among the railway companies of Britain. Isambard Kingdom Brunel, the engineer who had built the original line from London to Bristol, had left a legacy of a network of broad gauge (7 ft 0¼ in.) lines radiating out westwards from Paddington to the West Country, South Wales and the West Midlands. While the rest of the country's railways had opted to use George Stephenson's standard gauge of 4 ft 8½ in., the GWR, or 'God's Wonderful Railway', had gone its own way. Needless to say this caused terrible logistical problems at places where these two gauges met so the GWR made a decision to convert from broad gauge to standard gauge. This happened slowly, starting in the 1860s and by the beginning of the last decade of the 19th century the GWR had converted much of its network to standard gauge. The last route to be converted was the mainline from Paddington to Penzance via Bristol, completed on 23 May 1892.

The GWR also had style. It's express passenger trains were made up of fully lined brown and cream livered coaches hauled by steam locomotives finished in fully lined

BELOW: *Hauled by a 2-2-2 locomotive, the GWR's broad-gauge 'Cornishman' service bound for Penzance passes Uphill Junction, near Weston-super-Mare, Somerset, c.1890.*

'Middle Chrome Green' with polished brass domes, brass safety valves, brass whistles, brass window surrounds and copper capped chimneys. Each locomotive also had brass numerals attached to the cabsides and brass nameplates fixed to the wheel splashers. The wheel spokes and hubs, splasher fronts and frames were finished in 'Indian Red'.

From the beginning of the 20th century the GWR embarked upon the opening of many new routes, all designed to shorten journey times and improve connections, as follows:

1900	Patney & Chirton to Westbury, shortening the journey from Paddington to Weymouth by 14½ miles.
1903	Wootton Bassett to Patchway, shortening the journey from Paddington to South Wales by 33 miles.
1906	Castle Cary to Langport Curry Rivel Junction, shortening the journey from Paddington to Plymouth and Penzance by 20¼ miles.
1906/ 1908	Honeybourne to Cheltenham Malvern Road/Tyseley to Bearley, creating a new direct route from Birmingham to South Wales and Bristol.
1910	Birmingham Direct Line, built jointly with the Great Central Railway (see pages 19–20), shortening the journey from Paddington to Birmingham Snow Hill.
1913	Swansea District Lines, allowing trains from Paddington to Fishguard Harbour to avoid the congestion of Swansea. Seven years earlier the GWR had completed the construction of Fishguard Harbour which was then used by ferries to southern Ireland and, from 1909, by Cunard trans-Atlantic liners.

The GWR's terminus in London was at Paddington, designed by Brunel and completed in 1854. Electric lighting at the station was introduced in 1886 and the station was enlarged between 1913 and 1916. At Bristol, Temple Meads station, which it shared with the Midland Railway, was extensively enlarged in the 1870s.

The company's main locomotive works were at Swindon although construction was also carried out at Wolverhampton Works until 1908. William Dean was the Chief Locomotive Engineer at Swindon from 1877 to 1902, a period of transition from broad to standard gauge. Notable locomotives built during his term in office included the '3031' Class 4-2-2, the 'Duke', 'Bird', 'Bulldog', 'Badminton', 'Atbara' and 'Flower' Classes of 4-4-0, the '2600' Class 'Aberdare' 2-6-0 and the '2301' Class 'Dean Goods' 0-6-0 – a total of 260 of these versatile machines were built, with the last survivor being retired in 1957.

Dean was succeeded by George Jackson Churchward, the Chief Mechanical Engineer at Swindon, in 1902. He went on to design many groundbreaking locomotives including the 'City' Class 4-4-0, the two-cylinder 'Saint' Class 4-6-0, the four-cylinder 'Star' Class 4-6-0 and the unique *The Great Bear*, which was the first 4-6-2 (Pacific) locomotive to be built in Britain – the latter was not a success due to weight restrictions limiting its use to the Paddington to Bristol mainline only. Churchward retired in 1922 and was succeeded by Charles Collett who went on to introduce the highly successful four-cylinder 'Castle' and 'King' Class 4-6-0s for the enlarged GWR from 1923 onwards (see pages 64–65).

Many advances were made by the GWR during the latter part of the 19th century to its passenger train operations: slip coaches were introduced in 1869, 1st-Class sleeping cars in 1877, corridor trains in 1892, steam heating of coaches in 1893, 1st-Class restaurant cars in 1896 and 3rd-Class restaurant cars in 1903. By the beginning of the 20th century the GWR was operating restaurant car expresses from Paddington station to all corners of its empire; to Exeter, Torquay, Plymouth and Penzance, conveying slip coaches that served the numerous branch lines and seaside resorts of Devon and Cornwall; Weymouth; Bristol; Oxford, Worcester and Hereford; Swindon, Gloucester and Cheltenham Spa; Birmingham Snow Hill, Shrewsbury and Birkenhead; Newport, Cardiff, Swansea and Fishguard Harbour.

The GWR was adept at publicizing its own achievements and by the early 20th century the publicity department started promoting the company as 'The Holiday Line', producing posters to encourage holidaymakers to travel to Devon and Cornwall and publishing the *Holiday Haunts* annual guides to holiday resorts served by the railway – apart from the periods during the two world wars, this remained in print through to the British Railways' era of the 1960s.

Famous trains of the Great Western Railway

The Cornishman

Although not officially named as such, 'The Cornishman' was originally the premier train from Paddington to Penzance via Bristol during the broad gauge era. Running non-stop between London and Exeter via the Bristol avoiding line it was by far the longest such service in the world. By 1892 Brunel's broad gauge had been replaced by standard gauge and the train was discontinued in 1904 on the inauguration of the 'Cornish Riviera Limited'.

Cornish Riviera Limited

Until 1906 trains from Paddington to Devon and Cornwall had to travel the 'Great Way Round' via Bristol but with the opening of new lines between Patney & Chirton to Westbury in 1900 and from Castle Cary to Langport (near Taunton) in 1906 the journey was shortened by just over 20 miles. With the new, shorter route in mind the GWR had held a competition in 1904 to find a name for the daily premier express between Paddington and Penzance – thus was the 'Cornish Riviera Limited' born. Initially the train ran via Bristol but in 1906 it took the new, shorter route via Castle Cary. Slip coaches were included to serve other popular holiday destinations such as Weymouth, Ilfracombe, Newquay and St Ives. The train became so popular with holidaymakers that it ran in two portions on summer Saturdays until the First World War, when it was suspended. The train resumed service in 1919 and continued to be operated by the enlarged GWR after the 'Big Four Grouping' of 1923 (see pages 69–70 and 248–249).

Irish Mail via Fishguard

The Great Western Railway operated their own 'Irish Mail' train services between Paddington and Fishguard Harbour from 1906 to 1939. These trains connected with steamers bound for Rosslare and Cork in Ireland. Boat trains also connected with Cunard trans-Atlantic liners at Fishguard Harbour (en route to and from Liverpool) from 1909. However, Cunard soon chose Southampton as its main port of entry to the UK and these boat trains ceased to run. The opening in 1913 of the Swansea District Lines, thus avoiding Swansea, considerably speeded up these services.

Channel Islands Boat Train

The GWR started running passenger trains along the street tramway from Weymouth station to Weymouth Quay in 1889. At the quay passengers could embark on a GWR-owned ferry to the Channel Islands. Soon through trains between Paddington were being run to meet the ferry service, which continued to be operated by the GWR until 1948. A timetable example of these trains in 1902 shows a down boat train leaving Paddington on Tuesdays, Thursdays and Saturdays at 9.15 p.m. and, after travelling via Reading, Swindon, Trowbridge and Yeovil Pen Mill, arriving at Weymouth Quay at 2 a.m. the next day. The company-owned ferry left Weymouth Quay at 2.15 a.m., arriving in Guernsey at 7 a.m. The up train left Weymouth Quay at 4.10 p.m. and arrived back in Paddington at 8.20 p.m. On Mondays, Wednesdays and Fridays the London & South Western Railway (see page 39) ran its own 'Channel Islands Boat Train' between Waterloo and Southampton Docks. From 1923 these services continued to be operated by the enlarged Great Western Railway (see page 66) and the newly-formed Southern Railway respectively (see page 245).

ABOVE: *Introduced in 1904, the GWR's 'Cornish Riviera Limited' hauled by 'Star' Class 4-6-0 No 4062* Malmesbury Abbey *speeds through the West Country on its journey to Penzance.*

Highland Railway

The Highland Railway (HR) was created in 1865 by the amalgamation of the Inverness & Aberdeen Junction Railway and the Inverness & Perth Junction Railway – the former had opened between Inverness and Keith in 1858 and Inverness to Invergordon in 1862 while the latter had opened between Inverness and Perth via Forres in 1864. On its formation the HR controlled 242 route miles of railway. The 164½-mile route to Wick and Thurso in the Far North was completed in 1871 although acquisitions of the Sutherland Railway, the Duke of Sutherland's Railway and the Sutherland & Caithness Railway took until 1884.

Although the Dingwall & Skye Railway (D&SR) had opened westwards to Stromeferry in 1870, the final section to Kyle of Lochalsh had to wait for the HR to complete it, opening in 1897. Meanwhile the HR had already absorbed the D&SR in 1880.

The Highland Main Line was shortened in 1898 by the opening of a more direct route between Inverness and Aviemore via Carrbridge. This steeply graded route features the curving 28-arch 600-yd-long Culloden Moor Viaduct and the 445-yd-long steel Findhorn Viaduct. As well as serving its far-flung empire in the Highlands the HR also operated trains that conveyed through coaches between Euston and Inverness – these were especially well patronised during the grouse shooting season (12 August to 10 December) and over the Christmas and New Year periods. It can be fairly said that the towns and villages served along its mainline, such as Pitlochry, Blair Atholl and Aviemore, all owe their growth and popularity to the coming of the railway.

The company's headquarters and Lochgorm locomotive works were in Inverness. The first locomotive superintendent was none other than William Stroudley who, after four years in this post, left to join the London, Brighton & South Coast Railway (see page 41) in Brighton. His successor was David Jones who's 'Jones Goods' Class was the first 4-6-0 type of locomotive to operate in Britain. At the 'Big Four Grouping' on 1 January 1923 the HR and its 506 route miles became part of the newly-formed London Midland & Scottish Railway (see page 73). Much of the HR's network is still open for business today.

BELOW: *Dalwhinnie station, on the Highland Railway, Perth–Inverness mainline, Scotland, c.1910.*

OVERLEAF: *This Highland Railway poster of 1920 promoted its 'Royal, Quickest, and Only Direct Route' to the Highlands.*

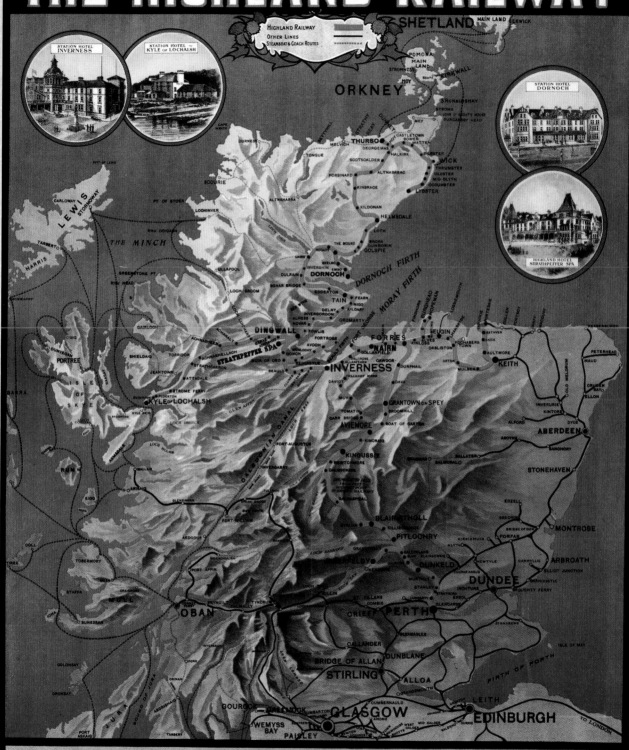

THE HIGHLAND RAILWAY

THE ROYAL, QUICKEST, AND ONLY DIRECT ROUTE
TO THE **HIGHLANDS** IS VIA PERTH AND DUNKELD.
FULL INFORMATION REGARDING TOURS, TRAINS, FARES, &c., MAY BE HAD FROM THE TRAFFIC MANAGER, HIGHLAND RLY., INVERNESS.

Tariff and Booklet descriptive of the Highland Railway Hotels may be had from the Hotels Manager, Highland Railway, Inverness.

Isle of Wight railways

By far the largest of England's island railways was to be found on the Isle of Wight where by 1900 there was a network of 56 route miles connecting Cowes, Ryde, Bembridge, Shanklin, Ventnor and Freshwater. The first to open, in 1862, was the Cowes & Newport Railway, followed by completion of the Isle of Wight Railway (IWR) between Ryde St John's and Ventnor in 1866. The next to open was the Ryde & Newport Railway in 1875. The Isle of Wight (Newport Junction) Railway was completed in 1879 but this went into receivership the following year and was bought by the Cowes & Newport Railway and the Ryde & Newport Railway, the three routes then being renamed Isle of Wight Central Railway (IWCR).

The short railway between Pier Head and St John's Road in Ryde was completed jointly by the London, Brighton & South Coast Railway and the London & South Western Railway in 1880. Following this the IWR opened a short branch from Brading to Bembridge in 1882 and the Freshwater, Yarmouth & Newport Railway opened in 1889, the latter being worked by the IWCR. The final chapter in this complicated story came in 1897 when the Newport, Godshill & St Lawrence Railway was opened, being extended to Ventnor West in 1900 and worked by the IWCR from the start, before being taken over lock, stock and barrel by that company.

The thriving network of railways on the Isle of Wight all became part of the newly formed Southern Railway in the 'Big Four Grouping' of 1923. Although highly popular with holidaymakers the railways all began to suffer from road motor bus competition by the 1930s. The Isle of Wight's railways all passed into British Railways ownership in 1948 and closures soon followed. Beginning in 1952, this finally ended in 1966 when the remaining steam-operated routes between Cowes and Ryde and Shanklin and Ventnor became victims of Dr Beeching's 'axe'. The section from Ryde Pier Head to Shanklin was electrified using redundant third-rail London Underground trains a year later and is still operational today. A 5½–mile section from Wootton to Smallbrook Junction is today operated by the Isle of Wight Steam Railway.

BOTTOM LEFT: 'Terrier' Class 0-6-0T No 11 waits to depart from Ventnor West with a train for Merstone in the summer of 1925.

BELOW: Produced c.1910 for the Isle of Wight Railway and the Isle of Wight Central Railway, this poster promoted the island as an attractive holiday destination.

Lancashire, Derbyshire & East Coast Railway

If completed as authorized by Parliament in 1891 the 170-mile east-west proposed route of the Lancashire, Derbyshire & East Coast Railway (LD&ECR) would have been the largest railway project to be built in Britain at the end of the 19th century. Its main purpose was to carry coal from the Derbyshire and Nottingham coalfields to proposed new docks at Warrington on the Manchester Ship Canal in the northwest and Sutton-on-Sea on the Lincolnshire coast in the east. However, due to lack of funds, only the 39½-mile section from Chesterfield to Lincoln and a 12-mile branch from Langwith Junction to Beighton Junction near Worksop were ever built. The mainline involved major civil engineering work including Boythorpe Viaduct at Chesterfield, the 370-ft-long Doe Lea Viaduct, two tunnels, including the troublesome 2,624-yd-long Bolsover Tunnel, several long rock cuttings and the 890-yd-long, 59-arch plus four trussed-steel spans Fledborough Viaduct over the River Trent. Supported financially by the Great Eastern Railway, which also wanted access to the coalfields, the fledgling LD&ECR opened between Chesterfield Market Place to Pyewipe Junction near Lincoln on 8 March 1897. The Beighton branch was completely opened on 30 May 1900. The headquarters of the railway was at Chesterfield Market Square station, a grand building with four curved platforms. The Great Central Railway purchased the unfinished LD&ECR at the beginning of 1907 with the ambitious project never completed.

The Achilles' heel of the Chesterfield to Lincoln route was always the notorious double-track Bolsover Tunnel. At nearly 1½ miles long it had always suffered badly from mining subsidence and a constant threat of flooding although much of the water was piped to supply the town of Bolsover. Concerns over its poor condition and also the nearby Doe Lea Viaduct led to the premature closure of the line between Chesterfield Market Place and Shirebrook North on 3 December 1951.

The remaining passenger service between Shirebrook North and Lincoln Central continued until 19 September 1955 when it ceased although summer excursion trains to Skegness continued to use the route until 1964. With the decline and eventual cessation of coal mining in the area the railway's lifeblood ebbed away and all that remains of the LD&ECR today is the section from Shirebrook, on the Robin Hood Line, to Tuxford which is used as a Network Rail test track. Chesterfield's grand Market Place station was sadly demolished in 1973 but impressive Fledborough Viaduct has survived and is now used by a footpath and cycleway.

The trackbed from the site of Fledborough station and across the viaduct to Pyewipe Junction is now a level traffic-free footpath and cycleway forming part of National Cycle Network Routes 647 (Fledborough to Doddington & Harby) and 64 (Doddington & Harby to Pyewipe Junction).

BELOW: *This poster was produced when the Lancashire, Derbyshire & East Coast Railway opened in 1897. Ambitious plans to link the west and east coasts of England failed to materialize and the unfinished railway was taken over by the Great Central Railway 10 years later.*

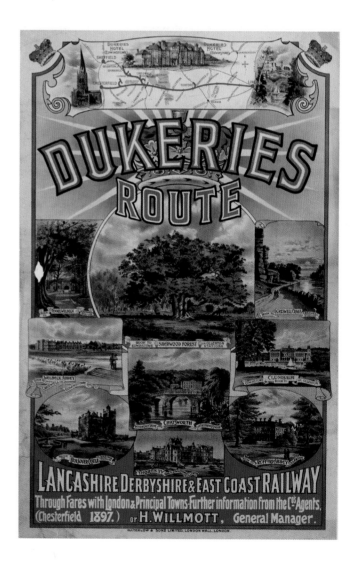

Lancashire & Yorkshire Railway

Serving one of the most densely populated and industrialized regions of Britain, the Lancashire & Yorkshire Railway (L&YR) was one of the most crowded railway networks in Britain. It was formed in 1847 from a merger of several railways including the Manchester & Leeds Railway and went on to expand its network throughout the rest of the 19th century with more takeovers. By the end of the century the L&YR's network stretched from Goole in the east to Liverpool and Southport in the west and Penistone in the south to Hellifield in the north. The company's main route across the Pennines was via the 2,885-yd-long Summit Tunnel between Rochdale and Todmorden – when completed in 1841 by the Manchester & Leeds Railway this was the longest railway tunnel in the world. At the

heart of the L&YR network was Manchester Victoria, one of Britain's largest railway stations, with 17 platforms including one that was the longest in the country. In Liverpool the company owned Exchange terminus station, a rather grand edifice with 10 platforms that was sadly closed in 1977.

Following the introduction of Bank Holidays in 1871, the company also heavily promoted passenger travel between industrialized Manchester and its environs and the West Lancashire coastal resorts such as Southport, Lytham St Annes and Blackpool. By the early 20th century Blackpool's and Southport's stations were filled with thousands of daytrippers from the cotton mill towns of Lancashire, most of them conveyed there by the Lancashire & Yorkshire Railway.

Designed by George Hughes, Lancashire & Yorkshire Railway 4-6-0 locomotive No 1514 is seen here at the head of a train at Southport Chapel Street station on 20 February 1921.

The L&YR's main locomotive works was at Miles Platting in Manchester until 1887 when the much larger Horwich Works was opened. By 1907 Horwich had produced 1,000 steam locomotives for the company and this continued under LMS and British Railways' ownership until 1957. The works finally closed in 1988.

The railway also owned the largest fleet of ships of any railway company in Britain at that time. By 1913 the company owned 26 steamers operating out of Liverpool and Goole to northern European ports and Ireland.

The Lancashire & Yorkshire Railway amalgamated with its bigger neighbour, the London & North Western Railway (LNWR) in 1922, a year before the LNWR became one of the main constituent companies that formed the London Midland & Scottish Railway. Much of the former L&YR network including Manchester Victoria station is still in use today.

Electrification

The L&YR was also at the forefront of railway electrification. Beating the North Eastern Railway by just one week, the railway became the first in Britain to operate a suburban electric service. A fourth rail system was used at 600 V DC with the first section opening between Liverpool Exchange and Crossens via Southport on 22 March 1904. With routes subsequently opened to Aintree (1906), Meols Cop (1909) and Ormskirk, the network of the L&YR's suburban electric lines radiating out from Liverpool had reached 37 miles by 1913. The Manchester to Bury route was electrified in 1916 and that from Bury to Holcombe Brook in 1918.

Liverpool Overhead Railway

Stretching for 6½ miles along Liverpool's waterfront, the standard gauge Liverpool Overhead Railway was completed in 1896 – at that time it was not only the world's first electric elevated railway but also the world's first railway to have an automatic electric signalling system. With 18 intermediate stations serving Liverpool's busy docks, the northern terminus was at Seaforth and the southern terminus was at Dingle, the latter approached through a tunnel. At its peak in the years preceding the First World War the 'Dockers' Umbrella', as it was affectionately known, carried around 20 million passengers a year. The railway remained untouched by the 'Big Four Grouping' of 1923 and Nationalization of the railways in 1948 but looming costly repairs coupled with Liverpool's docks downfall led to its closure at the end of 1956.

ABOVE: *Liverpool Overhead Railway driving cars provided excellent views for the driver, both at the front and through the overhanging side windows.*

RIGHT: *This poster was produced for the Liverpool Overhead Railway in the early 20th century to promote the panoramic views of the docks that can be seen from its trains.*

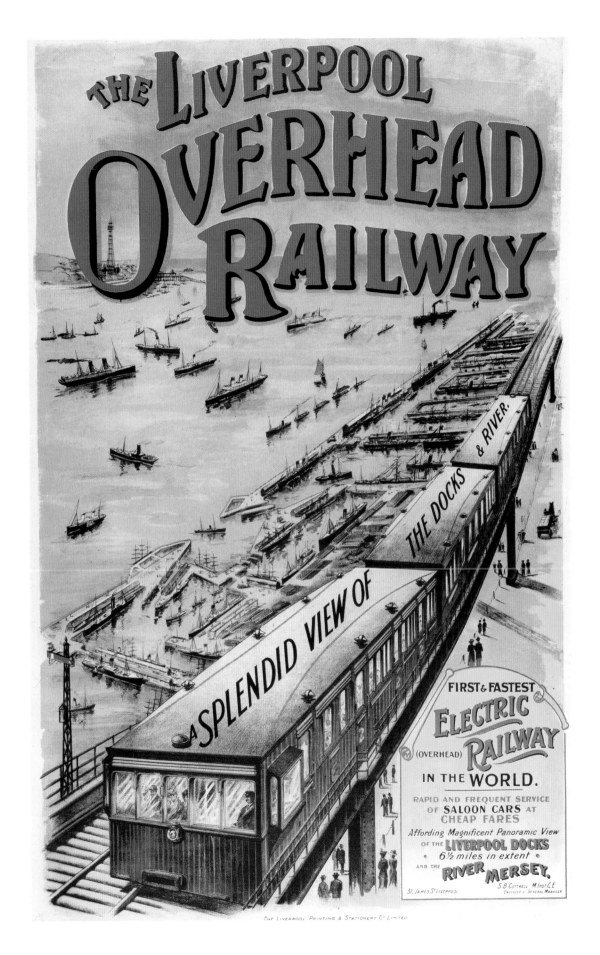

London & North Western Railway

What became one of Britain's, if not the world's, most successful railway companies of the late 19th century started life on 16 July 1846 with the amalgamation of the London & Birmingham Railway, the Grand Junction Railway and the Manchester & Birmingham Railway. Known as the London & North Western Railway (LNWR), the new company initially controlled 350 route miles of lines connecting Euston with Rugby, Birmingham, Wolverhampton, Crewe, Chester, Liverpool and Manchester. In Birmingham, Britain's second biggest city, the LNWR opened a new station in 1854 to replace the original London & Birmingham terminus at Curzon Street – at that time New Street station then had the largest single-span iron and glass arched roof in the world.

By the gradual acquisition of over 60 other railway companies the LNWR eventually controlled 2,667 route miles of railways linking London not only with the Midlands but also South Wales, North Wales and northwest England. Among these routes were the important links with Ireland and Scotland: the former via Holyhead and the latter via the West Coast Main Line to Carlisle and thence over Caledonian Railway metals to Glasgow and Edinburgh.

Advertising itself as the 'Premier Line' the railway introduced many innovations such as water troughs that enabled steam locomotives to collect water while travelling at speed, the first being installed at Mochdre in North Wales in 1860. The LNWR's main locomotive works were at Crewe and it was here that successive locomotive superintendents and chief mechanical engineers of the late 19th and early 20th centuries (Francis Webb, George Whale, Charles Bowen Cooke, Hewitt Beames and George Hughes) designed their groundbreaking locomotives for the company. Notable among these were Webb's 'Precedent' Class of 2-4-0, Whale's 'Precursor' Class 4-4-0 and 'Experiment' Class 4-6-0, Claughton's 'George the Fifth' Class 4-4-0 and 'Claughton' Class 4-6-0 – all fine locomotives that were designed to haul the LNWR's express passenger trains.

The LNWR's Wolverton Works also became the largest carriage works in Britain and by the end of the 19th century was building sleeping cars, corridor carriages with interconnecting gangway and restaurant cars.

During the First World War the works built ambulance trains for use in Britain and overseas.

The company also operated a fleet of ships on its Irish Sea routes from Holyhead. To connect Euston with Holyhead the LNWR introduced the 'Irish Mail' train in 1848. There were in fact two 'Irish Mail' services between Euston and Holyhead – the daytime service conveyed restaurant cars while the night service conveyed sleeping cars. Both trains included two Post Office sorting carriages – from as early as the 1870s these were also able to pick up mailbags at speed from lineside postal apparatus. These two services were continued by the London Midland & Scottish Railway in 1923, receiving the official name of 'The Irish Mail' in 1927 (see pages 77–78).

In addition to operating Anglo-Scottish restaurant car expresses and sleeper trains jointly with the Caledonian Railway (see page 11) along the West Coast Main Line (see page 60), the LNWR also ran boat trains between Euston and Fleetwood in conjunction with the Lancashire & Yorkshire Railway (see page 33) to connect with steamer services to and from Belfast. It also operated ocean liner expresses between Euston and Liverpool at a time when

Electrification

The LNWR pressed ahead with electrification of its London commuter routes in the early 20th century. With links to the District Railway and the new extension of the Bakerloo Line the railway embarked on a major electrification scheme for its inner-suburban network in North London that included lines from Broad Street to Richmond and Euston to Watford. With electricity generated at the company's Stonebridge Park power station the 630 V DC fourth rail system opened in stages between 1914 and 1922.

that port city was favoured by shipping companies such as Cunard Line and the White Star Line as the principal British port for their trans-Atlantic traffic.

A rare example of inter-regional workings was the 'Sunny South Express' which was introduced in 1905 jointly with the London, Brighton & South Coast Railway (see page 86). Operating during the summer months it carried holidaymakers from Liverpool and Manchester to South Coast resorts such as Brighton and Eastbourne. The train continued to be operated by the London Midland & Scottish Railway from 1923 to 1939. The LNWR also operated club trains in the years preceding the First World War – for an additional cost passengers could travel on regular trains in luxurious 12-wheel 1st Class coaches originally built by the company for the Euston to Liverpool ocean liner expresses. Destinations served by these 'Club Trains' included Manchester, Blackpool, Windermere and Llandudno. These trains continued to be operated by the London Midland & Scottish Railway from 1923 until 1939.

The LNWR amalgamated with the Lancashire & Yorkshire Railway on 1 January 1922 and a year later the much-enlarged company became the largest constituent company of the newly-formed London Midland & Scottish Railway.

LEFT: *This early 20th century poster shows a map of the LNWR's network with views of some of its destinations.*

FAR LEFT: *Raced by an early biplane, a LNWR 4-6-0 locomotive of the 'Experiment' Class breasts Shap Summit with a West Coast Route express, c.1910.*

London & South Western Railway

By the end of the 19th century the London & South Western Railway (LSWR) owned and operated a railway network that stretched from Waterloo to Padstow in North Cornwall – the latter destination had finally been reached in 1899, completing what became known as the 'Withered Arm' west of Exeter. Its main routes from Waterloo were as follows: Guildford and Portsmouth; Southampton, Bournemouth and Weymouth; Salisbury, Exeter, North Devon and North Cornwall. The company also operated an intensive service of commuter trains to stations in the leafy suburbs of southwest London, Surrey and east Hampshire. Giving it access to the business heart of London, the LSWR-backed Waterloo & City underground railway was opened in 1898.

Numerous secondary and seaside resort branch lines were opened by the LSWR in the later years of the 19th century and the early years of the 20th century. Among the last to be opened, in 1903, were the Meon Valley Railway between Alton and Fareham and the Axminster to Lyme Regis branch line.

With the Midland Railway the LSWR also jointly took over the ailing Somerset & Dorset Railway in 1891, the 114-mile route between Bournemouth West and Bath Queen Square – along with a branch to Highbridge – gave it access to the Midlands and the North of England, thus was the Somerset & Dorset Joint Railway formed (see pages 54–55).

The LSWR introduced the first non-stop service between Waterloo and Bournemouth in 1899. In 1911 the new 'T14' Class (or 'Paddleboxes') 4-6-0s were introduced on this service and the train was speeded-up so that the 108-mile journey was being achieved in 2 hours. It became one of the longest non-stop rail

journeys in Britain made without the use of water troughs – to overcome this problem, the LSWR had fitted their express locomotives with eight-wheeled tenders that had a capacity of 4,500 gallons of water. Introduced in 1919, the LSWR's new 'N15' Class ('King Arthur') 4-6-0s carried on this tradition and the Waterloo to Bournemouth non-stop service was continued by the newly-formed Southern Railway from 1923 (see page 110). Pullman cars had been used on the London & South Western Railway since the late 19th century – these were single cars attached to scheduled services but they had gone out of fashion by 1911.

Until the GWR opened its shorter route from Paddington to Plymouth (via Westbury and Castle Cary) in 1904 there was immense competition between that company and the rival LSWR to provide the fastest service between the two cities, both via Exeter, to connect with trans-Atlantic liners that called at Plymouth. Following a serious derailment at Salisbury in 1906, trains between Waterloo and Exeter were then forced to stop at that station – on 1 July that year 28 passengers were killed when an express train derailed on a sharp curve. The LSWR's 11 a.m. departure from Waterloo to Plymouth was the forerunner of what became known as the 'Atlantic Coast Express' which was introduced by the Southern Railway in 1927 (see pages 111–112).

The LSWR had been operating boat trains between Waterloo and Southampton Docks that connected with company-owned ferries to the Channel Islands since 1892. In that year the company had purchased the docks and went on to expand and modernize them, as did the LSWR's successor, the Southern Railway (see page 110), from 1923. The LSWR started operating ocean liner trains between Waterloo and Southampton Town & Docks station (also known as Southampton Terminus) in the late 19th century with passengers staying overnight at the grand South Western Hotel before boarding their ship – many of the passengers on the RMS Titanic stayed here in 1912 before taking their ill-fated voyage. By 1902 the LSWR was also operating the Channel Islands boat train on Mondays, Wednesdays and Fridays – the Great Western Railway operated a similar service from Paddington to Weymouth Quay, but on Tuesdays, Thursdays and Saturdays (see page 28). The LSWR's 'Channel Islands Boat Train' left Waterloo at 9.50 p.m. and arrived at Southampton Docks at 12.15 a.m. the next day, connecting with a company-owned ferry to the Channel Islands that left at 12.30 a.m. The up boat train left Southampton Docks at 5.15 a.m. and arrived at Waterloo at 7.37 a.m. These boat trains continued to be operated by the newly-formed Southern Railway from 1923 (see page 122).

The company's locomotive works were at Nine Elms, near Waterloo, until 1908 when they were transferred to a new site at Eastleigh in Hampshire. The locomotive superintendents and engineers of the late 19th and early 20th centuries were William Adams (1877–95), Dugald Drummond (1895–1912) and Robert Urie (1912–22).

LEFT: *The Daylight Bill of 1908 first set the twice-yearly changing of clocks in the UK. The LSWR was keen to point out that the sun sets about 20 minutes later in the West Country than in London!*

FAR LEFT: *Waterloo station, c.1900 – passengers embarking on the LSWR's 'American Line Express' bound for Southampton Docks.*

The most notable locomotives of this period that the LSWR built for express passenger work were the Class 'T9' 4-4-0s ('Greyhounds') that remained in service until the early 1960s, the Class 'T14' 4-6-0s ('Paddleboxes') and the Class 'N15' 4-6-0s ('King Arthurs'), the latter remaining in service until the late 1950s.

The First World War put the LSWR on the front line serving the vitally important company-owned Southampton Docks – its proximity to the great military centres of Southern England gave it supreme importance for the embarkation of troops and their supplies. This was all thanks to the far-sighted planning of the LSWR in the late 19th century when they modernized what was then a moribund concern, turning it into one of most modern port facilities in the world. Following the war, when the railways of Britain were put under Government control, the LSWR lived on until 1 January 1923 when it, with its network of 1,020 route miles, became one of the major constituent companies that formed the new Southern Railway (see page 110).

Electrification

Faced with a decline in passenger numbers on its Southwest London suburban network in the early 20th century, the London & South Western Railway (LSWR) lagged behind before it, too, implemented its own electrification scheme. Unlike the London, Brighton & South Coast Railway (see page 41) the LSWR opted for a third-rail system with a current of 600 V DC, the same as the North Eastern Railway's electrified lines in Tyneside. With great success electric multiple units started operating on the inner suburban services out of Waterloo in 1915 and by the outbreak of the First World War had been extended to Claygate in Surrey, making a total of 57 route miles. Following the 'Big Four Grouping' of 1923 the LSWR's third-rail system was chosen by the new Southern Railway for its massive mainline electrification programme.

Hauled by Class 'T9' 4-4-0 No 338, a LSWR express from Waterloo roars through Earlsfield station, c.1903.

London, Brighton & South Coast Railway

Up until 1860 the London, Brighton & South Coast Railway (LBSCR) – then with 170 route miles of railway – used London Bridge station as its London terminus but in that year the new 'Brighton' side of Victoria station was opened by the Victoria Station & Pimlico Railway – a consortium of four strange bedfellows in the shape of the Great Western Railway, London & North Western Railway, East Kent Railway and the LBSCR. By 1865 the LBSCR had expanded by opening a further 177 route miles of railways in South London, Sussex and Surrey but soon faced bankruptcy following the banking collapse of 1867. It recovered from this near disaster and went on to expand its suburban services in South London and by the late 1880s operated the largest such network in Britain. By the end of the 19th century the company's empire stretched from London Victoria in the north to Eastbourne in the south and from Hastings in the east to Portsmouth in the west.

The pioneering LBSCR had been successfully operating Pullman services since 1875 – the 'Pullman Limited' that had been operating between Victoria and Brighton since 1881 featured three new 35-ton 12-wheel vehicles that were the first electrically-lit railway carriages in the country. During the late 19th century, years before the advent of air travel, the only way to travel between London and Paris was by boat train. Compared to the current Eurostar service through the Channel Tunnel, the journey was leisurely and involved a ferry journey between Dover or Folkestone and Calais. In 1906 the LBSCR introduced new luxury Pullman cars and within a few years these were included in their boat trains from Victoria station. They were the predecessors to the famous all-Pullman 'Golden Arrow' boat train introduced by the Southern Railway in 1929 (see pages 119–120).

Introduced by the LBSCR in 1908, the all-Pullman 'Southern Belle' was dubbed at that time the most luxurious train in the world. The seven new 12-wheel Pullman cars, including a buffet car with cooking facilities, for this service were the first to be built in Britain as others, such as the Midland Railway's examples (see page 46), had previously had to be imported from the USA. The cars were painted in umber and cream and this became the standard colour scheme for all Pullman cars used throughout Britain. The journey between Victoria and Brighton was achieved in just 1 hour making the train the fastest by far on the LBSCR and within six months of introduction the train was making two return journeys between the capital and Brighton. The train proved so popular that in 1910 it was making four return trips each day with either one of Marsh's 'Atlantics' 4-4-2 or a Marsh/Billington 'Baltic' 4-6-4 tank locomotive at its head. The service was disrupted by the onset of the First World War in 1914 and finally withdrawn in 1917. The 'Southern Belle' was reintroduced after the war – more so than any other railway company in Britain, the LBSCR excelled in operating Pullman trains. The 'Southern Belle' continued to be operated by the newly-formed Southern Railway from 1923 (see page 123). After coming under Government control during the First World War, the LBSCR, with its network 457 route miles, went on to become one of the main constituent companies of the newly-formed Southern Railway on 1 January 1923.

Electrification

The early years of the 20th century found the LBSCR suffering from an acute shortage of steam locomotives – the problem caused by an inefficient locomotive department at Brighton Works. In light of this the electrification of its intensely operated suburban services in South London had been mooted in 1900 but it took until 1909 before the first route, between Victoria and London Bridge stations, was up and running. The overhead power supply for London's first overground electric railway was the same as that used on the Midland Railway's new route from Lancaster to Morecambe, 25-cycle 6,600 V AC. The new route, dubbed the 'Elevated Electric', was a great success and other lines soon followed but the outbreak of the First World War delayed the electrification of the rest of the LBSCR's South London suburban lines which was only completed in 1921, by which time there were 24½ route miles in place. Despite plans to extend electrification on the mainlines to the south coast the London & South Western Railway's third-rail system eventually won over under new Southern Railway management and the last 'Elevated Electric' train ran in 1929.

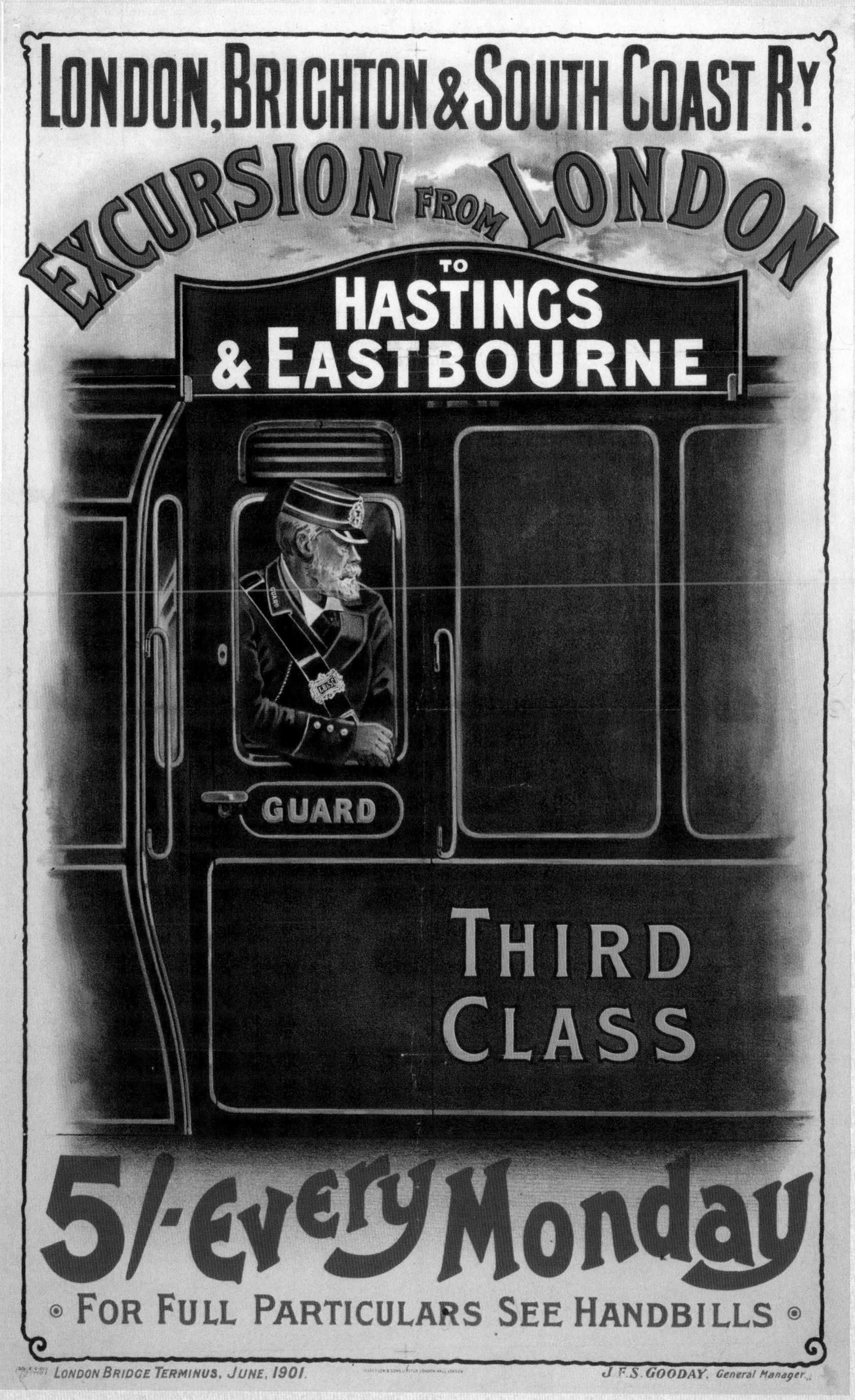

Midland & Great Northern Joint Railway

With its headquarters at Melton Constable in Norfolk, the Eastern & Midlands Railway (E&MR) was formed in 1883 by the amalgamation of three existing local railway companies. Following takeovers of other companies and the opening of the Melton Constable to Cromer line it soon owned an extensive railway network that stretched from Peterborough and Little Bytham in the west to Cromer, Norwich and Great Yarmouth in the east. For the first time the Great Eastern Railway had a serious rival, with many of the two companies' routes being in direct competition with each other.

However the overstretched E&MR soon fell on hard times and was taken over in 1893 by the Great Northern Railway and the Midland Railway. This joint enterprise became the Midland & Great Northern Joint Railway (M&GNJR) and, with a route mileage of 173 miles, allowed the Midland Railway access for the first time to Norwich and the towns, villages and ports of North Norfolk. The M&GNJR was the longest joint railway in Britain, much of it single-track, but during the busy summer months it was stretched to capacity carrying holidaymakers from the Midlands to the seaside resorts of North Norfolk.

In turn, the M&GNJR became jointly owned by the newly formed London & North Eastern Railway and the London, Midland & Scottish Railway in the 'Big Four Grouping' of 1923. Although the network was kept busy during the Second World War the post-war years brought a rapid decline in traffic, lost to ever-increasing competition from road transport. The 'Muddle & Get Nowhere Railway' as it was by then known was living on borrowed time and in 1958 British Railways announced its complete closure. Despite strong local opposition the end came for passenger services on 2 March 1959 – Cromer to Melton Constable was the only section to remain open, only to be closed on 6 April 1964 following publication of the 1963 'Beeching Report'.

FAR LEFT: *Poster produced for the LBSCR in 1901 promoting rail excursions from London to Hastings and Eastbourne.*

BOTTOM LEFT: *Built by Beyer-Peacock in 1886, M&GNJR Class 'A' 4-4-0 No 31 heads a long passenger train in the 1920s.*

BELOW: *With a dubious reference to Sandringham (which it did not serve), this M&GNJR poster of the 1920s promotes the railway's holiday destinations.*

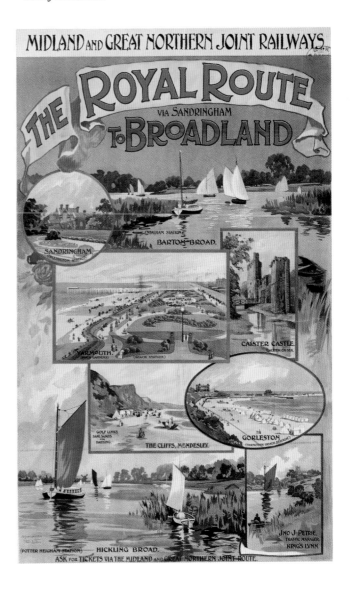

Midland Railway

By 1 January 1923, when it became one of the major constituent companies of the newly-formed London Midland & Scottish Railway (LMS), the Midland Railway (MR) operated 2,171 route miles of railway in England and Wales – it was the third-largest railway company in Britain. In addition to this it had a 50 per cent share of the Midland & Great Northern Joint Railway (see page 43, at 173 route miles, the longest joint railway in Britain), a one-third share of the Cheshire Lines Committee (see page 43, at 143 route miles, the second-largest joint railway in Britain) and a 50 per cent share of the Somerset & Dorset Joint Railway (see pages 54–55, at 114 route miles, the third-largest joint railway in Britain). Including these joint railways, the MR's network stretched from Yarmouth and Cromer in the east to Swansea in the west, and from Bournemouth in the south to Carlisle in the north.

The MR's empire was centred on Derby where it had its headquarters and railway works. Here, successive locomotive superintendents and chief mechanical engineers followed a strict 'small engine policy' that necessitated the common practice of double-heading heavily loaded trains. However, the MR built some very successful locomotives, many of which survived in service well into the British Railways' era. Of particular note are Samuel Johnson's Class 115 4-2-2s (introduced in 1896 and nicknamed 'Spinners'), which were capable of hauling expresses in the late 19th century at speeds of 90 mph, and his Class 1000 4-4-0 compounds (introduced 1902), which were the mainstay of express trains and survived until the early 1950s. At the other end of the scale, over

RIGHT: *Poster produced for the Midland Railway, c.1900, promoting the company's routes and destinations.*

BELOW: *Designed by Samuel Johnson, Midland Railway 4-4-0 No 332 crosses Ambergate Viaduct in Derbyshire with an express on 15 June 1911.*

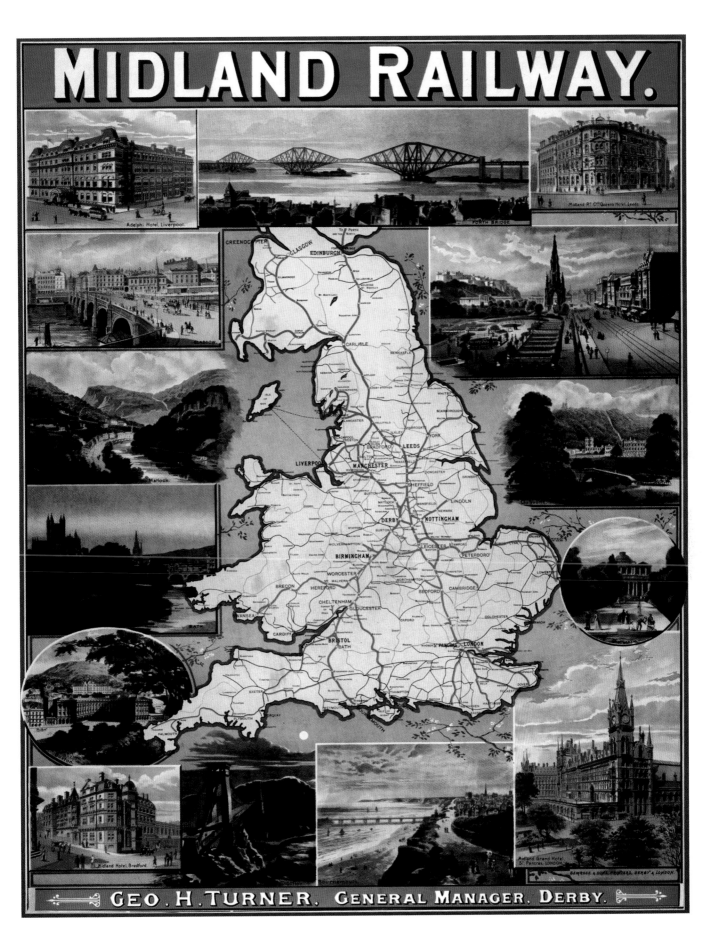

900 of his 0-6-0 goods locomotives were built between 1875 and 1908, some of them surviving until the early 1960s. Johnson retired in 1904 and was replaced by Richard Deeley as Chief Mechanical Engineer at Derby who went on to improve the 4-4-0 compounds but then fell out with MR management over their 'small engine policy' and resigned in 1909. He was succeeded by Henry Fowler who went on to become Chief Mechanical Engineer for the LMS in 1925 where he finally broke out of the 'small engine policy' by introducing the 'Royal Scot' Class 7P 4-6-0s, the Somerset & Dorset Joint Railway Class 7F 2-8-0s and the articulated 'Garratt' Class 2-6-0+0-6-2s.

The MR's London terminus was at St Pancras, which was designed by William Barlow and completed in 1868 – saved from demolition in the 1960s, the station is now the London terminus of the Eurostar high-speed trains to Paris and Brussels. The completion of the Settle–Carlisle Line in 1876 was a triumph for the MR but it was completed three years late and cost 70 per cent more than the original estimate. This famous route includes 23 viaducts (the longest at Ribblehead has 24 arches) and 13 tunnels (the longest, Blea Moor, is 1½ miles long) while the summit of the line, at Ais Gill, (1,169 ft above sea level) is reached from the south by a 15-mile-long ruling gradient of 1-in-100. To cope with the extra traffic generated by the Settle–Carlisle Line the station at Carlisle Citadel was considerably enlarged and, for the first time, allowed Midland Railway restaurant car and sleeper trains to run directly from St Pancras to Glasgow St Enoch via the Glasgow & South Western Railway (G&SWR – see page 17) and to Edinburgh via the North British Railway's (NBR – see page 47) Waverley Route.

The MR was also at the forefront of operating luxury passenger trains and was the first railway company in Britain to introduce Pullman cars. Built as a kit of parts in the USA by the Pullman Car Company of Chicago, these clerestory-roofed balconied bogie coaches entered service in 1874 between Bradford and St Pancras. They were not particularly popular with the travelling public who were used to the privacy of compartment coaches and were soon transferred to the London, Brighton & South Coast Railway (see page 41) where they were more successful on that company's route from Victoria to Brighton.

In the early years of the 20th century the Midland Railway was also operating an overnight sleeper service between St Pancras and Stranraer Harbour in Scotland, via

Electrification

While the Midland Railway (MR) experimented successfully with electrification of its route from Lancaster Green Ayre to Morecambe and Heysham in 1908 this line remained unique in the company's network. Like the London, Brighton & South Coast Railway's electric commuter lines that opened a year later in South London the MR used an overhead power supply at 25-cycle 6,600 V AC. The MR's original electric multiple units remained in service until 1951 after which the route was converted to 50-cycle 6,600V AC, reopening in 1953. Later used as a test bed for the standard 25 kV 50-cycle system that was introduced on the West Coast Main Line by British Railways, the Lancaster Green Ayre to Morecambe line closed in 1966.

G&SWR metals and the Portpatrick & Wigtownshire Joint Railway (in which the MR had an interest). At Stranraer Harbour the train, affectionately known as 'The Paddy', connected with steamer sailings to and from Larne (for Belfast) in Northern Ireland. The route was via Leeds, Carlisle, Dumfries and the 'Port Road' to Stranraer through the wilds of Galloway. This train continued to be operated by the London Midland & Scottish Railway from 1923 (see page 82). A boat train connecting with steamer services to and from Belfast at Heysham was inaugurated by the Midland Railway as early as 1904. Running to and from St Pancras, the unnamed train ran in competition with the London & North Western Railway's boat train that ran between Euston and Fleetwood. These two trains were combined by the newly-formed London Midland & Scottish Railway from 1923 (see page 88) with Euston as the London terminus. The MR also operated P&O ocean liner trains between St Pancras and Tilbury via the London, Tilbury & Southend Railway, which it had taken over in 1912.

Before the age of the car, privately-owned horse-drawn carriages were regularly transported around Britain by train. They were usually conveyed in special carriage trucks attached to scheduled passenger trains. By the beginning of the 20th century early motor cars were also being carried in the same manner with the MR being one of the first companies to offer this service.

North British Railway

The North British Railway (NBR) had become the largest railway company in Scotland by the end of the 19th century, its tentacles stretching as far south as Carlisle via the Waverley Route, as far north and west as Fort William via the West Highland Line and as far north and east as Kinnaber Junction on the route to Aberdeen. However the NBR's densest networks were in the industrial Central Belt, serving the Linlithgow and Lanarkshire coalfields, and in the Fife coalfields. Having overcome the Tay Bridge disaster of 1879 the NBR opened a new bridge over the Firth of Tay in 1887 and had a 35 per cent stake in the new Forth Bridge which opened in 1890. It also operated jointly with the North Eastern Railway (see page 49) and the Great Northern Railway (see page 24) the Anglo-Scottish services on the East Coast Main Line (see page 14) between King's Cross, Edinburgh and Aberdeen.

Opening throughout in 1862, the North British Railway's Waverley Route between Edinburgh and Carlisle only came into its own as a third Anglo-Scottish route 14 years later, when the Midland Railway's Settle–Carlisle line opened in 1876 (see page 46). The opening of the latter enabled through running of trains between St Pancras and Scotland, thus avoiding the West Coast Main Line (see page 60) which was controlled by the London & North Western Railway and the Caledonian Railway. Jointly-owned coaching stock for use on this route was built by the Midland Railway and lettered 'M. & N.B.' (Midland & North British) – these services between St Pancras and Edinburgh were the predecessors to the 'Thames-Forth Express' and 'The Waverley' restaurant car expresses later introduced by the LMS/LNER and British Railways respectively (see pages 88 and 205–206).

In February 1873 the NBR was the first railway in Britain to introduce a sleeping car on a train that ran between Glasgow Queen Street, Edinburgh and King's Cross via the East Coast Main Line. Prior to the First World War the Midland Railway and the North British Railway were also operating overnight sleeper trains via the Settle-Carlisle/ Waverley Route with through coaches between St Pancras and Edinburgh, Aberdeen, Perth, Inverness and Fort William.

The NBR had also backed the building of the West Highland Railway between Glasgow and Fort William which opened in 1894. This highly scenic line was a triumph of late Victorian engineering with its 198-mile route clinging to mountainsides, skirting lochs and crossing miles of featureless and inhospitable bogs. Built by Robert McAlpine (or 'Concrete Bob') the 38¼-mile Mallaig Extension between Fort William and Mallaig opened in 1901. A showcase for McAlpine's use of concrete, this highly scenic line features the famous 21-arch Glenfinnan Viaduct. Both the WHR and the Mallaig extension were absorbed by the NBR in 1908.

The NBR's locomotive works were at Cowlairs in Glasgow. Notable locomotive superintendents of the time were Dugald Drummond (1874–82), Matthew Holmes (1882–1903) and William Reid (1903–19) and many of their locomotives had a very long working life stretching into the British Railways' era. Some of Holmes' Class 'J36' 0-6-0s (introduced 1888) survived until 1967 and Reid's Class 'J35' (introduced 1906) and Class 'J37' (introduced 1914) 0-6-0s both continued in revenue-earning work until the 1960s – the last was withdrawn in 1967 – while his versatile 'Glen' Class 4-4-0s (introduced 1913) were used extensively on the West Highland Line until the late 1950s.

Despite being a Scottish railway company the NBR also operated branch lines in Northumberland and the Carlisle to Silloth line in Cumberland. From small beginnings in 1844 the NBR network had grown to 2,739 route miles by the time of the 'Big Four Grouping' in 1923 when it became a major constituent company of the newly-formed London & North Eastern Railway (LNER). Much of the NBR's former rail network is still open for business today apart from the missing section of the Waverley Route between Tweedbank and Carlisle which closed in January 1969.

ABOVE: *NBR Class 'H' 4-4-2 Liddesdale hauls the 'Queen of Scots' Pullman train through Princes Street Gardens, Edinburgh, c.1912.*

OVERLEAF: *Early 20th century NBR poster promoting 'Summer Tours to the Trossachs and Loch Katrine'.*

SUMMER TOURS VIA ABERFOYLE

TROSSACHS, LOCH KATRINE

AND

CIRCULAR TOUR OF **EDINBURGH** AND **TROSSACHS**

The various stages of the journey are as follows:—

TRAIN
EDINBURGH (Waverley) TO STIRLING
STIRLING TO BUCHLYVIE
BUCHLYVIE TO ABERFOYLE.

COACH
ABERFOYLE TO FOOT OF LOCH KATRINE.

STEAMER
UP LOCH KATRINE.

COACH
HEAD OF LOCH KATRINE TO INVERSNAID.

STEAMER
INVERSNAID TO BALLOCH

TRAIN
BALLOCH TO COWLAIRS OR GLASGOW (Queen Street) OR COWLAIRS TO EDINBURGH (Waverley).

For full Details as to hours &c. see the NORTH BRITISH RAILWAY COMPANY'S TIME TABLES. The Route may be reversed at the option of the Passenger. Passengers holding Tourist Tickets may break the journey at any point on the Route.

CIRCULAR TOUR OF **GLASGOW** AND **TROSSACHS**

The various stages of the journey are as follows:—

TRAIN
GLASGOW (Queen Street) TO ABERFOYLE.

COACH
ABERFOYLE TO FOOT OF LOCH KATRINE.

STEAMER
UP LOCH KATRINE.

COACH
HEAD OF LOCH KATRINE TO INVERSNAID.

STEAMER
INVERSNAID TO BALLOCH.

TRAIN
BALLOCH TO GLASGOW (Queen St.)

For full Details as to hours &c. see the NORTH BRITISH RAILWAY COMPANY'S TIME TABLES. The Route may be reversed at the option of the Passenger. Passengers holding Tourist Tickets may break the journey at any point on the Route.

In addition to the romantic "CAMPSIE GLENS" and the far famed "CLACHAN of ABERFOYLE" this New Tourist Route, includes views of Highland Scenery of surpassing interest and beauty, which are now for the first time rendered accessible to ordinary Travellers

The Coaches between ABERFOYLE and "LOCH KATRINE run by the new road across the shoulder of BEN VENUE to the upper end of LOCH ACHRAY and through the famous PASS of the TROSSACHS.

LOCH LOMOND

THE NEW TOURIST ROUTE
Between GLASGOW EDINBURGH & TROSSACHS
IS VIA ABERFOYLE
Ask for "Trossachs Tickets Via Aberfoyle"

THE FARES BY THIS ATTRACTIVE ROUTE IN NO CASE EXCEED THOSE BY OTHER ROUTES

North Eastern Railway

The North Eastern Railway (NER) comprised four constituent companies: York, Newcastle & Berwick Railway, York & North Midland Railway, Leeds Northern Railway and the Malton & Driffield Railway. At its formation in 1854 the NER was the largest railway company in Britain, owning 720 route miles along with various canals and dock installations. The company went on to totally dominate northeast England by absorbing 25 more railways and three dock companies between 1857 and 1922, giving it a network of just under 1,757 route miles before it became the largest of the English constituent companies of the newly-formed London & North Eastern Railway in 1923.

The route northwards from Darlington to Gateshead via the Team Valley was opened throughout in 1872 and the East Coast Main Line between York and Newcastle that we know today was complete. At its northern end,

Newcastle Central station, reaching over the Tyne via Robert Stephenson's High Level Bridge, had already been opened in 1850. However, trains entering the station were forced to reverse direction until the opening of the King Edward VII Bridge across the river in 1906. Down south the small terminus station at York was totally inadequate with trains from London to Newcastle also required to reverse out of the station before continuing their journey northwards. With its 13 platforms and

BELOW: Featured on this North Eastern Railway's poster from the early 1920s, the Royal Border Bridge at Berwick-upon-Tweed is one of the most iconic structures on the East Coast Main Line.

OVERLEAF: Poster produced for the North Eastern Railway in the early 1920s promoting circular tours on the most scenic sections of the railway.

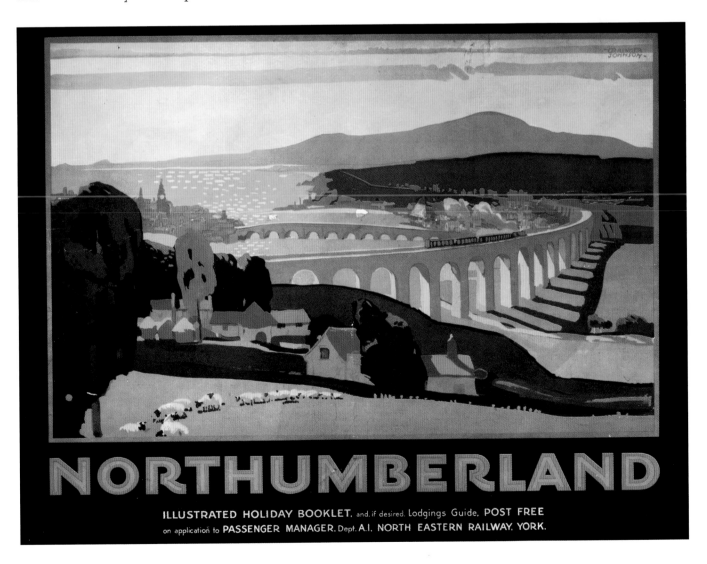

NORTHUMBERLAND

ILLUSTRATED HOLIDAY BOOKLET. and, if desired. Lodgings Guide. POST FREE
on application to PASSENGER MANAGER. Dept. A.I. NORTH EASTERN RAILWAY. YORK.

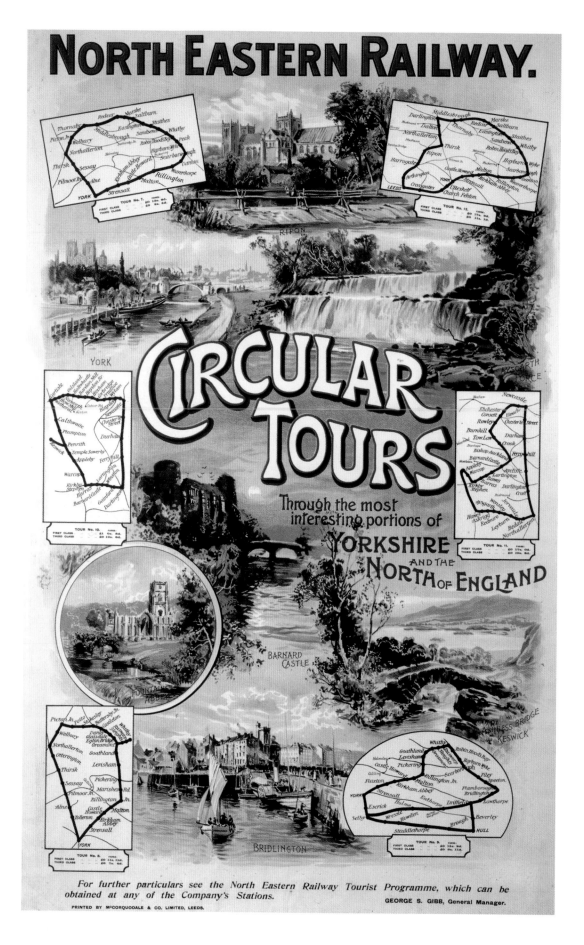

Electrification

By the end of the 19th century it had become rather fashionable for Newcastle businessmen to commute to work from their elegant homes on the coast. Resorts such as Whitley Bay and Tynemouth were within easy reach of the city centre along the existing steam-operated network but by 1903 competition from new electric street trams had seen railway passenger numbers enter a steep decline. Faced with this loss of income the NER took the bold decision to fight back by electrifying a near-circular route out from Newcastle Central via the coastal towns of Tynemouth, Whitley Bay and Monkseaton to the former Blythe & Tyne Railway's terminus at Bridge Street. The railway was electrified with a third rail at 600 V DC and new electric multiple units, built at the NER's workshops in York, began operating services on 29 March 1904. The electrified lines remained in operation until the 1960s when the by then archaic system was replaced by diesel multiple units. Using overhead current collection the Tyne & Wear Metro opened in 1980 along the same routes. Vincent Raven (the NER's innovative Chief Mechanical Engineer from 1910 to 1922) had completed the electrification of the coal-carrying line between Newport and Shildon in 1916 and had also advocated the electrification of the York to Newcastle mainline – a prototype mainline electric locomotive had been built at Darlington in 1922, but the scheme was shelved by the new LNER the following year.

overall curving arched roof, the present station at York was opened by the NER in 1877 and, at the time, was the largest in the world.

From its inception the NER had set up its headquarters at Gateshead in Newcastle where the company established its own locomotive, carriage and wagon works. Under successive locomotive superintendents – chiefly Edward Fletcher and Wilson Wordsell – the works turned out many classic steam locomotive types and in 1904 introduced the ground-breaking electrified North Tyneside suburban railway (see below). Wordsell was replaced by Vincent Raven in 1910 by which time locomotive construction had been transferred to Darlington. The highlights of Raven's reign at Darlington were his Class 'Z' 'Atlantic' 4-4-2 and 'Pacific' 4-6-2 locomotives – a forerunner of the famous LNER Class 'A1', two of the latter were built by the NER in 1922. Raven's Class 'Q6' freight locomotives remained active until the end of steam haulage in the northeast in 1967. Gateshead Works closed completely in 1932.

Until 1923 the company had a total monopoly on the railway routes serving the collieries, iron ore mines and iron and steel-making regions of Northumberland, County Durham and Yorkshire – in its heyday before the First World War the NER carried a larger tonnage of coal and mineral traffic than any other railway in Britain. Its major dock installations at Tyne Dock, Hartlepool, Middlesbrough and Hull handled vast amounts of goods ranging from coal, iron and steel exports and grain, timber and fruit imports. The company also operated its own fleet of steamships for the North Sea trade with Scandinavia and northern Europe. It was also responsible for operating the Anglo-Scottish expresses on the East Coast Main Line (see pages 14–15) between Doncaster and Berwick-upon-Tweed using East Coast Joint Stock that was jointly owned with the North British Railway and the Great Northern Railway.

ABOVE: *The North Eastern Railway was at the forefront of mainline electrification. Here Bo-Bo electric locomotive No 8 is seen on trial with a dynamometer car and long coal train at Newport, 12 October 1921.*

North London Railway

The North London Railway (NLR) operated a network of commuter lines in north London stretching from Poplar and East and West India Docks in the east to Richmond and Kew Bridge in the west. The section of line from Willesden Junction to Richmond via Camden Town and Hampstead Road was owned jointly with the Midland Railway and London & North Western Railway (LNWR). The NLR's terminus was at Broad Street (convenient for the City of London), reached by a line from Dalston Junction and Shoreditch, which had opened in 1865 and was extended in 1891 and 1913. It suffered damage during a Zeppelin bombing raid in 1915 and also extensive damage during the Blitz in the Second World War after which it was not fully repaired. In 1986 it became a victim of Dr Beeching's 'axe', one of only two of London's termini to close in the 20th century. It has since been demolished.

The railway's main workshop was at Bow in east London. Here a series of 4-4-0Ts were built between 1863 and 1876, all designed by the locomotive superintendent William Adams who went on to work for the London & South Western Railway (see page 39) until 1895.

The LNWR took over the working of the NLR in 1909, electrifying the Broad Street to Kew Bridge section in 1916, before finally absorbing it in 1922. Today, the main west-to-east route of the NLR forms part of London Overground's North London Line while other sections to the east are used by the Docklands Light Railway and the East London Line.

RIGHT: *Early 20th century NLR poster promoting the company's 'open air route' from Broad Street to Hampstead.*

BELOW: *Seen here at Bow in the early 20th century, NLR 4-4-0T No 31 hauls a passenger train bound for Broad Street.*

North Staffordshire Railway

Nicknamed 'The Knotty' (the company's coat of arms featured a knot), the North Staffordshire Railway (NSR) operated a network of routes centred on Stoke-on-Trent, ranging from Crewe and Market Drayton in the west to Burton-on-Trent in the east and from Colwich in the south to Macclesfield in the north. By 1913 the company had a route mileage of 216 miles serving the industrialized Potteries and surrounding district. While freight traffic was the lifeblood of the railway – mostly coal and the vast output of china and pottery goods produced in the area – the NSR also heavily promoted the scenic quality of its routes, especially the line between North Rode and Uttoxeter via Rudyard along the beautiful Churnet Valley which they named 'Staffordshire's Little Switzerland'. Along this route the railway opened a hotel at Rudyard Lake (also NSR-owned) and successfully developed the surrounding area, attracting up to 20,000 on peak weekends and bank holidays in the summer – all carried there by its trains.

Built under a Light Railway Order, the Leek & Manifold Valley Light Railway was worked by the NSR from opening in 1904. This 8-mile 2-ft-6-in.-gauge line once ran along the pretty Manifold Valley in Staffordshire. Depending more or less entirely on summer daytrippers and milk traffic for its livelihood the Leek & Manifold made a connection with the NSR's standard gauge terminus at Waterhouses. The railway

became part of the newly-formed London Midland & Scottish Railway (LMS) in 1923 but with ever-increasing competition from road transport it closed in 1934. The LMS donated the trackbed to Staffordshire County Council and it was reopened as a footpath and bridleway in 1937. Now known as the Manifold Way it is today a popular destination for walkers and cyclists.

With its network of 220 route miles, the NSR became a constituent company of the London Midland & Scottish Railway in the 'Big Four Grouping' of 1923. Closed to passengers in 1965, a section of the Churnet Valley line has since reopened as a heritage railway known as the Churnet Valley Railway while a section of the railway trackbed at Rudyard Lake is now used by a miniature railway.

RIGHT: *Early 20th century poster promoting the North Staffordshire Railway-owned Rudyard Lake and its nearby amenities.*

BELOW: *Resplendent in its crimson livery, a NSR train is seen entering Stone Junction station in 1915.*

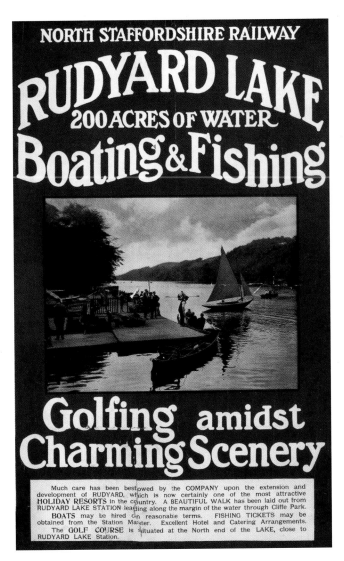

Somerset & Dorset Joint Railway

With a 114-mile network stretching from Bournemouth to Bath along with branches from Evercreech Junction to Burnham-on-Sea, Edington Junction to Bridgwater and Glastonbury to Wells, the Somerset & Dorset Joint Railway (S&DJR) was Britain's third-longest joint railway. Formerly the Somerset & Dorset Railway, it had been jointly owned by the Midland Railway and the London & South Western Railway (LSWR) since 1876 – the building of the Bath Extension over the Mendip Hills in the years immediately before had virtually bankrupted the original company, hence the joint takeover.

The Bath Extension allowed through trains to travel over the London & North Western Railway and Midland Railway between the North of England and the Midlands and Bournemouth but working trains over the steeply-graded, single-track railway was, to say the least, a major problem. In an effort to remedy this many sections of the railway had been doubled, including the widening of many viaducts, by 1905. Despite these improvements there were still several pinch-points, the worst one being the 4½ miles of single-track line through the smoky confines of Devonshire and Combe Down tunnels between Bath and Midford. At Templecombe, an important interchange point where the S&DJR met the LSWR mainline, trains were forced to reverse out of or into the station, a time-consuming

business that lasted right through to the closure of the route in 1966.

The forerunner of what later became known as the 'Pines Express' (see pages 83 and 195–196), a Manchester to Bournemouth restaurant car train, first started running on weekdays throughout the year from 1 October 1910. It ceased running during the First World War but was reinstated after the War and by 1922 the train included through coaches from Bournemouth West and Swanage to Liverpool Lime Street and Manchester London Road, the 248½-mile journey from Bournemouth to Manchester taking 6 hrs 25 min. This train continued to be operated by the London Midland & Scottish Railway and the Southern Railway from 1923. In addition to these north–south mainline trains, the S&DJR also operated excursion trains along its branch to the seaside resort of Burnham-on-Sea, a practice that continued long after the official passenger closure of the line from Highbridge in 1951.

In the 'Big Four Grouping' of 1 January 1923 the S&DJR came under the joint ownership of the newly-

RIGHT: S&DJR 4-4-0 No 15 heads a passenger train along the mainline near Blandford Forum in the early 20th century.

BELOW: Seen here in the early 1920s, Glastonbury & Street station was once served by trains from Wells, Burnham-on-Sea and Evercreech Junction.

formed London Midland & Scottish Railway and the Southern Railway. During the summer months in the 1930s the mainline was particularly busy with up to 12 long distance holiday trains making the journey between Bath and Bournemouth on Saturdays in addition to the local passenger services – the holiday trains did not stop at Templecombe, usually officially running non-stop between Bath and Poole although unofficially they stopped at Evercreech Junction to either divest themselves of or add a pilot engine after or before the arduous journey over the Mendips.

On Nationalization of the railways in 1948 the S&DJR (or the 'Slow & Dirty') came under the management of the newly-formed Southern Region of British Railways. The Wells branch closed in 1951 and the Bridgwater branch in 1952. Then in 1958 the route north of Templecombe was transferred to the Western Region. The rot then set in, the working of through trains over the route ceased in September 1962 followed by closure of the entire S&DJR on 7 March 1966.

I was lucky enough to live in Gloucester in my childhood and, as my father did not own a car, we always travelled by train for our annual summer holidays. I must have travelled over the S&DJR many times but those journeys recorded in my trainspotting notebooks cover the period 1961 to 1965. On 19 August 1961 we travelled down to Swanage via the S&DJR at a time when through trains to and from the North of England still used this route. My notebook records 53 steam locomotives spotted during the whole trip including six ex-LMS Fowler Class 2P 4-4-0s and two ex-S&D Class 7F 2-8-0s on the S&DJR section. The final leg of the trip from Poole to Swanage was behind Class M7 0-4-4T 30110.

My second trip was on 3 August 1963 and this time we travelled down to Lyme Regis over the S&DJR route as far as Templecombe. The train engine from Bath Green Park to Templecombe was BR Standard Class 5 No 73054 and this time I spotted 15 steam locomotives on this stretch

of the journey including two ex-S&D Class 7F 2-8-0s. My last trip over the S&DJR was on 6 September 1965 in the company of my friend Peter Hughes when closure of this route was looming. The train engine from Bath to Templecombe was BR Standard Class 5 No 73068 and en route I spotted 48760 and 47506 at Norton Hill Colliery, 80037 at Shepton Mallet and 80041 at Evercreech Junction. There were nine steam locomotives on shed at Templecombe (82G) and we then travelled back to Evercreech Junction behind 80138. Here we changed trains and then travelled to Highbridge in a one-coach train hauled by 41249 (the only other passenger was a vicar), before returning to Evercreech Junction behind 41216. The journey back to Bath was behind 80041 and we found time to visit Green Park shed (82F) where I spotted 15 steam locomotives of which three Ivatt Class 2 2-6-2Ts were stored out of use. This steam heaven ended just six months later!

South Eastern & Chatham Railway

The South Eastern & Chatham Railway (SE&CR) was formed in 1899 by the loose amalgamation of two competing railway companies that operated in southeast England – the South Eastern Railway (SER) and the London, Chatham & Dover Railway (LC&DR).

The latter half of the 19th century had brought mixed fortunes for the SER with a combination of poor management and cut-throat competition from not only its rival near-bankrupt northern neighbour, the LC&DR, but also from the London, Brighton & South Coast Railway to its west.

Despite its poor record for punctuality and passenger comfort, the LC&DR had a more redeemable quality as being one of the safest railways in Britain, being an early user of the Westinghouse air brake system and fail-safe signalling. However the banking collapse of 1867 coupled with shady financial dealings between the railway and its contractors, Peto & Betts, led to its downfall with the company becoming bankrupt in 1867. Although refinanced the LC&DR continued to struggle on through the rest of the 19th century as many of its routes were destinations also served by its rival, the SER.

The marriage of the two rivals in 1899 was not a complete amalgamation as each company still retained its own board of directors and both companies remained in existence until the 'Big Four Grouping' of 1923. With the competition eliminated the new SE&CR thrived and with the exception of the independent Kent & East Sussex Railway and East Kent Light Railway it not only controlled the entire rail network in Kent and the important continental traffic via the cross-Channel ports but also the Hastings mainline in east Sussex and the important west–east cross-country route across Surrey and Kent between Reading, Redhill and Tonbridge. In London its termini were at Cannon Street, Charing Cross, Ludgate Hill, Holborn Viaduct and Victoria – it shared the latter station with the London, Brighton & South Coast Railway. Until 1916 Holborn Viaduct was a through station, serving Farringdon and King's Cross via Snow Hill Tunnel – because of its proximity to Holborn Viaduct, Ludgate Hill was finally closed in 1929.

Following the success of its western neighbour, the London, Brighton & South Coast Railway, in operating luxury Pullman trains the former SER had dabbled with its own version of a luxury train. In 1892 it introduced the 'Hastings Car Train' using American-built luxury coaches but the train was not a success and was soon withdrawn. Then, in 1898, it tried again on the same route but this time with improved Pullman-type coaches built in Britain. The train continued to run successfully under new SE&CR management until the outbreak of the First World War in 1914, when it was withdrawn. But the SE&CR did not give up and after the war a new luxury Pullman train between Victoria and Kent was introduced in 1921. Known as the 'Thanet Belle', the train ran non-stop between London and Margate, ending or starting its journey at Ramsgate Harbour. The train continued to be operated by the Southern Railway from 1923 (see page 123).

Locomotive building for the new company was concentrated at the SER's Ashford Works, after the LC&DR's works at Longhedge, Battersea, closed in 1911. Locomotive Superintendents at Ashford were Harry Wainwright (1899–1913) and Richard Maunsell (1913–22) – Maunsell went on to become the Chief Mechanical Engineer for the newly-formed Southern Railway (see page 110) from 1923 to 1937.

The SE&CR had a complete monopoly of railway services to the Channel ports and it operated its own fleet of steamers that served destinations in Northern France and Belgium. A total of 11 cross-channel ships were built for the company between 1899 and 1914 but by then the clouds of war were looming and the company's ships were soon fully occupied with carrying troops to the battle fronts of northern Europe. During the First World War, when the railways of Britain came under Government control, the SE&CR was stretched to the limit, its network providing enormous logistical support to the military by transporting troops and armaments for the battlefront in one direction and returning casualties in the other. By the end of the war the railway network of 638 route miles was worn out and inevitable change was soon on the way in the form of the 'Big Four Grouping' of 1923. On 1 January of that year the SE&CR became one of the three main constituent companies of the newly-formed Southern Railway.

RIGHT: *SE&CR poster of 1905 promoting its luxury Pullman-type 'American Car Trains' between London and Hastings.*

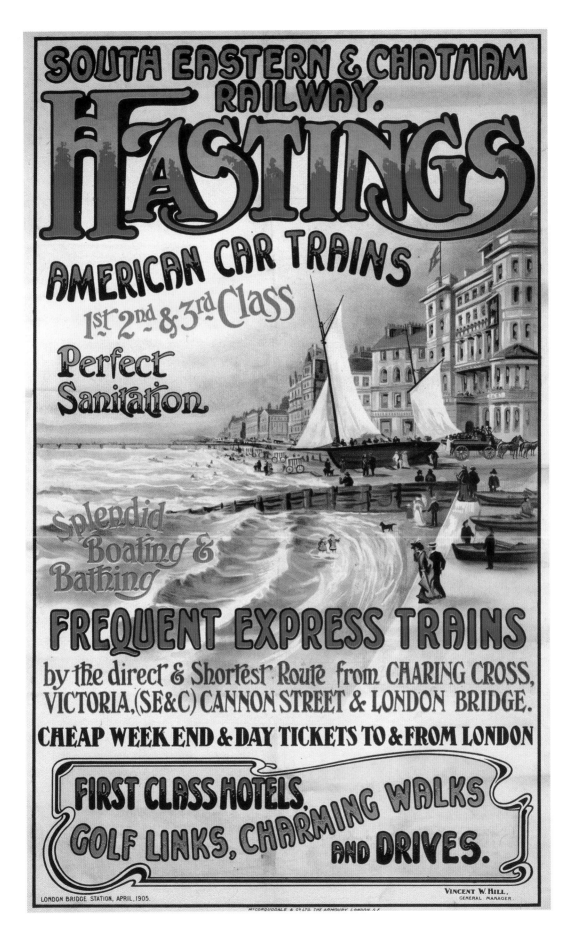

Taff Vale Railway

The Taff Vale Railway (TVR) opened between Cardiff Docks and Merthyr Tydfil in 1841. The 24½-mile single-track route was doubled between 1845 and 1861. The TVR went on to lease two other local railways and in 1889 purchased six more. With the purchase of the Cowbridge & Aberthaw Railway in 1894 and the Aberdare Railway in 1902 the TVR ended up with a route mileage of 124½ serving hundreds of collieries in the Rhondda, Taff and Aberdare Valleys. Although coal was its lifeblood the railway also operated an intensive service of passenger trains between the valleys, Cardiff and the seaside resorts, such as Penarth, along the Welsh side of the Bristol Channel coastline. At summer weekends and bank holidays excursion trains filled to bursting with daytrippers would make the journey down the valleys to the seaside. The company became a constituent of the enlarged GWR in 1923. During its lifetime the TVR became one of the most profitable railway companies in South Wales, rewarding its shareholders each year with handsome dividends. The TVR's mainlines from Cardiff to Pontypridd thence to Treherbert, Aberdare and Merthyr are all still open for business today.

RIGHT: *Featuring the resort of Penarth with pier and steamship* Lorna Doone, *this early 20th century poster was produced for the Taff Vale Railway and Bristol Channel Passenger Service Ltd to promote rail and ferry services to resorts on both sides of the Bristol Channel.*

BELOW: *A 4-4-2T of the Taff Vale Railway impressively decorated to haul the Royal Train in 1888.*

West Coast Route

The West Coast Main Line (WCML) between Euston and Glasgow via Crewe was completed in 1848. The route was operated jointly by the London & North Western Railway (LNWR) between Euston and Carlisle and by the Caledonian Railway (CR) between Carlisle and Glasgow. It was the first Anglo-Scottish railway route to be completed, beating the rival East Coast Main Line (ECML) by two years.

In 1862 the LNWR and the CR introduced joint coaching stock for Anglo-Scottish trains that was built by the former company at Wolverton Works. The coaches were lettered WCJS – West Coast Joint Stock – and by the 1890s included corridor passenger coaches with lavatories, luggage vans, fish vans and Travelling Post Offices.

One of the most famous long-distance expresses in the world, the 'Royal Scot' was first introduced by the LNWR and the CR in 1862. Departing at 10 a.m. from Euston the train travelled the length of the WCML to Glasgow, a distance of 401¼ miles. By the early 20th century it was being hauled between Euston and Carlisle by one of the L&NWR's crack express

locomotives such as the 4-4-0 'Precursor' or the later 4-6-0 'Claughton'. The train required banking assistance on the climb to Shap before arriving at Carlisle where a Caledonian Railway locomotive, such as a 4-6-0 'Cardean', took over for the journey to Glasgow Central. Banking assistance was also needed for the train over Beattock Summit. This famous train continued to be operated by the London Midland & Scottish Railway from 1923 (see page 85).

The early afternoon departures from Glasgow and Euston along the WCML had long been known unofficially as 'The Corridor' – the train was so nicknamed as it was one of the first Anglo-Scottish expresses on the WCML operated by the LNWR and the CR to use luxurious 12-wheeled corridor coaches, introduced in 1908. The train also carried through coaches for Aberdeen and

Edinburgh which were attached or detached at Law Junction and Symington respectively. The train must have made a fine sight with its chocolate and cream coaches and the pale blue livery of the 'Caley' locomotive. The train continued to be operated by the London Midland & Scottish Railway from 1923 (see 'Mid-Day Scot', page 81).

The CR first introduced a sleeping carriage in October 1873 on a limited stop mail train that operated three days a week between Glasgow and Euston. The ancestry of the true Anglo-Scottish sleeping car train goes back to the famous Railway Races to the North of 1897 (see page 15) when the two rival West Coast and East Coast railway companies competed for the fastest journey time between London and Aberdeen – the latter trains were lightly loaded and built for speed. But these high-speed and potentially dangerous races were soon curtailed and speed restrictions were placed on all daytime WCML and ECML expresses, a situation that lasted until 1932. However, the speed restrictions did not apply to night-time services and by the turn of the century the unofficially named 'Night Limited' sleeping car train, with a 11.50 p.m. departure from Euston, was reaching Glasgow Central in 8 hours.

Its success was such that the train grew longer, hence heavier and slower. In the years leading up to the First World War travellers on the down service were compensated for the slower journey as a restaurant car was attached at Carlisle, enabling them to enjoy breakfast before their arrival at Glasgow Central. The train continued to be operated by the London Midland & Scottish Railway from 1923 (see 'Night Scot', page 82).

Another important service on the WCML was the unofficially named 'West Coast Postal' between Euston and Aberdeen which started life in 1885. Officially named the 'North Western T.P.O. Down' and the 'North Western T.P.O. Up', the train carried mail sorting coaches fitted with exchange apparatus and parcels vans along the 540-mile route in the dead of night. The down train left Euston at 8.30 p.m. and, after stops at Rugby, Tamworth, Crewe, Preston, Carlisle, Carstairs, Stirling and Perth, arrived at Aberdeen at 7.35 a.m. the next day. The short black and white film, *Night Mail* (1936), featured the Euston to Glasgow mail train hauled by 'Royal Scot' Class 4-6-0 No 6115 *Scots Guardsman*. The verse commentary was written by W. H. Auden with music composed by Benjamin Britten – over 80 years later it is still considered a masterpiece.

In this specially posed photograph, LNWR Class 'N19' 2-4-2 No 2054 Queen Empress heads a London to Glasgow express of West Coast Joint Stock at Whitmore, 24 June 1895.

1923 to 1947
THE 'BIG FOUR'

Government control of Britain's railways during the First World War continued for nearly three more years after the end of the conflict. The war had brought Britain's 120 railway companies to their knees, they were in a bad shape both financially and physically. There was also a duplication of routes with many railway companies competing directly with each other, losses were mounting and the coalition government under the premiership of David Lloyd George wanted to introduce a more efficient and economical working of Britain's railway system. Some voices in Parliament, many of them members of the fledgling Labour Party, called for Nationalization and worker participation but this was rejected in favour of what became known as the 'Big Four Grouping'. Receiving Royal Assent on 19 August 1921 the 1921 Railways Act grouped the 120 railway companies into four larger regional companies, taking effect from 1 January 1923. The only exception being London's railways, the amalgamation of which which was delayed until the 1933 London Passenger Transport Act.

The 'Big Four' railway companies

Great Western Railway (GWR)
London Midland & Scottish Railway (LMS)
London & North Eastern Railway (LNER)
Southern Railway (SR)

Some railways were excluded from the grouping including 15 narrow-gauge railways and 18 standard-gauge light railways, many of which were managed by Colonel H. F. Stephens from his modest office in Tonbridge.

The 'Big Four' inherited and further developed a network of feeder bus services but by the late 1920s the legality of these was in some doubt and the railway companies were forced to sell off their majority holdings in companies such as Crosville and the Bristol Tramways & Carriage Company. However, they did continue with their minority shareholdings in over 30 bus and coach companies.

The 'Big Four' also inherited the multitude of shipping services operated previously by many of the constituent companies and also pursued other transport interests by forming airlines – the LMS, SR and GWR formed Railway Air Services (the predecessor to British European Airways) while the SR and GWR owned Channel Island Airways. Even the Thomas Cook travel company was sold to the 'Big Four'.

From 1923 to the outbreak of the Second World War the 'Big Four' made enormous strides in railway technology, culminating in the high-speed steam trains of the 1930s. All this sadly came to an abrupt end on 30 August 1939, two days before the outbreak of war, when the Government-controlled Railway Executive Committee (REC) once again took over control of Britain's railways. The war left a terrible legacy for the railways, their rundown state and lack of investment meant that the REC remained in control until Nationalization on 1 January 1948 (see pages 124–125).

LEFT: *Just three months after the birth of the 'Big Four', 4 April 1923, brand new LNER Class A1 4-6-2 No 1473 (later named* Solario) *heads an express bound for King's Cross through Doncaster.*

BELOW: *Poster produced in 1924 by the LMS showing engineers laying track. Original painting by Stanhope Forbes, co-founder of the Newlyn School of Art.*

LMS THE PERMANENT WAY
RELAYING
by Stanhope Forbes R.A.

Great Western Railway

Out of all the 120 companies that made up the 'Big Four' the Great Western Railway (GWR) was the only one to retain its original name in the grouping of 1923. With a total route mileage of 3,566 the newly-enlarged GWR controlled large swathes of South and Mid-Wales, the West Country, the Cotswolds, the Thames Valley and the West Midlands. It had already absorbed 23 other railway companies including the 295¼ route miles of the Cambrian Railways, the 124½ route miles of the Taff Vale Railway, the 63¼ route miles of the Midland & South Western Junction Railway and the 59¾ route miles of the Brecon & Merthyr Railway. The GWR operated 15 joint lines with the London Midland & Scottish Railway, two with the Southern Railway and one with the London & North Eastern Railway. The company also became the owner of three narrow-gauge lines in Wales: the Corris Railway, the Vale of Rheidol Railway and the Welshpool & Llanfair Light Railway.

The GWR's terminus in London was at Paddington station which was considerably enlarged during the 1930s and from where express trains started their journeys to the far-flung corners of the company's network – Weymouth, Bristol, Barnstaple, Exeter, Plymouth and Penzance; Cardiff, Swansea and Fishguard; Birmingham, Birkenhead and Aberystwyth. Slip coaches were added to the formation of many of these trains, thus allowing passengers to reach intermediate stations while the train continued on its

journey without stopping. To haul the company's express trains the GWR built the highly-successful 'Castle' Class 4-6-0s (introduced in 1923), and the more powerful 'King' Class 4-6-0s (introduced in 1927) at Swindon Works, all designed by Charles Collett, the company's Chief Mechanical Engineer. After the war 30 of Frederick Hawksworth's 'County' Class 4-6-0s were built at Swindon along with the versatile 'Modified Hall' Class 4-6-0s.

In addition to the GWR's daytime services the company also operated sleeping cars in its overnight trains between Paddington and Plymouth, Penzance, Carmarthen, Fishguard and Birkenhead and between Plymouth and Manchester. Initially these were for 1st Class passengers but in 1928 sleeping cars were introduced for the use of 3rd Class customers. Boat trains were also operated between London and Weymouth (for the Channel Islands), Plymouth Millbay Docks (for trans-Atlantic liners) and Fishguard (for Rosslare in the Irish Republic).

Strangely, Pullman car trains were a very rare sight on the Great Western Railway although one all-Pullman train, the short-lived 'Torquay Pullman', was operated by the company from July 1929 to September 1930. Pullman cars were also introduced on 'Ocean Liner Expresses' in May 1929 – these trains connected with trans-Atlantic liners that called into Plymouth on their journey to

Southampton, thus getting their passengers into London 4 hours earlier. These trains ran as required between Plymouth Millbay Docks and Paddington with the Pullman cars being included in the train's make-up for 1st Class passengers. This, too, was discontinued in September 1930 and the GWR ended its short-lived love affair with Pullman cars, instead building its own luxurious 'Ocean Saloon' carriages, which were introduced in 1931. These paved the way for new luxury 'Centenary' coaches which were built at Swindon for the 'Cornish Riviera Express' and introduced in 1935.

A scheduled car-carrying service was introduced in 1924 by the GWR between Severn Tunnel Junction and Pilning High Level as an alternative to the erratic Aust Ferry across the River Severn. Passengers were conveyed in separate carriages while the cars travelled on open bogie trucks attached to the rear. Cars were usually filthy at the end of their journey despite being covered by a tarpaulin while being conveyed through the dripping tunnel by a steam engine!

The GWR also excelled in publicity, extensively promoting the places served by the railway. During the 1920s and '30s the company's publicity department employed some of the finest illustrators and designers of the period to produce artwork for its posters. They also published numerous books about the railway, for 'Boys of all Ages', rambling guides and jigsaws – altogether one million of these had been made by Chad Valley of Birmingham by 1939. Introduced in 1906, the company's *Holiday Haunts* was an annual guide to holiday resorts served by the railway which included lists of hotels and boarding establishments, selling 200,000 copies each year.

LEFT: *Poster featuring a 'King' Class 4-6-0 produced for the GWR in 1939 promoting the company's speedy services to the West of England. Original artwork by Charles Mayo.*

BELOW: *In this 1930s' photograph a 'King' Class 4-6-0 hauling a Taunton to Paddington express overtakes 'Castle' Class 4-6-0 No 4083 Abbotsbury Castle on the slow line near Reading.*

The Bristolian

Paddington to Bristol

'The Bristolian' express was introduced in 1935 to mark the centenary of the GWR. Travelling non-stop between Paddington and Bristol the lightweight train of only seven carriages including a buffet car was initially hauled by 'King' Class 4-6-0s and was timed to take 1 hr 45 min for the outward journey of 118¼ miles via Bath and for the return journey of 117½ miles via the Badminton cut-off. A few months after its introduction the 'Kings' were replaced by 'Castle' Class 4-6-0 locomotives. Before the Second World War, when the train was temporarily suspended, the down 'The Bristolian' left Paddington at 10 a.m. and the up train left Bristol at 4.30 p.m. It was reinstated by the Western Region of British Railways in 1954 (see page 239).

Cambrian Coast Express

Paddington to Aberystwyth/Pwllheli

With major improvements to the route between Paddington and Birmingham (shortening the distance by 19¼ miles) completed in 1910, a new weekday restaurant car express between Paddington and West Wales via Birmingham had been introduced by the Great Western Railway in 1921, two years before the company had taken control of the Cambrian Railways. With portions for Aberystwyth and Pwllheli that were attached or detached at Machynlleth, the train was officially named the 'Cambrian Coast Express' in 1927. Initially the train ran only on summer Fridays and Saturdays with a departure from Paddington at 10.10 a.m. and a fast run to Birmingham Snow Hill broken by a stop at Leamington. Motive power between Paddington and Wolverhampton Low Level was normally provided by a 'Castle' Class loco. At Wolverhampton the 'Castle' was taken off to be replaced by a couple of outside-frame 'Duke' Class 4-4-0s for the run to Welshpool and beyond via the Abbey Foregate avoiding line at Shrewsbury – from 1938 the new 'Manor' Class 4-6-0s started to take over this leg of the journey. The 'Cambrian Coast Express' was withdrawn on the outbreak of the Second World War and reinstated by the Western Region of British Railways in 1951 (see pages 240–241).

Channel Islands Boat Train

Paddington to Weymouth Quay

The 'Channel Islands Boat Train' between Paddington and Weymouth Quay had been operated by the GWR since the early 20th century (see page 28). A similar service was also operated by the Southern Railway on alternate days between Waterloo and Southampton Docks (see page 116).

GWR-owned ferries carried passengers between Weymouth and the Channel Islands and by the 1930s, with rail traffic increasing to Weymouth Quay, the company added more passing loops and sidings to the street tramway which served the station. In 1933 the station was enlarged with a second platform and track added to accommodate extra trains. The 'Channel Islands Boat Train' was suspended on the outbreak of the Second World War and not restored until 1946. The train continued to be operated by the newly-formed Western Region of British Railways from 1948 to 1960 (see page 245).

Cheltenham Flyer

Paddington to Gloucester Central and Cheltenham Spa St James'

During the 1920s and 1930s there was fierce rivalry not only between the British 'Big Four' railway companies but also among railways throughout the world to lay claim that they ran the fastest scheduled passenger service in the world. For many years the GWR had run an afternoon express service between Cheltenham Spa and Paddington but the introduction of Collett's 'Castle' Class 4-6-0s in 1923 led to a rapid acceleration of these trains, one of which was named the 'Cheltenham Spa Express' – it soon earned the nickname the 'Cheltenham Flyer'. Timings were increasingly accelerated until 1929 when the 77¼ miles between Swindon and Paddington was scheduled to take only 70 minutes at an average speed of 66.2 mph. In 1931 the timing for Swindon to Paddington was further accelerated to an average speed of 69.2 mph but by now the tantalising 70 mph average speed was within the GWR's grasp.

On 6 June 1932 Driver Ruddock and Fireman Thorp of Old Oak Common shed handed the GWR publicity department a glittering prize when they shattered all previous timings and broke all railway speed records.

ABOVE: *Luggage label used by lucky passengers on the 'Cheltenham Flyer'.*

BELOW: *This official GWR print of 1934 shows 'Castle' Class 4-6-0 No 5000* Launceston Castle *hauling the 'Cheltenham Flyer' over the River Thames at Maidenhead.*

Headed by No 5006 *Tregenna Castle*, the 'Cheltenham Flyer' left the town of its name promptly at 2.30 p.m. and after a leisurely journey through the Cotswolds reached Swindon for its final stop before Paddington. At 3.48 p.m. *Tregenna Castle* and its six coaches left Swindon and then the fireworks started – the train accelerating continuously until Didcot (24.2 miles from Swindon) was passed in 18 min 55 sec at a speed of over 90 mph. This high speed was maintained for mile after mile and despite a slight slowing past Twyford the train was still travelling at 84.4 mph just two miles short of Paddington which was reached in 56 min 47 sec from Swindon at an average speed of 81.6 mph. Three months later the 'Cheltenham Flyer' was accelerated again and was rescheduled to take only 65 minutes between Swindon and Paddington at an average speed of

71.3 mph – it was now officially the fastest scheduled train service in the world. Within a few years the GWR had lost this title to high-speed diesel trains in the USA and Germany and the world-beating service for the gentry of Cheltenham Spa was soon consigned to the history books. Although this world-famous train was withdrawn on the outbreak of war in 1939, never to return to its exciting high-speed schedule, the 'Cheltenham Spa Express' was reintroduced by the Western Region of British Railway in 1956 (see pages 246–247).

An unidentified GWR 'Castle' Class 4-6-0 approaches Paddington station with the up 'Cheltenham Flyer', c.1934. With a start-to-stop speed between Swindon and Paddington booked at 71.3 mph, the 'Flyer' could rightfully claim to being the 'World's Fastest Train' – a claim proudly carried by the train's headboard.

Cornish Riviera Limited

Paddington to Penzance

ntroduced by the Great Western Railway in 1904, the 'Cornish Riviera Limited' was suspended during the First World War before being reinstated in 1919. In 1923 the introduction of new carriages and the 'Castle' Class 4-6-0 locomotives brought a much-needed improvement to service. Then in 1927 the introduction of the more powerful 'King' Class 4-6-0 locos allowed even heavier trains to reach Plymouth in 4 hours and two years later through coaches were added for Falmouth and St Ives. New track layouts bypassing Westbury and Frome, which opened in 1933, further reduced travelling time to and from the West Country.

In 1935 new luxury 'Centenary' carriages were introduced and the regular 10.30 a.m. departure from Paddington carried reserved seat passengers only and ran (officially) non-stop to Truro – in fact a stop was made at Newton Abbot for a pilot engine to be attached and the train then halted at Devonport to change engines, the 'King' being too heavy to cross the Royal Albert Bridge. On summer Saturdays such was the demand for the train that it ran 'non-stop' to St Erth

ABOVE: *The stylish luggage label used by passengers on the 'Cornish Riviera Express'.*

BELOW: *This early 1920s postcard depicts the 'Cornish Riviera Express' at speed behind new 'Castle' Class 4-6-0 No 4073 Caerphilly Castle. This milestone locomotive was designed by Charles Collett and built at Swindon Works in 1923. Withdrawn from service in 1960, it has since been preserved.*

with passengers for Falmouth and Helston being conveyed in a relief express.

By 1939 the 'Limited' normally consisted of eight portions: the main portion with restaurant car for Penzance, one through coach each for St Ives, Falmouth, Newquay, Kingsbridge, the Taunton slip with coaches for Ilfracombe and Minehead and two Weymouth coaches slipped at Westbury. By then a stop at Exeter was being made in place of a previous slip coach. Slipping coaches was a practice much favoured by the GWR – slip coaches were detached from the train while at speed and brought to a stop by an onboard brakeman. The consequence of shedding coaches en route was that when the time came to tackle the steep gradients of South Devon the train weighed much less. The train continued to run, combined for a short time with the 'Torbay Express' (see page 72)

during the Second World War but via Bristol and with consequently slower timings. The pre-war schedules were only regained in 1955 by the Western Region of British Railways (see pages 248–249).

RIGHT: *The GWR's Holiday Haunts guide of 1947. Very fetching cover artwork by Frank Soar.*

BOTTOM RIGHT: *'King' Class 4-6-0 No 6025* King Henry III *heads a 'Holiday Haunts Express' to the West Country in 1938.*

BELOW: *GWR poster of 1928 promoting* The Cornish Riviera *and a new illustrated book of the same name by celebrated travel writer S. P. B. Mais. Original artwork by L. Burleigh Bruhl.*

Holiday Haunts Express

From 1906 until the outbreak of the Second World War, the Great Western Railway published *Holiday Haunts*, an annual guide to holiday resorts served by the railway which included lists of hotels and boarding establishments. The guide, costing 6d (2½p), was almost 700 pages long and over 200,000 copies were printed each year. To help popularize and give people an opportunity to inspect prospective 'digs', special trains were operated in the 1930s at cheap fares on Sundays during the spring. These trains were appropriately named the 'Holiday Haunts Express' and ran from principal towns and cities on the GWR network to such destinations as Penzance, Minehead, Weymouth, Paignton and Newquay. Fares ranged between 5s (25p) and 10s (50p) and sufficient time was allowed at the destination for passengers to book rooms for a holiday stay later in the year. The train was suspended during the Second World War, but the *Holiday Haunts* series of guides continued to be published by the GWR after the war and British Railways from 1948 until the early 1960s.

Torbay Express

Paddington to Kingswear

Although an express had been run by the Great Western Railway between Paddington and Torbay for many years before the First World War it was only officially named 'The Torbay Express' in 1923. As was common with GWR practice the train carried coaches which were slipped at Taunton for onward conveyance to Ilfracombe – in the summer months this four-coach portion had the distinction of including a restaurant car. With 'King' or 'Castle' 4-6-0s in charge the train was achieving mile-a-minute status between Paddington and Exeter by the late 1930s. The Old Oak Common locomotive would begin or end its journey on the heavily graded single-track section between Goodrington Sands to Kingswear (now the Paignton & Dartmouth Steam Railway) – set alongside the picturesque River Dart the latter station possessed a turntable large enough to take the 'King' Class.

The train continued to operate during the Second World War, initially combined with the 'Cornish Riviera Express' via Bristol but this proved too heavy and the train soon resumed its previous separate but much slower identity. Normal running returned after the war but the pre-war schedules were not achieved until the 1950s by which time it was being operated by the Western Region of British Railways (see pages 266–267).

BELOW: *Hand-coloured GWR poster of the 1920s promoting South Devon and the company's 'Torbay Express', which is seen here travelling at speed behind a 'King' Class 4-6-0 along the scenic coastal stretch between Dawlish and Teignmouth.*

GREAT WESTERN RAILWAY

THE TORBAY EXPRESS

GLORIOUS SOUTH DEVON

London Midland & Scottish Railway

With a network of 7,331 route miles the London Midland & Scottish Railway (LMS) was by far the largest of the 'Big Four'. It controlled the West Coast Main Line between Euston and Glasgow and routes in North Wales, the Midlands, the North West of England and large swathes of Scotland extending up to Inverness, Thurso and Wick. In England and Wales the LMS was formed by the amalgamation of the London & North Western Railway (including the Lancashire & Yorkshire Railway), the Midland Railway (including the Northern Counties Committee and the Dundalk, Newry & Greenore Railway in Northern Ireland and the London, Tilbury & Southend Railway), the North Staffordshire Railway and the Furness Railway. Scottish railway companies that became part of the LMS were the Caledonian Railway, the Highland Railway and the Glasgow & South Western Railway. The LMS also operated 21 joint lines (total mileage 585) of which the largest were the Midland & Great Northern Joint Railway in Norfolk and the Somerset & Dorset Joint Railway. It also became the owner of the narrow-gauge Leek & Manifold Valley Light Railway.

Principal London termini were at Euston and St Pancras but the LMS also owned Broad Street station and shared Fenchurch Street station with the LNER until Nationalization in 1948. The company operated restaurant car services on all its principal routes and sleeping car trains between London and Glasgow, Edinburgh, Oban, Inverness and Aberdeen as well as Holyhead and cities in the north of England. Boat trains were operated between Euston and Holyhead, Liverpool, Fleetwood, Heysham and Stranraer as well as from St Pancras to Tilbury, from Glasgow St Enoch to Greenock Princes Pier and from Inverness to Kyle of Lochalsh.

The company's locomotive works were at Crewe, Derby and Horwich. However Crewe Works, with its own steel-making plant, was by far the most important works and at its peak in the 1930s employed over 20,000 people. To haul their express trains the LMS built 'Royal Scot' Class 4-6-0s (introduced in 1927) and 'Patriot' Class 4-6-0s (introduced in 1930), both designed by the company's Chief Mechanical Engineer, Henry Fowler – the 'Royal Scots' were built at Derby and the North British Locomotive Works in Glasgow, while the 'Patriots' were built at Crewe and Derby. William Stanier became Chief Mechanical Engineer in 1932 and he went on to design 'Princess Royal' 4-6-2s (introduced in 1933), 'Jubilee' Class 4-6-0s (introduced in 1934) and the streamlined 'Coronation' Class 4-6-2s (introduced in 1937) – all built at Crewe. Built as mixed traffic locomotives, Stanier's Class 5 4-6-0s, introduced in 1934, were often seen at the head of express trains right across the extensive LMS network – a total 842 of these versatile machines had been built by 1951. Nearly half were built at Crewe, Derby and Horwich while the rest came from the Vulcan Foundry and Armstrong Whitworth.

A visit to Crewe and Crewe Works at the beginning of August 1962 was a highly successful foray. I travelled by train from Gloucester Eastgate to Birmingham New Street and then caught a train to Crewe via Wolverhampton High Level, making the same journey back home at the end of the day. My trainspotting notebook for this trip covers eight pages (three columns per page) and is too extensive to go into much detail here. Highlights of my trip included 10 'Coronation' Class Pacifics, 26 'Jubilee' Class 4-6-0s, 8 'Royal Scot' Class 4-6-0s and 4 BR Standard Class 7 'Britannias'. I also recorded 'Western' Class diesel-hydraulics D1037–D1051 under construction in the works. There were also some vintage service locos at the works, including L&YR 0-6-0ST No 51412 (built 1895) and L&YR 0-6-0s No 52093 (built 1890) and No 52312 (built 1895). LNWR Class G2 0-8-0 No 49395 (built 1904) was also in the works awaiting preservation. It was quite a day!

Blackpool & Fylde Coast Express

Euston to Blackpool Central

Introduced by the LMS after the 'Big Four Grouping', the 'Blackpool & Fylde Coast Express' ran between Blackpool Central and Euston, leaving the former station in the morning and returning from the latter in the late afternoon. With stops at Fylde Coast stations, Preston and Crewe the restaurant car train was normally hauled by a 'Jubilee' or 'Patriot' Class 4-6-0. The down train also conveyed through coaches for Barrow-in-Furness. The train lost its name on the outbreak of war in 1939. Sadly, the Preston & Wyre Joint Railway's line from Kirkham & Wesham to Blackpool Central closed on 2 November 1964.

Bon Accord

Glasgow Buchanan Street to Aberdeen

The 'Bon Accord' was named after the motto of the city of Aberdeen which, in English, translates as 'good agreement'. (Bon Accord was also the name of an unfortunate Aberdeen football team that suffered, in 1885, the worst defeat (36–0) in any British senior football match!) From 1937 the train was one of four named express trains that once ran between Glasgow Buchanan Street and Aberdeen along the former Caledonian Railway's route via Forfar. Of these four the 'Bon Accord' and the 'St Mungo' (see page 86) were timed to cover the 153 miles in 3 hours (Mondays to Fridays only). With a load of only seven coaches and a restaurant car the LMS 'Jubilee' 4-6-0s usually employed put up a spirited performance leaving Glasgow at 10.05 a.m. and running non-stop to Perth. The train then ran non-stop to Stonehaven via Forfar before arriving in Aberdeen at 1.05 p.m. The return run had the same two intermediate stops arriving back in Glasgow at 6.20 p.m. The service was suspended during the Second World War but reinstated by the Scottish Region of British Railways in 1949 (see page 210).

The Comet

Euston to Manchester London Road/Liverpool

'The Comet' restaurant car express between Euston and Manchester London Road was introduced by the London Midland & Scottish Railway in 1932. The up service had an early evening departure from Manchester with one intermediate stop at Stafford. From there to Euston it travelled at just over a mile-a-minute to Euston and was one of the fastest scheduled runs on the LMS. The slower down service left Euston just before mid-day and had intermediate stops at Crewe and Stockport. Both trains were normally hauled by a 'Royal Scot' Class 4-6-0 but strangely only the down train (loading up to 14 coaches) included through coaches for Liverpool, which were detached at Crewe. The train was withdrawn for the duration of the Second World War but was reintroduced by the London Midland Region of British Railways in 1949 (see page 177).

Coronation Scot

Euston to Glasgow Central

Not to be outdone by the LNER's 'Coronation' (see page 91), the London Midland & Scottish Railway introduced its own Anglo-Scottish streamlined train in 1937. Confusingly named the 'Coronation Scot' the train was hauled by streamlined versions of William Stanier's new 'Coronation' Class 4-6-2s. No 6200 *Coronation* briefly held the world speed record for steam traction when it reached 114 mph during a test run south of Crewe on 29 June of that year. Departure for both up and down trains was at 1.30 p.m. and, with one intermediate stop at Carlisle, Euston and Glasgow Central were both reached in 6½ hours with both trains booked to pass each other at Preston. Initially both locomotive and nine coaches were finished in a matching blue with horizontal white lines and a 'speed whisker' at the front. Unlike the LNER's train the 'Coronation Scot' made use of standard coaching stock until more luxurious versions were introduced in 1939. The livery was also changed at the same time with the locos and coaches painted in LMS red and gold lining. This new train was shipped across the Atlantic to appear at the New York World's Fair in April 1939 but got trapped in the USA when the Second World War broke out in September. The loco, No 6220 *Coronation*, was eventually returned to Britain during the war but the set of coaches, used as accommodation for US army officers, remained in the USA until after the war. Following the war the train was not reinstated and Stanier's 'Coronation' Pacifics soon had their streamlined casing removed.

LEFT: *The inaugural 'Blackpool & Fylde Coast Express' departs from Blackpool Central station on its journey to Euston, 9 July 1934. The train is hauled by brand new 'Jubilee' Class 4-6-0 No 5556 (later named* Nova Scotia*).*

BELOW: *Streamlined LMS 'Coronation' Class 4-6-2 No 6222* Queen Mary *picks up water from Dillicar Troughs while hauling the 'Coronation Scot' soon after the train's inauguration in July 1937.*

The Devonian

Bradford Forster Square to Paignton/Kingswear

One of just a small number of named inter-company cross-country trains, 'The Devonian' was first introduced between Bradford and Paignton/Kingswear by the London Midland & Scottish Railway in 1927. During the winter months it was an express between Bradford Forster Square and Bristol where three coaches were then detached and taken forward by a slow GWR stopping train to Paignton. During the summer months the entire train of LMS coaches and restaurant car ran between Bradford and Paignton with a portion of five or so coaches being forwarded to Kingswear. Locomotives were changed at Bristol and such was the demand on summer Saturdays that 'The Devonian' ran as several separate trains. Although discontinued during the Second World War the train was reinstated by the LMS in October 1946 and continued to be operated by the London Midland Region from 1948 (see pages 178–179).

RIGHT: *'The Devonian' with its train of LMS coaches hauled by GWR 'Castle' Class 4-6-0 No 5003* Lulworth Castle *heads along the coastal railway route in South Devon towards its destination of Paignton, 1930s.*

The Grampian

Glasgow Buchanan Street to Aberdeen

Introduced between Glasgow and Aberdeen via Forfar as 'The Grampian Corridor' by the Caledonian Railway (see page 11) in the early 20th century, this service continued to be operated by the newly-formed London Midland & Scottish Railway from 1923 with newer LMS coaching stock and refurbished Pullman cars until the outbreak of the Second World War. This named train was reintroduced by the Scottish Region of British Railways in 1962 (see page 212).

The Granite City

Glasgow Buchanan Street to Aberdeen

First introduced by the Caledonian Railway in 1906 (see page 11), the luxurious 'The Granite City' restaurant car train was reinstated by the London Midland & Scottish Railway in 1933 and the name given to the 10.05 a.m. departure from Glasgow Buchanan Street, returning at 5.35 p.m. from Aberdeen. During the Second World War the train continued to run although the name was quietly dropped. It was reintroduced by the Scottish Region of British Railways in 1949 (see page 213).

The Irish Mail

Euston to Holyhead

Amail train had operated between Euston and Holyhead since 1848 (see page 37) but it was only given the official name of 'The Irish Mail' by the London Midland & Scottish Railway in 1927. At this time both the daytime and night-time services between Euston and Holyhead were amongst the heaviest to be operated on Britain's railways – the introduction of Henry Fowler's 'Royal Scot' Class 4-6-0s in the same year saw these locomotives hauling up to 17 bogie coaches unassisted along the North Wales coastline, the same engine and crew working the train for the entire 263 miles between Euston and Holyhead. Only the daytime service survived for the duration of the Second World War with the night service being reinstated in 1946. At this stage the daytime service became a summer-only working. The train continued to be operated by the London Midland Region of British Railways from 1948 (see pages 181–182).

BELOW: *1930s LMS poster featuring the Britannia Tubular Bridge over the Menai Straits, promoting 'The Irish Mail' between Euston and Holyhead. Original artwork by Norman Wilkinson.*

OVERLEAF: *The 1st Class breakfast and luncheon menu for passengers on 'The Irish Mail', dated 20 January 1934. The conductor in charge was W. M. Dean.*

THE BRITANNIA TUBULAR BRIDGE
MENAI STRAITS
by Norman Wilkinson R.I.

LMS

The train which left Euston on August 1st, 1848, was called The Irish Mail, and has been so named ever since. It started at 8-45 p.m. that night, and that is its time today. But the Britannia Bridge was not yet built and passengers and mail bags had to take coach from Bangor by Telford's Suspension Bridge to Anglesey where another train awaited them.

By June, 1850 the Britannia Bridge was opened to traffic, and today Robert Stephenson's mighty engineering feat stands as a memorial to the consummate skill of the Victorian generation of engineers. Today the Irish Mail provides a day and night service to Ireland, covering the journey between Euston and Kingstown (Dun Laoghaire) in a little over 9 hours.

M'Corquodale & Co., Ltd., London.   E.&.O. 5330/71.

Stay at LMS Hotels

LONDON	...	Midland Grand Hotel
		Euston Hotel
BIRMINGHAM	...	Queen's Hotel
LIVERPOOL	...	Adelphi Hotel
		Exchange Hotel
MANCHESTER	...	Midland Hotel
MORECAMBE	...	Midland Hotel
GLASGOW	...	Central Hotel
		St. Enoch Hotel
EDINBURGH	...	Caledonian Hotel
*GLENEAGLES	...	Gleneagles Hotel
TURNBERRY	...	Turnberry Hotel
STRATFORD-		
ON-AVON		Welcombe Hotel
*STRATHPEFFER		Highland Hotel
†DORNOCH	...	Dornoch Hotel

* Open May to September.
† Open Easter to November.

THE · IRISH · MAIL

menu

breakfast   luncheon

3/6

Tea   Coffee   Cocoa

Malted Milk

•

Grape Fruit
or
Porridge & Cream

Fried Filleted Plaice

Kippered Herring

•

Bacon & Egg

Calf's Liver   Grilled Tomatoes
or
Cold Ham

•

Honey, Jam, Marmalade

FIRST CLASS

3/6

Grape Fruit
or
Thick Ox-tail

•

Fried Fresh Haddock
Tomato Sauce

•

Roast Mutton, Onion Sauce
or
Game Pie

Baked & Mashed Potatoes

Brussel Tops

•

Fresh Pineapple Condé

•

Cheese,   Celery,   Etc.

•

Coffee per Cup, 4d.

20-1-34

In the general interest passengers are requested to refrain from smoking immediately prior to, and during the service of meals. Passengers are requested to see that their bills are written out in their presence and to pay no money without one. It will be appreciated if patrons will report any unusual service or attention on the part of Dining Car Attendants to Arthur Towle, Controller, L M S Hotel Services, St. Pancras, N.W.1. This will enable the Management to recognise exceptional efficiency, which they desire to encourage in their service.

The A.B.C. Railway Guide can be consulted on
application to the Conductor.

wine list

		Bot.	½ Bot.
CHAMPAGNE			
318	Lanson, Extra Quality, Extra Dry	17 6	9 6
365	Perrier Jouët, Finest Extra Quality	17 6	9 6
315	Veuve Clicquot, Dry (Old Landed)	19 6	10 6
356	Deutz & Geldermann, Gold Lack, 1923	21 0	11 0
OTHER FRENCH SPARKLING WINES			
259	Sparkling Muscatel, "Golden Guinea"	15 0	8 0
122	Ackerman-Laurance, Dry Royal	15 0	8 0
BORDEAUX (RED)			
30	Bordeaux Supérieur	4 0	2 0
31	Médoc	4 6	2 6
32	Margaux	6 0	3 6
282	Château Margaux. Grand Vin, 1916	9 0	5 0
BORDEAUX (WHITE)			
52	Graves	4 0	2 0
252	Clos du Gravier, Extra Dry	4 6	2 6
54	Haut Sauternes	5 6	3 0
179	Graves Dry Royal, 1st Growth Podensac	7 0	4 0
185	Château Carbonnieux (Château bottled)	9 0	5 0
BURGUNDY (RED)			
56	Macon	5 0	2 6
59	Beaune	7 0	4 0
60	Pommard	7 6	4 0
BURGUNDY (WHITE)			
74	Chablis	5 0	3 0
BRITISH EMPIRE WHITE WINES			
762	South African Hock Type, Paarl Amber	5 0	3 0
757	Australian Highercombe Amber	6 0	3 6
760	South African Dry Dominion (Sp'kling)	12 6	7 0
RHINE AND MOSELLE STILL WINES			
598	Still Hock	5 0	3 0
599	Still Moselle	5 0	3 0
615	Nierstein	6 6	3 6
661	Zeltinger	7 0	4 0
603	Liebfraumilch	7 6	4 0
SHERRY			
4	Amontillado, Pale Dry (per glass, 1/-)		
1	Fine Rich (per glass, 1/-)		
PORT			
15	Ruby (per glass, 1/-)		
400	Vintage Character (per glass, 1/6)	— 5 0	
401	Finest Old Tawny (per glass, 1/6)	— 5 0	

		Bot.
GORDON		
"SHAKER-BOTTLE" COCKTAILS		
Piccadilly, Martini, Dry Martini, Manhattan		
Bronx		1 6
WHISKY		
138 "**Royal Scot**"		
(finest procurable)		- 10
Other Proprietary Brands		1 0
GIN		
Finest Unsweetened		- 10
Booth's Old Matured Dry		1 0
Gin and Bitters		1 0
Gin and Vermouth		1 0
Vermouth, French or Italian		1 0
COGNAC		
Fine Old Cognac		1 6
		liqueur Glass
134 Cognac Vieux Maison (35 years old)		1 6
207 Hine's Grande Champagne		
(25 years old)		2 0
LIQUEURS, ETC.		
Crème de Menthe; Curaçao; Cherry Brandy		1 0
Kümmel ; Bénédictine ; Grand Marnier		1 6
Cointreau		1 6
Drambuie "Scotland's Own Liqueur"		1 0
BEER, CIDER,		
AERATED WATERS, ETC.		
Bass' No. 1 Barley Wine per nip		1 0
Bass' or Worthington's Pale Ale per rep. pint		- 11
Guinness, Son & Co.'s Stout	,,	- 11
" Red Tower " Lager	,,	- 11
Graham's Golden Lager	,,	- 11
Barclay's "London" Lager	,,	- 11
Lager, Genuine Pilsner	,,	- 11
Cider	per bottle	1 0
Bulmer's "Pomagne" per bot. 4/- per ½ bot.		2 6
Ross & Co.'s Dry Ginger Ale per bottle		- 8
"Schweppes" Sp'kl'g Grape Fruit	,,	- 8
Schweppes' Aerated Waters	,,	- 5
Schweppes' Soda Water small bottle		- 5
Sparkling Buxton per bot. 1/- split		- 8
Apollinaris	split	- 6
Perrier per bot., 1/- split		- 6
Still Malvern	per bottle	- 8
Vichy Celestins	,,	1 6

SPLITS

Lanson Champagne, 5/- · Bordeaux Supérieur, 1/- · Graves, 1/- · Sauternes, 1/6 · Hock, 1/6
Moselle, 1/6 · Burgundy Red, 1/6 · Burgundy White, 1/6
Sherry No. 1 2/6 · Port No. 400 & 401 2/6

LIGHT REFRESHMENTS WHEN TABLE D'HOTE MEALS ARE NOT AVAILABLE.

Tea or Coffee, Bread and Butter or Cake or Toast	0 9	Tea or Coffee, Two Poached or Boiled Eggs	2 0	Sandwiches each 0 6
Tea or Coffee with Bread and Butter and either Toast, Cake or Jam	1 0	Tea or Coffee, Fish or Plate of Cold Meat, Salad, &c	3 6	Glass of Hot or Cold Milk 0 3

Conductor in Charge W. M. DEAN

The Lakes Express

Euston to Windermere/Workington

Hardly justifying the title of express, 'The Lakes Express' was introduced between Euston and the Lake District as a summer-only train by the London Midland & Scottish Railway in 1927. Within a few years a weekend service with the same name had also been introduced in the winter. In its pre-war years the restaurant car train carried portions for Preston and Blackpool (detached or attached at Wigan), Barrow-in-Furness, Whitehaven and Workington (detached or attached at Lancaster) and Windermere (detached or attached at Oxenholme) before the remainder of the train continued to Keswick and Workington via Penrith – the latter portion arrived in Workington over half an hour before the portion that had been detached at Lancaster! The Keswick and Workington portion was hauled by ancient 19th century ex-LNWR locos westwards from Penrith. The train lost its name during the Second World War but this was reinstated by the London Midland Region of British Railways in the summer of 1950 (see page 183).

The Lancastrian

Euston to Manchester London Road

Given its name officially in 1928, 'The Lancastrian' provided a fast restaurant car service primarily between Manchester and London and, until the Second World War, the up service also conveyed through coaches from Colne and Rochdale which were attached to the up train at Wilmslow – between here and Euston the train ran non-stop via Macclesfield and Stoke-on-Trent, usually behind a 'Royal Scot' Class 4-6-0. The down service travelled via Crewe and Stockport, the exact opposite to the 'The Mancunian' (see below). The train lost its name on the outbreak of the Second World War and was only reinstated by the London Midland Region of British Railways in 1957 (see page 184).

The Mancunian

Euston to Manchester London Road

Introduced by the LMS in 1927, 'The Mancunian' offered a restaurant car service with a morning departure from Manchester and an early evening departure from Euston. As with 'The Lancastrian' (see above and page 184) the up and down trains took different routes but in the case of 'The Mancunian' it travelled down via Stoke-on-Trent and up via Crewe and Wilmslow. Motive power on the up train was usually a 'Royal Scot' 4-6-0 but on the down train haulage was usually provided by a 'Jubilee' or 'Patriot' 4-6-0. Strangely, the through coaches from Colne and Rochdale attached to the up 'The Lancastrian' at Wilmslow were conveyed back by down 'The Mancunian' and detached at Wilmslow. The train was discontinued during the Second World War but revived by British Railways in 1949 (see page 185).

LMS PASSENGER EXPRESS
THE SYMBOL OF COMFORTABLE TRAVEL
NORMAN WILKINSON. R.I.

The Manxman

Euston to Liverpool Lime Street

The Isle of Man had long been a popular destination for holidaymakers and to cater for this traffic 'The Manxman' restaurant car express was introduced by the London Midland & Scottish Railway in 1927. Running only during the summer months the restaurant car train provided connections with steamers to and from the island at Liverpool. The train also carried a through coach to Swansea Victoria, detached at Stafford for the long journey via Shrewsbury and the Central Wales Line, and through coaches for Southport, detached at Liverpool. The train was discontinued on the outbreak of the Second World War but reintroduced by the London Midland Region of British Railways in 1951 (see page 186).

Merseyside Express

Euston to Liverpool Lime Street

Originally brought in by the London Midland & Scottish Railway in 1927 as the 'London–Merseyside Express', this restaurant car train was renamed 'The Merseyside Express' a year later. The down train conveyed through coaches for Southport which were detached at Edge Hill but on the up service they were attached at Lime Street. The name was discontinued during the Second World War but was revived in 1946. The train continued to be operated by the London Midland Region of British Railways from 1948 (see pages 187–188).

BELOW: *The up 'Merseyside Express' hauled by 'Royal Scot' Class 4-6-0 No 6117* Welsh Guardsman *takes on water from Whitmore Troughs, c.1930. Original painting by the F. Moore collective studio of artists.*

The Mid-Day Scot

Euston to Glasgow Central

The early afternoon departures from Glasgow and Euston along the West Coast Main Line had long been known unofficially as 'The Corridor' (see page 60). In the years before the 'Big Four Grouping' the train was operated jointly by the London & North Western Railway and the Caledonian Railway.

The train continued to be operated by the London Midland & Scottish Railway from 1923, receiving the name 'The Mid-Day Scot' in 1927. From 1932, the new Stanier 'Princess Royal' Pacifics took over haulage of this heavy restaurant car train which regularly loaded up to 15 coaches throughout between Euston and Glasgow – previously 'Royal Scot' Class 4-6-0 locomotives were changed at Crewe. During this period 'The Mid-Day Scot' was greatly accelerated and also conveyed through coaches for Glasgow, Edinburgh and Aberdeen – the Glasgow portion was detached at Carlisle while the rest of the train ran to Lockerbie where it was split again into its separate portions. The down train also attached a through GWR coach destined for Glasgow at Crewe that had travelled from as far away as Penzance. 'The Mid-Day Scot' continued to be operated during the Second World War, albeit with a slower schedule and minus the through coaches for Aberdeen and Edinburgh, and thence from 1948 by the newly-formed London Midland and Scottish regions of British Railways (see page 189).

BELOW: *LMS 'Princess Royal' Class 4-6-2 No 6203* Princess Margaret Rose *heads the up 'The Mid-Day Scot' over Dillicar Troughs in the Lune Gorge, Westmorland, on 29 July 1936.*

The Night Scot

Euston to Glasgow Central

'The Night Scot' sleeper train was introduced by the LMS in 1927. Running between Euston and Glasgow Central the train was hauled by 'Royal Scot' Class 4-6-0s until the introduction of more powerful 'Princess Royal' Class Pacific locomotives in the 1930s. Departing from Euston at 11.45 p.m., the down train stopped at Rugby, Crewe and Carlisle where a restaurant car was added to the formation, thus enabling passengers to partake of breakfast before their arrival, at 9.35 a.m., in Glasgow. In the up direction the train departed from Glasgow at 10.45 p.m. and ran non-stop to Crewe before arriving at 7.15 a.m. at Euston. Although the train lost its name on the outbreak of war in 1939, it continued to operate with demand often necessitating the running of three separate trains.

The Paddy

Euston to Stranraer Harbour

Affectionately, but unofficially, known as 'The Paddy', this overnight sleeper train was introduced by the Midland Railway between St Pancras and Stranraer (for the ferry to Larne in Northern Ireland) in the early 20th century (see page 46). In 1923 the London Midland & Scottish Railway transferred the London terminus of this train from St Pancras to Euston. The train continued to be operated through the Second World War – such was the demand then that two trains were laid on – and then, from 1948, by the London Midland and Scottish regions of British Railways, receiving its official name of 'The Northern Irishman' in 1952 (see page 193).

The Palatine/The Peak Express

St Pancras to Manchester Central

Introduced by the London Midland & Scottish Railway in 1938, 'The Palatine' was one of a pair of named restaurant car expresses – the other was 'The Peak Express' – that operated over the former Midland Railway route between St Pancras and Manchester Central via Derby. The former departed from Manchester at 10 a.m. and returned from St Pancras at 4.30 p.m. while the latter train left St Pancras at 10.30 a.m. and returned from Manchester at 4.25 p.m. Hauled by one of Stanier's 'Jubilee' Class 4-6-0 locomotives, 'The Palatine' also carried a through coach to and from Liverpool which was attached or detached at Chinley. Both named trains were discontinued during the Second World War and only 'The Palatine' was later reintroduced by the London Midland Region of British Railways (see page 194).

ABOVE: *LMS 4-4-0 Compound No 926 approaches Chinley North Junction with an up express from Manchester to St Pancras, 2 April 1932.*

Pines Express

Manchester London Road/Mayfield to Bournemouth West

Running from Manchester to Bournemouth via Birmingham New Street, Gloucester Eastgate, Bath Queen Square and thence over the Somerset & Dorset Joint Railway (S&DJR), an unnamed restaurant car express was first introduced by the Midland Railway in 1910 (see page 54). The train continued to be operated by the newly-formed London Midland & Scottish Railway from 1923 and was given the name 'Pines Express' in 1927. By the 1930s the southbound weekday train left Manchester London Road at 10.10 a.m. and first called at Crewe where it collected through coaches from Liverpool Lime Street to Bournemouth and Southampton. It then called at Wolverhampton High Level and Birmingham New Street before reaching Cheltenham Lansdowne where the Southampton coach was detached for its onwards journey via the single-track Midland & South Western Junction Railway. The main train then called at Gloucester Eastgate and thence to Bath Queen Square via the Mangotsfield avoiding line. From here the train reversed direction for

the journey over the Mendip Hills to Evercreech Junction before arriving at 4.37 p.m. at Bournemouth West. On summer Fridays and Saturdays the train ran in two portions, one of which took an alternative route to avoid the congestion of Birmingham. All in all this was quite a journey, the highlight of which was the double-heading of steam locomotives over the steeply-graded and partly single-track S&DJR line across the Mendips. The train continued to run until the outbreak of the Second World War in September 1939. The 'Pines Express' was later restored in October 1946 and continued to be operated by the newly-formed London Midland and Southern regions of British Railways from 1948 (see page 195).

BELOW: *Double-headed over the Mendip Hills south of Bath by ex-MR Class 2P 4-4-0 No 509 and a LMS Stanier Class 5 4-6-0, the 'Pines Express' heads towards its destination of Bournemouth West, c.1947.*

The Royal Highlander

Euston to Aberdeen/Inverness

The ancestry of this Anglo-Scottish sleeping car train goes right back to the famous 'Railway Races to the North' of 1897 (see page 15) when the two rival West Coast and East Coast railway companies competed for the fastest journey time between London and Aberdeen. Although the latter trains were lightly loaded and built for speed 'The Royal Highlander', introduced by the LMS in 1927, was a very different animal. Loading up to 13 coaches the train carried sleeping cars to and from Aberdeen, Inverness and Perth with the train splitting or joining at the latter city. Between Perth and Inverness the train was always double-headed for the gruelling journey over Druimuachdar and Slochd summits – the introduction of LMS Stanier 'Black Five' 4-6-0s from the mid-1930s greatly improved performances. Such was its popularity during the summer months that up to three separate trains were run each night. Although the name

was dropped during the Second World War the service continued to operate, such was the demand from service personnel that it ran as two separate trains. The end of hostilities in 1945 immediately brought a marked improvement in the schedule with LMS 'Coronation' Class Pacifics in charge for the overnight run between Euston and Perth. This train, albeit then unnamed, continued to be operated by the newly-formed London Midland and Scottish regions of British Railways from 1948 (see page 199).

BELOW: *Railway photographer Henry Casserley and his new wife Kathleen pose in front of 'Royal Scot' Class 4-6-0 No 6115 Scots Guardsman before leaving on their honeymoon to Scotland on 'The Royal Highlander' overnight sleeper train on 17 March 1931. Henry, along with his wife, spent most of the honeymoon taking photographs of obscure Scottish branch lines!*

Royal Scot

Euston to Glasgow Central/Edinburgh Princes Street/Aberdeen

ntroduced by the London & North Western Railway and the Caledonian Railway in 1862 (see page 60), the 'Royal Scot' became the premier daytime restaurant car express between Euston and Glasgow Central of the London Midland & Scottish Railway from 1923. The introduction of the Fowler-designed 7P 'Royal Scot' Class 4-6-0s in 1927 led to a greatly improved service with heavier loadings. However, even these powerful locos still needed assistance over Shap and Beattock summits – a situation which was only remedied in 1933 with the introduction of Stanier's 8P 'Princess Royal' Class Pacifics. By then the train had officially become non-stop but in reality it still stopped at Carlisle for a crew change. 'Coronation' Class Pacifics took over in 1937, a duty they were to retain until the end of steam haulage. Before the onset of the Second World War the train also conveyed through coaches for Edinburgh and Aberdeen. The train continued to operate during the war, sometimes loading up to 17 coaches minus the restaurant car, but with much slower schedules. Such was the demand from service personnel that two trains needed to be run, one conveying through coaches for Thurso – this was the longest through passenger working in Britain, with a journey time of around 21 hours. From 1948 the train continued to be operated by the London Midland and Scottish regions of British Railways (see pages 200–201).

BELOW: *A stylish LMS poster of 1937 promoting the company's 'Royal Scot' express service between Euston, Glasgow and Edinburgh. Original artwork by Bryan de Grineau who also produced artwork for Hornby and Meccano catalogues.*

The Saint Mungo

Glasgow Buchanan Street to Aberdeen

'The Saint Mungo' express between Aberdeen and Buchanan Street came into service in 1937 but only two years later it was discontinued on the outbreak of the Second World War. The service was later revived by the Scottish Region of British Railways (see page 214).

Sunny South Express

Manchester London Road and Liverpool Lime Street to Brighton, Eastbourne and Hastings

Introduced jointly by the London & North Western Railway and the London, Brighton & South Coast Railway in 1905 (see page 37), the 'Sunny South Express' restaurant car train for holidaymakers in the North of England escaping to south coast resorts continued to be operated on summer weekends by the LMS and the Southern Railway (SR) between 1923 and 1939. Locomotives were changed at Willesden Junction with the SR-hauled train taking the West London Line to the South Coast via Kensington and Clapham Junction. The train was suspended on the outbreak of war in 1939, never to return.

RIGHT: *LNWR 'Precursor' Class 4-4-0 No 301 heads the 'Sunny South Express' past Kenton, near Harrow in the 1920s.*

BELOW: *This LMS poster, seen at Manchester Victoria on 26 June 1930, advertised holidays at South Coast resorts which were served from Liverpool and Manchester on summer weekends by the 'Sunny South Express'.*

The Thames-Clyde Express

St Pancras to Glasgow St Enoch

The alternative and more scenic route from London to Glasgow was via the ex-Midland Railway line from St Pancras to Carlisle via Leeds and the Settle–Carlisle line and then to Glasgow St Enoch via Dumfries over the ex-Glasgow & South Western Railway route. In 1927 the LMS gave the name 'The Thames-Clyde Express' to its 10 a.m. restaurant car departure from St Pancras to Glasgow St Enoch and the 9.30 a.m. departure in the opposite direction. Although serving major population centres in the East Midlands and Yorkshire the route was much longer and harder to work than the alternative West Coast Main Line, consequently the journey was much longer. Before the Second World War the eight-coach train was usually hauled between St Pancras and Leeds by a Stanier 'Jubilee' Class 4-6-0 locomotive – at Leeds the train reversed direction with a Holbeck shed 'Jubilee' then normally in charge for the demanding Settle–Carlisle section of the journey. This named train ceased to run during the Second World War but was reintroduced by the London Midland and Scottish regions of British Railways in 1949 (see page 203).

Thames-Forth Express

St Pancras to Edinburgh Waverley

The London Midland & Scottish Railway and the London & North Eastern Railway gave the name the 'Thames-Forth Express' in 1927 to a daytime restaurant train running between St Pancras and Edinburgh Waverley via the Settle–Carlisle Line and the Waverley Route. Both routes were very demanding for the crews of steam locomotives especially the long, hard slog up to Ais Gill Summit (1,169 ft above sea level) on the former and up to Whitrope Summit (1,006 ft above sea level) on the latter. The train also conveyed through coaches for Halifax which were detached at Sheffield. The 'Thames-Forth Express' was discontinued during the Second World War but was reinstated minus its name in 1945. The unnamed train continued to be operated by the London Midland and Scottish regions of British Railways from 1948 (see 'The Waverley' pages 205–206).

The Ulster Express

Euston to Fleetwood/Heysham Harbour

A boat train connecting with steamer services to and from Belfast at Heysham was inaugurated by the Midland Railway as early as 1904 (see page 46). Running to and from St Pancras the unnamed train ran in competition with the London & North Western Railway's boat train that ran between Euston and Fleetwood (see page 37) in conjunction with the Lancashire & Yorkshire Railway. From 1923 the newly-formed London Midland & Scottish Railway combined these two trains into one service between Euston and Fleetwood. With new 'Royal Scot' 4-6-0s in charge the name 'The Ulster Express' was bestowed on this service in 1927. The following year the train was diverted to run to and from Heysham Harbour and by the outbreak of the Second World War had been considerably accelerated – the entire 234¼-mile journey of the down train from Euston to Morecambe Promenade was being achieved in 4 hr 12 min – at the Promenade terminus the train had to reverse direction behind a different locomotive for the final, short journey to Heysham Harbour. The name was dropped for the duration of the war but reinstated by the London Midland Region of British Railways in 1949 (see page 204).

The Welshman

Euston to Llandudno/Porthmadog/Pwllheli

'The Welshman' was a summer-only restaurant car express that linked London with the seaside resorts of North Wales, beginning in 1927. The train divided at Llandudno Junction with one portion heading north for Llandudno while the rest of train went west to Bangor before heading south to Caernarfon and then along the single-track line to Afon Wen. Here it divided again, with one portion heading west to Pwllheli and other going east to Porthmadog. It was suspended during the Second World War but revived by the London Midland Region of British Railways in 1950 (see page 208).

LLANDUDNO
ON THE SUNNY NORTH WALES COAST
EXPRESS SERVICES AND CHEAP TICKETS BY LMS
ILLUSTRATED GUIDE FROM LLANDUDNO PUBLICITY ASSOCIATION. TOWN HALL, LLANDUDNO

London & North Eastern Railway

The second largest of the 'Big Four', the London & North Eastern Railway (LNER) had a network of 6,671¾ route miles and controlled the East Coast Main Line from King's Cross to Edinburgh, East Anglia and Lincolnshire, the Great Central route from Marylebone to Sheffield, Yorkshire, North East England and Eastern Scotland. The major English constituents of the LNER were the Great Central Railway, the Great Eastern Railway, the Great Northern Railway, the Hull & Barnsley Railway and the North Eastern Railway. In Scotland the Great North of Scotland Railway and the North British Railway also became part of the LNER. The LNER also operated 21 joint lines with the LMS and one with the GWR.

The LNER's termini in London were at King's Cross, Liverpool Street and Marylebone – King's Cross served express trains to Leeds, York, Newcastle, Edinburgh and Aberdeen; Liverpool Street served trains to East Anglia; Marylebone served trains to Sheffield and Manchester. Under the leadership of Chief Mechanical Engineer Nigel Gresley, the company went on to build world-beating locomotives to haul its express trains: A1/A3 Class

(introduced in 1922/1928) and streamlined A4 4-6-2s (introduced in 1935), P2 Class 2-8-2s (introduced in 1934) and V2 2-6-2s (introduced in 1936) at Doncaster Works, while Darlington Works also built some V2s and the majority of B17 Class 4-6-0s (introduced in 1928) and the North British Locomotive Company also built some A3s. During the Second World War the LNER also introduced the highly versatile Thompson B1 Class 4-6-0s (introduced in 1942), which continued to be constructed by British Railways until 1952.

Sleeper trains were operated between London and Newcastle while Scottish destinations included Edinburgh, Glasgow, Aberdeen and Fort William. The company also operated boat trains between King's Cross and Tyne Commission Quay near Newcastle and also between Liverpool Street and Parkeston Quay near Harwich.

BELOW: *The great man himself, Sir Nigel Gresley, stands in front of brand new streamlined Class 'A4' 4-6-2 No 4498 on 30 October 1937. This iconic locomotive, now preserved, was named after him in honour of his achievements as Chief Mechanical Engineer of the LNER.*

The Aberdonian

King's Cross to Aberdeen

The successor to the famous East Coast Route's King's Cross to Aberdeen fast overnight service of the late 19th century (see page 15), 'The Aberdonian' was introduced in 1927 by the London & North Eastern Railway. Between King's Cross and Edinburgh the heavily-loaded train including sleeping cars was hauled by one of Gresley's A3 Pacifics, but with the inclusion of a dining car the train was weighing in at around 500 tons by 1939. North of Edinburgh the train was hauled over the winding and heavily graded section north to Aberdeen by Gresley's powerful new Class 'P2' 2-8-2 locomotives, which were introduced in 1934. During the summer the train ran in two sections with the Inverness and Fort William portions being named the 'Highlandman' and the main Aberdeen portion also conveying a sleeping car for Lossiemouth.

During the Second World War 'The Aberdonian' was one of only four British named trains to hold on to its title but even heavier loads and wartime conditions took its toll on the schedules with 13½ hours being allowed for the down journey to Aberdeen. The train continued to run after the war and from 1948 it was operated by the Eastern, North Eastern and Scottish Regions of British Railways (see page 129).

Cambridge Buffet Expresses

King's Cross to Cambridge

Officially known as the 'Garden Cities and Cambridge Buffet Expresses', a series of five express trains began operating between King's Cross and Cambridge in 1932. Each train included an open buffet car which dispensed hot snacks and beverages and for this reason the trains were nicknamed by Cambridge students as 'Beer Trains'. With intermediate stops at Welwyn Garden City, Letchworth Garden City (hence the rather long name of the train) and Hitchin, they provided a rapid and comfortable journey between the university city and the capital. Journey times including stops were a very respectable 72 minutes for the up services and three minutes longer for the down services. A wide choice of motive power was used for these trains including ex-Great Northern Railway 'C1' Class Atlantics and more modern 'B17' Class 4-6-0s. The five trains were suspended on the outbreak of the Second World but later reinstated by the Eastern Region of British Railways (see page 132).

RIGHT: *An LNER poster of the 1930s promoting rail travel to Cambridge. Original artwork by Fred Taylor.*

TRINITY COLLEGE

CAMBRIDGE

ON THE

LONDON & NORTH EASTERN RAILWAY

OF ENGLAND & SCOTLAND

The Coronation

King's Cross to Edinburgh Waverley

The 1930s were the golden age of high-speed rail travel. Worldwide, railway companies were introducing luxurious trains that competed with each other for the title of the world's fastest train. First on the scene was the GWR's 'Cheltenham Flyer' (see page 67) but this was soon eclipsed in 1935 when the London & North Eastern Railway introduced its streamlined 'Silver Jubilee' (see page 106) non-stop service between King's Cross and Newcastle. Introduced in July 1937 to commemorate the coronation of King George VI, the LNER's 'Coronation' went one step further by introducing the first high-speed streamlined service between London and Scotland. Much heavier than the 'Silver Jubilee', this train called at York and Newcastle before reaching Waverley in 6 hours. Unlike the German and American streamlined trains which were diesel hauled, the LNER's train was hauled by Nigel Gresleys 'A4' 4-6-2s of which five, all named after countries of the British Empire, were allocated for this service. Both locomotive and the nine coaches (four twin articulated coaches and a streamlined 'beaver tail' observation car – the latter only carried in the summer) were colour co-ordinated with the engine finished in a deep 'garter blue' and the stock

BELOW: *Stylish poster produced by the LNER in 1937 to promote its new streamlined train, 'The Coronation', seen here crossing the Royal Border Bridge at Berwick-upon-Tweed. Original artwork by Tom Purvis.*

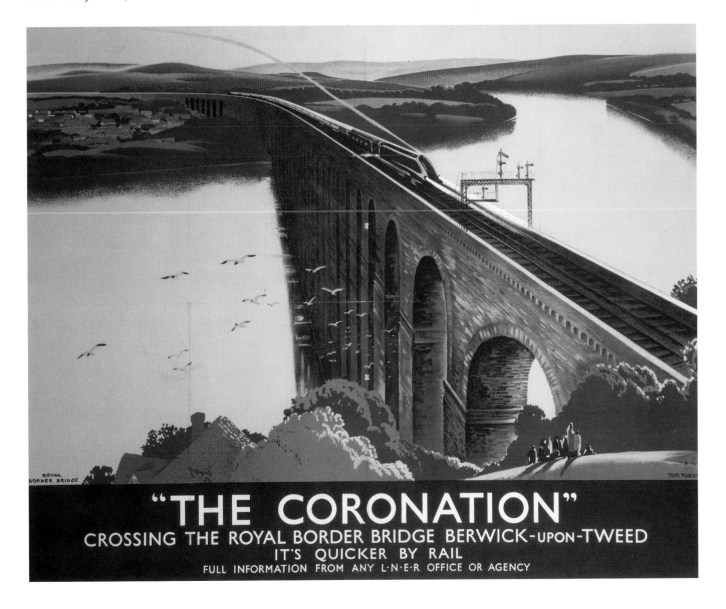

ROYAL BORDER BRIDGE

TOM PURVIS

"THE CORONATION"
CROSSING THE ROYAL BORDER BRIDGE BERWICK-UPON-TWEED
IT'S QUICKER BY RAIL
FULL INFORMATION FROM ANY L·N·E·R OFFICE OR AGENCY

finished in a two-tone blue. The latest in air conditioning, double-glazing and sound-proofing was incorporated into the coaches while the two kitchen cars provided meals served at the customers' seats.

The down train left King's Cross at 4 p.m. while the up train left Waverley at 4.30 p.m. and both proved to be very popular with travellers. One highlight of the down train was that it ran between King's Cross and York at an average speed of just under 72 mph, making it then the fastest scheduled train in the British Empire. One of Nigel Gresley's streamlined 'A4' Pacifics, No 4468 *Mallard* went on to break the world record for steam traction on 3 July 1938 with a speed of 126 mph – this record has never been broken. Sadly the onset of the Second World War in September 1939 brought an abrupt end to the highly popular 'Coronation' high-speed luxury service. The articulated coach sets were then stored at remote locations in Scotland but the train never returned in its pre-war guise. After the war some of the articulated coaches were used on the 'Fife Coast Express' in Scotland (see page 211).

(see page 211)

RIGHT: Dated 22 November 1937, the dinner menu for 3rd Class passengers on the 'The Coronation' included six courses for 4 shillings and 6 pence (in today's money 22½p).

RIGHT BELOW: Named after Dominions of the British Empire, these five brand new LNER 'A4' Class 4-6-2 locomotives, seen here lined up at King's Cross shed on 3 July 1937, were used mainly to haul the 'The Coronation' and 'West Riding Limited' expresses.

BELOW: The stylish interior of the observation car which was air-conditioned, sound-proofed and fitted with double-glazing.

BOTTOM: The two-tone blue streamlined 'beaver tail' observation car was positioned at the rear of the 'The Coronation' express.

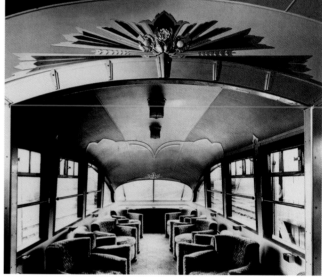

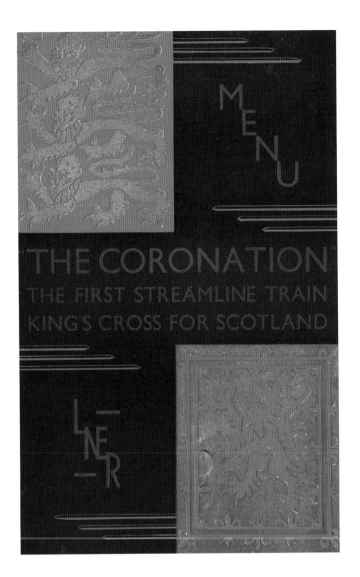

MENU

DINNER 4/6

English or Scotch Meat
Only Served on this Car

Honey Melon
Tomato Cocktail

Clear Pot au Feu
Thick Saubise

Fried Slip Sole   Mushroom Sauce

Tournedos Beef Francaise
Boiled Chicken and Ham   Parsley Sauce
Cauliflower   Boiled Potatoes

Gooseberry Fool
Maids of Honour

Cheese etc.

Coffee 4d.

Monday, November 22, 1937   Third-Class

À LA CARTE

SOUPS			GRILLS	
Clear Pot au Feu	0 6		Chop, Steak or Cutlets	3 0
Thick Saubise	0 6		(Above served with Vegetables)	
If not followed by a second course per portion	1 0		**COLD MEATS**	
			Chicken and Ham with Salad ...	3 0
FISH			**SWEETS**	
Fried Slip Sole, Mushroom Sauce with Potatoes	2 6		As per Menu ... ... per portion	0 6
			Fruit Salad and Cream per portion	1 0
MEAT DISHES (Hot)				
Tournedos Beef Francaise	2 6			
Boiled Chicken and Ham, Parsley Sauce	3 0		Dessert ... ... per portion	1 0
Above served with Vegetables			Roll or Bread and Butter	0 2
SUNDRIES			Roll or Biscuits, Butter and Cheese per portion	0 6
Honey Melon	0 6			
Tomato Cocktail	0 6		Sandwich ... ... **each**	0 4

The Company will be obliged if patrons desirous of making any comments regarding the catering
or service on this car will write to The Hotels Superintendent, Southern Area, London and North
Eastern Railway, Liverpool Street Station, London, E.C.2.

The Day Continental

Liverpool Street to Harwich Parkeston Quay

The successor to the pre-First World War 'Flemish Continental', 'The Day Continental' was introduced by the London & North Eastern Railway in 1947. It was one of a trio of post-war luxury restaurant car expresses (the others were the 'Scandinavian' and the 'Hook Continental' – see pages 101 and 144) that connected with cross-channel ferries to and from the Hook of Holland and Esbjerg at Parkeston Quay in Harwich. 'The Day Continental' service was continued by the Eastern Region of British Railways from 1948 (see page 134).

East Anglian

Liverpool Street to Norwich

To coincide with the new high-speed streamlined 'Coronation' (see page 91) on the East Coast Main Line the London & North Eastern Railway introduced a similar streamlined train on the Liverpool Street to Norwich route in 1937. Luxuriously equipped, the two six-coach sets for this new train – named 'The East Anglian' – were each hauled by one of two specially streamlined 'B17' Class 4-6-0s, No 2859 *East Anglian* and No 2870 *City of London*. However, there the similarity ended as the trains were scheduled to take a leisurely 2¼ hours for the 115-mile journey – the streamlining was purely a cosmetic publicity stunt by the LNER and the travelling public were not taken in by it. The train was withdrawn on the outbreak of the Second World War but was reinstated in 1946. The streamlining on the two 'B17s' was soon to disappear and the train was usually worked by normal 'B17' or 'B1' Class 4-6-0s. This train continued to be operated by the Eastern Region of British Railways from 1948 (see page 135).

BELOW: *'B17' Class 4-6-0 No 2859* East Anglian *and classmate No 2870* City of London *were fitted with streamlined casings at Doncaster in 1937 for working the 'East Anglian' express between Liverpool Street and Norwich.*

Eastern Belle

Liverpool Street to various East Anglian destinations

Usually hauled by a 'B17' 4-6-0, the seven-coach all-Pullman 'Eastern Belle' was introduced for tourists in the summer of 1929 by the London & North Eastern Railway. The train started and ended its journey at Liverpool Street, visiting a different destination each weekday – these included Cromer, Sheringham, Lowestoft, Hunstanton and Skegness. The train was suspended on the outbreak of the Second World War, and did not reappear after the war.

BELOW: *Seen here c.1930 hauled by brand new 'B17' Class 4-6-0 No 2811* Raynham Hall, *the 'Eastern Belle' was a luxury Pullman train that operated in the summer between Liverpool Street and various destinations in Eastern England.*

Fife Coast Express

Glasgow Queen Street to St Andrews

A summer-only train for holidaymakers was introduced by the North British Railway from Glasgow Queen Street to Crail on the East of Fife coastal line in 1910. Suspended during the First World War, the train was reintroduced after the war and was named the 'Fife Coast Express' by the London & North Eastern Railway in 1924.

The train, by now extended to serve St Andrews, operated daily in the summer and served the popular coastal resorts along the east coast of Fife. The Second World War put an end to this service for holidaymakers but it was reintroduced by the Scottish Region of British Railways in 1949 (see page 211).

Flying Scotsman

King's Cross to Edinburgh/Glasgow/Perth/Aberdeen

The 'Special Scotch Express' between King's Cross and Edinburgh Waverley became officially known as the 'Flying Scotsman' in 1924, although it had been running since 1862, and one of Gresley's 'A1' locos, No 4472, was also named in honour of the train. To reduce the journey time between King's Cross and Edinburgh some of the Class 'A1' locos (later rebuilt as Class 'A3') were fitted with larger tenders not only containing more coal but also with a corridor linking the engine to the first coach of the train. The latter allowed a crew changeover halfway through the journey and so the 'Flying Scotsman' became a non-stop restaurant car service in May 1928 – complete with a host of on-board facilities such as a cocktail bar and hairdressers. The speed limitation agreement introduced in 1895 between the West Coast and East Coast mainlines' operators was abolished in 1932 and the gloves were finally off. By 1938, with new 'A4' streamlined Pacifics now in charge of the train, the journey time for the 'Flying Scotsman' had been reduced to 7 hr 20 min in both directions. The train of 14 coaches weighing just over 500 tons conveyed through coaches for Glasgow Queen Street, Perth and Aberdeen. The austerity measures of the Second World War brought an end to high-speed rail travel and it took some years before pre-War schedules were being attained again. During the war it was common for the train to load up to 20 coaches, weighing over 700 tons, all hauled singlehandedly by a surefooted 'A4' Pacific. From 1948 the Eastern, North Eastern and Scottish regions of British Railways continued to operate the train (see pages 140–141).

FAR LEFT: *Nearly new 'A4' Class 4-6-2 No 4492 Dominion of New Zealand exits Potters Bar Tunnel in Hertfordshire with the down 'Flying Scotsman' in 1937.*

BELOW: *The 'Flying Scotsman' 10 a.m. departure for Edinburgh was always the highlight of each day at King's Cross station. Here the world-famous train gets ready to depart on its 400-mile non-stop journey behind LNER 'A1' 4-6-2 No 4475 Flying Fox, c.1930. To the left is classmate 4-6-2 No 2547 Doncaster departing on an earlier train.*

OVERLEAF: *This rare 1932 poster was produced for the LNER to promote rail travel on the 'Flying Scotsman'.*

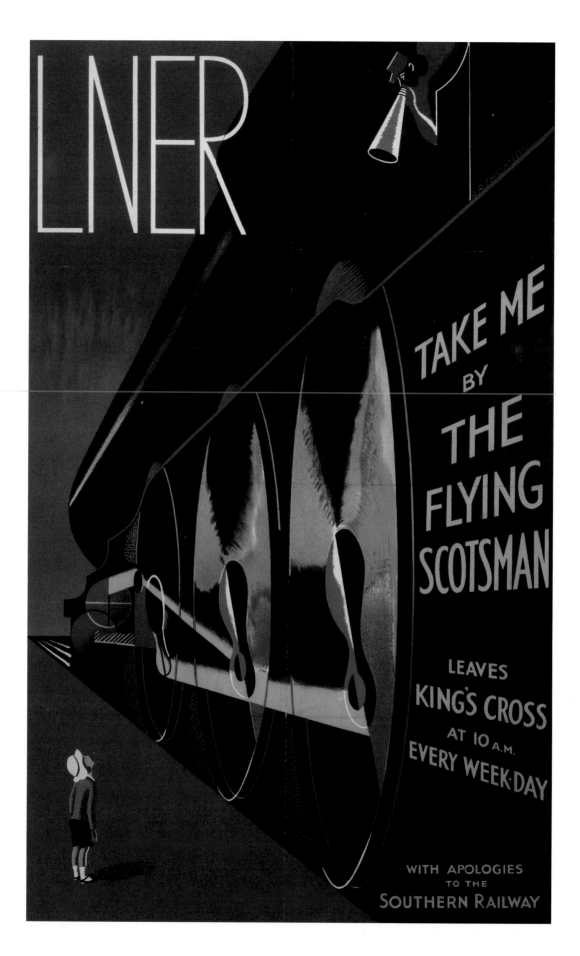

Harrogate Pullman/West Riding Pullman/ The Yorkshire Pullman

King's Cross to Newcastle Central via Leeds and Harrogate
King's Cross to Hull/Leeds/Bradford/Harrogate

Using Pullman coaches that were previously operated by the Great Eastern Railway (see page 22), the luxurious 'Harrogate Pullman' was introduced between King's Cross and Newcastle via Leeds and Harrogate by the London & North Eastern Railway in 1923. It was renamed the 'West Riding Pullman' in 1928 and again, in 1935, as 'The Yorkshire Pullman'. In 1928 the train had stopped running north of Harrogate, being replaced by the new 'The Queen of Scots' Pullman train which operated between Kings Cross and Edinburgh/Glasgow via the same route (see pages 104 and 153). A portion serving Hull (detached or attached at Doncaster) and Bradford (detached or attached at Leeds) was also added to the new 'The Yorkshire Pullman' when it was introduced in 1935 (see pages 109 and 170–171).

BELOW: *LNER 'A3' 4-6-2 No 4472 Flying Scotsman is seen at the head of the 'Harrogate Pullman', c.1930. Built at Doncaster in 1923, this world-famous locomotive has recently been restored to working condition.*

OVERLEAF: *Poster produced c.1930 promoting the LNER's 'Harrogate Pullman' express between King's Cross, Yorkshire and Newcastle. Original artwork by George Harrison.*

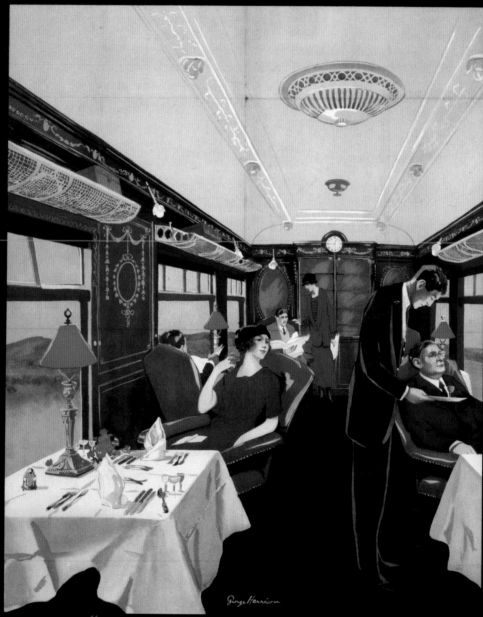

The Hook Continental

Liverpool Street to Harwich Parkeston Quay

The Great Eastern Railway created this service in the early 20th century (see page 19). The express service between Liverpool Street and Harwich Parkeston Quay – for ferries to the Hook of Holland, Zeebrugge and Flushing (the latter being introduced in 1927) – was continued by the newly-formed London & North Eastern Railway from 1923. The LNER introduced a new luxury 13-coach train (including two Pullman coaches and a restaurant car) on this route in 1924 – officially named 'The Hook Continental' in 1927, the down train left Liverpool Street in the evening with the up train returning the next morning. Timings were tight especially for the up train which had to battle its way through heavy morning commuter traffic into the capital. Haulage was initially by ex-Great Eastern Railway '1500' Class 4-6-0s but these were replaced by newer 'B17' Class 4-6-0s from 1928 onwards. Yet another new luxury set of coaches was introduced to this service in 1936 and this included two Pullman cars, two restaurant cars and a kitchen car in total weighing nearly 500 tons. Other boat trains with Pullman cars that were operated by the LNER on this route were 'The Antwerp Continental', 'The Flushing Continental' and 'The Scandinavian'.

The Second World War naturally brought an end to all of these Continental services but the luxurious 'The Hook Continental' was reintroduced in late 1945. It was continued by the newly-formed Eastern Region of British Railways from 1948 (see page 144).

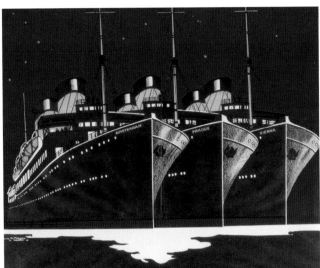

ABOVE : *Poster produced in 1935 for the LNER promoting the Harwich to Hook of Holland nightly service on three new luxury ships.*

The Master Cutler

Marylebone to Sheffield Victoria

For many years between the two world wars the former Great Central Railway (see page 20) mainline between Sheffield Victoria and Marylebone was served by a popular up morning restaurant car express service to London and an early evening down service. Known unofficially as 'The Sheffield Special', it was discontinued during the Second World War but was revived by the LNER in the autumn of 1947 with the title 'The Master Cutler'. In its early years the train was normally hauled by a 'B17' Class 4-6-0 – the up train travelled via the direct line through Amersham while the down train was sent via the GW/GC Joint Line through High Wycombe, Princes Risborough and the GCR line from Ashendon Junction to Grendon Underwood Junction to avoid the heavy early evening commuter traffic. The train continued to be operated by the newly-formed Eastern Region of British Railways from 1948 (see pages 146–147).

The Night Scotsman

King's Cross to Edinburgh Waverley/Glasgow/Perth/Aberdeen

'The Night Scotsman' sleeping car train had been operated along the East Coast Main Line by the London & North Eastern Railway since 1923. It conveyed sleeping cars and through coaches for not only Edinburgh Waverley but also Glasgow Queen Street, Perth and Aberdeen, all detached at Edinburgh. Stops were made on the down journey at Grantham, York and Newcastle. The up train strangely was not named and conveyed through sleeping cars and coaches from Dundee, Inverness and Perth. Both were very heavy trains, usually loading up to 14 coaches, which were normally hauled by an 'A3' Pacific locomotive. The train became so popular that by 1932 it no longer carried passengers to and from Edinburgh who had to follow in a slightly later unnamed train. The busiest times of year were undoubtedly during Christmas and New Year and in late July and early August during the grouse-shooting season in Scotland. The train continued to operate throughout the Second World War, albeit with a slower schedule, but only ran between London and Edinburgh. The immediate post-war years saw the as then unnamed up service also being given the title 'The Night Scotsman'. It continued to be operated by the Eastern, North Eastern and Scottish regions of British Railways from 1948 (see page 148).

BELOW: *With original artwork by Robert Bartlett, this LNER poster of 1932 promotes the company's overnight sleeping car service to Scotland. 'The Night Scotsman' is seen here hauled by a stylized 'A3' Class 4-6-2 locomotive.*

Northern Belle

King's Cross to various destinations in Scotland

ntroduced by the London & North Eastern Railway in 1933, the 'Northern Belle' was a self-contained luxury summer-only cruise train that took well-heeled passengers on a week-long rail tour of the Scottish Highlands. Departure from King's Cross was on a Friday evening, returning the following Friday morning. The train was made up of 14 coaches, including restaurant cars and sleeping cars, and was hauled between London and Edinburgh by an 'A3' Pacific or, later, by a streamlined 'A4'

Pacific. The train was discontinued on the outbreak of war in 1939. In more recent times, 'The Royal Scotsman' luxury cruise train (introduced in 1985) performs a similar task.

BELOW: *The 'Northern Belle' luxury cruise train to Scotland departs from King's Cross behind 'A4' Class 4-6-2 No 4467* Wild Swan *on a Friday evening in June 1939, the last month of its operation.*

The Queen of Scots

King's Cross to Glasgow Queen Street via Leeds and Harrogate

In 1923 the newly-formed London & North Eastern Railway had taken over the luxurious Pullman cars that were originally used by the Great Eastern Railway (see page 22) on services out of Liverpool Street. These were put into service on the new 'Harrogate Pullman' (see page 99) that operated between King's Cross, Leeds, Harrogate and Newcastle from the summer of that year. In 1928, when this train stopped running north of Harrogate, the LNER introduced a new all-Pullman train along the 450-mile route between King's Cross and Glasgow Queen Street via Leeds, Harrogate, Newcastle and Edinburgh Waverley. With ex-Great Northern Railway Ivatt Atlantics and, later, 'A3' Class Pacifics usually in charge of the train, it wasn't a particularly fast service with both the up and down trains taking 9½ hours to complete the journey. This was eventually cut to just under 9 hours in 1932. Discontinued during the Second World War, 'The Queen of Scots' was reintroduced by the Eastern, North Eastern and Scottish regions of British Railways from 1948 (see pages 153–155).

RIGHT: *An LNER poster of 1935 promoting travel on 'The Queen of Scots' Pullman train between King's Cross and Glasgow Queen Street. Original artwork by Septimus E Scott.*

BELOW: *The down 'The Queen of Scots' Pullman train is seen here at speed passing Potters Bar in Hertfordshire in 1933 behind LNER Class C1 4-4-2 No 4435.*

THE QUEEN OF SCOTS PULLMAN

leaves GLASGOW *(Queen Street) at* 10·5 a.m. week-*and* EDINBURGH *(Waverley) at* 11·15 a.m. days

for KING'S CROSS, LONDON.

Through connexion for the Continent via Victoria.

Scarborough Flier

King's Cross to Scarborough/Whitby

Running only during the summer months, the first through restaurant car express between London and the Yorkshire resort town of Scarborough was introduced by the London & North Eastern Railway in 1923. It was officially named 'Scarborough Flier' [sic] in 1927. Over the following years the train was speeded up until in 1935 the schedule was cut to 3 hours for the non-stop run between King's Cross and York, making it one of the fastest trains in Britain. Haulage for that part of the journey was usually behind an 'A3' Pacific. Locomotives were changed at York where a through coach to or from Whitby was detached or attached. Such was the popularity of the train that on summer Saturdays extra, unnamed, restaurant car services were operated to Scarborough and Whitby respectively. Suspended during the Second World War, the train was reintroduced as 'The Scarborough Flyer' by British Railways in 1950 (see page 156).

BELOW: *The first of its class to be fitted with a high-pressure boiler, LNER 'A3' 4-6-2 No 2743* Felstead *is seen here hauling the 'Scarborough Flier' at Hadley Wood in Hertfordshire in 1933.*

The Silver Jubilee

King's Cross to Newcastle Central

Named by the LNER to honour King George V's 25 years of reign, 'The Silver Jubilee' was Britain's first streamlined high-speed train when it went into regular service between King's Cross and Newcastle on 30 September 1935. Hauled by Gresley's new streamlined 'A4' Pacifics, the train consisted of two pairs of articulated coaches separated by a triplet articulated set (including restaurant car), making seven coaches in all. Both locomotives and coaches were finished in a two-tone silver and grey livery with stainless steel embellishments. The four 'A4' locos specially built to haul the train were appropriately named *Silver Link*, *Quicksilver*, *Silver King* and *Silver Fox*. Setting new standards in speed, luxury and reliability the train was so popular that an extra coach, as part of an articulated triplet set, was later added. On the train's trial run, three days before it went into regular service, No 2509 *Silver Link* twice reached 112½ mph and maintained a speed of 100 mph for 43 consecutive miles.

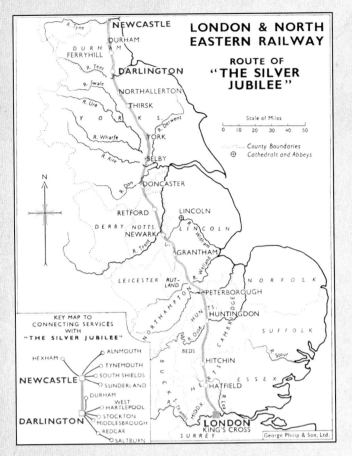

LONDON & NORTH EASTERN RAILWAY

ROUTE OF "THE SILVER JUBILEE"

Scale of Miles
0 10 20 30 40 50

⊕ County Boundaries
⊕ Cathedrals and Abbeys

KEY MAP TO
CONNECTING SERVICES
WITH
"THE SILVER JUBILEE"

George Philip & Son, Ltd.

With a 2-minute stop at Darlington, the total journey time for both up and down trains was exactly 4 hours, giving an average speed of just over 67 mph for the 268-mile journey – the up train left Newcastle at 10 a.m. and the down train left King's Cross at 5.30 p.m. This was all pretty amazing especially as there were severe speed restrictions – at Peterborough, Selby and York – en route. After four years of 100 per cent reliability the onset of the Second World War on 1 September 1939 brought an abrupt end to this service. Two of the articulated coach sets were later used after the war on the 'Fife Coast Express' (see page 211) in Scotland.

FAR LEFT: *The inaugural service of the LNER's 'The Silver Jubilee' high-speed streamlined train to Newcastle departs behind 'A4' 4-6-2 No. 2509 Silver Link from King's Cross on 30 September 1935.*

LEFT: *The route of 'The Silver Jubilee'.*

BELOW: *The seat plan of 'The Silver Jubilee'.*

OVERLEAF: *With original artwork by Frank Newbould, this LNER poster of 1935 promotes Britain's first streamlined train, 'The Silver Jubilee'.*

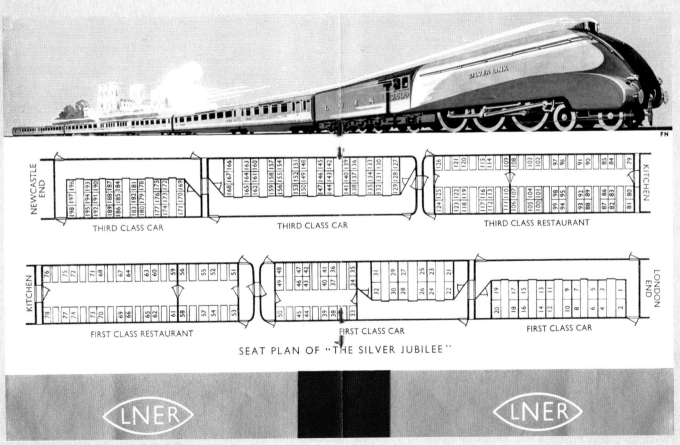

SEAT PLAN OF "THE SILVER JUBILEE"

West Riding Limited

King's Cross to Leeds Central/Bradford Exchange

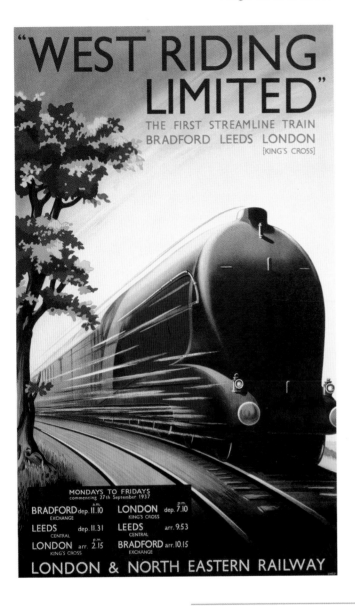

The 'West Riding Limited' was a streamlined high-speed restaurant car express introduced between King's Cross, Bradford Exchange and Leeds on 27 September 1937. For this new service, which was hauled by new 'A4' Pacifics, the company built a set of articulated coaches that were similar in construction to those used on their 'Coronation' high-speed express (see page 91). Emerging new from Doncaster Works only three months before, 'A4' Pacific No 4492 *Dominion of New Zealand* hauled the inaugural train which left Leeds at 11.33 a.m. – having already arrived from Bradford behind two tank engines – arriving at King's Cross at 2.15 p.m. The down train left London at 7.10 p.m. and arrived at Leeds at 9.53 p.m. and Bradford at 10.15 p.m. The service was suspended on the outbreak of war in 1939 but was reinstated as 'The West Riding' by British Railways in 1949 (see page 167).

LEFT: *An LNER poster of 1938 promoting the 'West Riding Limited', the first streamlined train to operate between King's Cross and Yorkshire. Original artwork by Charles 'Shep' Shepherd.*

The Yorkshire Pullman

King's Cross to Hull/Leeds/Bradford/Halifax/Harrogate

The London & North Eastern Railway introduced this all-Pullman restaurant car in 1935, as the successor to the 'West Riding Pullman' (see page 99). Timings were altered following the introduction of the streamlined 'West Riding Limited' in 1937 (see above) and the train continued to run until the outbreak of the Second World War.

'The Yorkshire Pullman' was reinstated in 1946 – the heavy 11-coach express, now with portions to and from Bradford and Hull, was usually hauled between King's Cross and Leeds by a Gresley 'A3' Pacific. From 1948 it was operated by the Eastern and North Eastern regions of the newly-formed British Railways (see pages 170–171).

Southern Railway

The smallest of the Big Four, the Southern Railway (SR) was the largest operator of passenger services with its busy commuter routes into South London. With a total network of 2,115½ route miles the constituent companies that formed the SR were the London & South Western Railway, the South Eastern Railway, the London, Chatham & Dover Railway and the London, Brighton & South Coast Railway. The SR controlled railway routes in South East and Southern England, the Isle of Wight and Dorset, East and North Devon and North Cornwall. The SR's major joint line was the Somerset & Dorset Joint Railway between Bath and Bournemouth that it shared with the LMS. It also became the owner of the narrow-gauge Lynton & Barnstaple Railway in North Devon but sadly this little gem closed in 1935.

The SR's termini in London were at Cannon Street, Charing Cross, Holborn Viaduct, London Bridge, Victoria and Waterloo. Third-rail electrification of routes from Waterloo, Holborn Viaduct and Victoria gathered pace in the 1920s and by the outbreak of the Second World War in 1939 had spread as far as Brighton, Hastings, Eastbourne, Sevenoaks, Maidstone, Portsmouth and Reading. The onset of war halted plans by the company for any further electrification.

Apart from the 'Night Ferry' which was introduced in 1936 between Victoria and Paris, the SR did not operate any sleeper trains. Boat trains were operated between London and Dover, Folkestone and Southampton Docks. Steam locomotives were also hampered by the lack of any water troughs across the network but the company countered this by fitting larger 8-wheel tenders with increased water capacity.

To haul its express passenger train the SR continued to build the ex-LSWR 'N15' ('King Arthur') Class 4-6-0s until 1926 and went on to construct the powerful 'Lord Nelson' Class 4-6-0s (introduced in 1926) and 'Schools' Class 4-4-0s (introduced in 1930) at Eastleigh Works. Oliver Bulleid's innovative 'Merchant Navy' Class 4-6-2s (introduced in 1941) were also built at Eastleigh while his 'Light Pacifics' of the 'Battle of Britain' and 'West Country' Classes (introduced in 1945) were nearly all built at Brighton Works. Many of Bulleid's Pacific locomotives continued in service until the end of steam in 1967.

Atlantic Coast Express

Waterloo to Torrington, Ilfracombe, Bude, Padstow and Plymouth

Until the GWR opened its shorter route from Paddington to Plymouth (via Westbury and Castle Cary) in 1904 there was immense competition between that company and the rival London & South Western Railway to provide the fastest service between the two cities. The latter's 11 a.m. departure from Waterloo to Plymouth was the forerunner of what became known as the 'Atlantic Coast Express' ('ACE'), which was introduced in 1926 by the Southern Railway (SR) and contained through carriages to many destinations in Devon and North Cornwall – the name of the train was selected in a competition organised by SR among its employees, the winner being a guard from Woking.

Trains between Waterloo and Exeter had always been forced to stop at Salisbury following a serious derailment at the station in 1906. It was here that locos were usually changed but with the introduction of the 'Lord Nelson' 4-6-0s in 1926 through running of locos became the order of the day. However, due to the lack of water troughs on the SR, the Salisbury stop continued to be included until the end of steam to take on water and a crew change. By the outbreak of the Second World War

LEFT: *Probably the most well-known railway poster is this 1930s Southern Railway example, promoting holiday travel to the South Coast.*

BOTTOM LEFT: *The new light green livery of the Southern Railway shows up well in this hand-tinted photograph of the 12.30pm Bournemouth express about to leave Waterloo station behind 'Schools' Class 4-4-0 No 927 Clifton, c.1935.*

BELOW: *Proof copy of a poster produced for the SR in 1935 showing the 'Atlantic Coast Express' at speed behind 'Lord Nelson' Class 4-6-0 No 850 Lord Nelson. Original artwork by Charles 'Shep' Shepherd.*

the down 'ACE' consisted of through coaches to Sidmouth, Exmouth, Ilfracombe, Torrington, Bude, Padstow and Plymouth.

Halted by the Second World War, the 'ACE' resumed service soon after the end of the war with Oliver Bulleid's new 'Merchant Navy' Pacifics in charge of the heavily loaded train as far as Exeter. Beyond Exeter the various portions were taken on to their destinations behind his new 'Battle of Britain'/'West Country' Class Light Pacifics. The train continued to be operated by the Southern Region of British Railways (see pages 217–218) from 1948.

BELOW: *The celebrated travel writer S. P. B. Mais describes the journey of the 'Atlantic Coast Express' in this book illustrated by Anna Zinkeisen and published by the Southern Railway in the 1930s.*

THE ATLANTIC COAST EXPRESS

By S. P. B. MAIS

MY object in this book is quite simple. It is to make you look out of the carriage window. You may object to this that you can't possibly read a book and look out of the window at the same time. Well, here for once, you can. This book will help you to look out of the window.

You may say that you see no point in looking out of the carriage window because you know every point of interest already.

If you're so sure about that I would ask you to spot the photographs of scenes taken from the carriage window that are included in this book and if you can accurately place them all you needn't worry to read any more.

You may say that you won't look out of the carriage window because there is nothing particular to see. May I say, Sir, that I have travelled through many countries at many seasons of the year, but I have never been more moved by the beauty of what I have seen from the carriage window than I was on that golden early morning on the last day of December when I looked down from the moor bathed in sunlight, with fields all about me white with rime, on two sinuous snake-like ribbons of white billowy mist that traced out the course of the rivers Tavy and Tamar, five hundred feet below the railway line. It was as majestic as Switzerland.

Nothing to see ?

ACE

S. P. B. Mais tells what can be seen from the compartment window of the

ATLANTIC COAST EXPRESS

PRICE *and ANNA ZINKEISEN adds her whimsical illustrations* PRICE
1/- *Published by the* 1/-
SOUTHERN RAILWAY

Bournemouth Belle

Waterloo to Bournemouth West

The success of all-Pullman trains previously operated by the London, Brighton & South Coast Railway (see page 41) led the Southern Railway to experiment with a similar train between Waterloo and Bournemouth. The 'Bournemouth Belle' first ran in 1931 but only operated on summer Sundays until 1936 when it became a regular daily working and, apart from its suspension during the Second World War, continued to run until its demise in 1967.

In its pre-war years the 'Belle' was usually hauled by a 'Lord Nelson' 4-6-0 and travelled non-stop between Waterloo and Southampton before calling at Bournemouth Central and terminating at Bournemouth West. Following the end of the war the train was reinstated in 1946 but this time it was hauled by one of Bulleid's new 'Merchant Navy' Class 4-6-2s. So popular was the train that it often extended to 12 carriages with a total weight of around 500 tons, a weight just within the 'Merchant Navy's' excellent capabilities. On Nationalization of the railways in 1948 the train continued to be operated by the Southern Region of British Railways (see pages 219–220).

RIGHT: *With artwork by Marton, this 1936 Southern Railway poster promotes travel on the 'Bournemouth Belle' Pullman train.*

BELOW: *The 'Bournemouth Belle' hauled by air-smoothed 'Merchant Navy' Class 4-6-2 No 21C15* Rotterdam Lloyd *passes through Winchfield in Hampshire in 1947.*

Bournemouth Limited

Waterloo to Bournemouth Central/West, Swanage and Weymouth

Introduced in 1911 by the London & South Western Railway (see page 38), the Waterloo to Bournemouth 2-hour expresses continued to be operated by the Southern Railway from 1923. By then the trains were normally hauled by a 'N15' Class ('King Arthur') 4-6-0 until the arrival of new 'V' Class ('Schools') 4-4-0s in 1930. These trains were the forerunners of the 'Bournemouth Limited' express which was introduced with new corridor coaches and a restaurant car in 1929. The train also carried portions for Weymouth and Swanage which were detached for their onward journeys at Bournemouth Central – the Swanage portion was detached from the Weymouth portion at Wareham – while the main train continued on to terminate at Bournemouth West. The arrival of the new 'Schools'

Class in 1930 saw another speed-up of this train between Waterloo and Bournemouth Central with up and down trains scheduled to take 116 minutes and 118 minutes respectively, which was an awesome feat for a 4-4-0. The 'Bournemouth Limited' was withdrawn on the outbreak of the Second World War, never to return to its former pre-war glory (see 'Royal Wessex', page 234).

RIGHT: Southern Railway poster of 1938 promoting the company's new carriages that had been introduced on the 'Bournemouth Limited' express. It is featured here hauled by 'Schools' Class 4-4-0 No 932 Blundell's.

BELOW: With a quote from Shelley thrown in for good measure, this SR poster of 1938 extolls the delights of the New Forest that can reached quickly from London by the new 'Bournemouth Limited' express.

"We wandered to the Pine Forest that skirts the ocean's foam —"
Shelley.
TO HAMPSHIRE & THE NEW FOREST QUICKLY BY THE NEW "BOURNEMOUTH LIMITED"

SOUTHERN RAILWAY

BOURNEMOUTH LIMITED

CORRIDOR COMPARTMENT & RESTAURANT CAR · FIRST CLASS

SALOON AND CORRIDOR COMPARTMENT · THIRD CLASS

"SHEP."

TRY THE LATEST AND MOST LUXURIOUS RAILWAY CARRIAGES YET DESIGNED FOR ORDINARY FARES SOUTHERN RAILWAY

SOUTHERN RAILWAY ADVERTISING.   23.Ad.4720/⁵⁰⁰⁄₁₉₃₈   PRINTED IN ENGLAND AT THE BAYNARD PRESS, LONDON.

Brighton Belle

Victoria to Brighton

Replacing the steam-hauled 'Southern Belle (see page 123), the all-Pullman 'Brighton Belle' was introduced by the Southern Railway on 1 January 1933 upon the completion of the Victoria to Brighton third-rail electrification. Three new sets of five-car all-Pullman electric multiple units were supplied by Metropolitan-Cammell of Birmingham for this service. In common with many other Pullman coaches the non-driving cars all received female names such as 'Hazel', 'Doris', Audrey', 'Vera', Gwen', and 'Mona'. Usually made up of two five-car sets, the train made three return journeys, each taking 1 hour, between Victoria and Brighton on weekdays (Mon–Sat), while a reduced service operated on Sundays. The 'Brighton Belle' was suspended on the outbreak of the Second World War but reinstated in 1946 and continued to be operated by the newly-formed Southern Region of British Railways from 1948 (see pages 221–222).

RIGHT: *Southern Railway poster of 1934 promoting the company's new 'Brighton Belle' electric Pullman train.*

BELOW: *The third-rail electric Pullman 'Brighton Belle' in all its glory.*

Channel Islands Boat Train

Waterloo to Southampton Docks

First introduced by the London & South Western Railway in 1892 (see page 39), the 'Channel Islands Boat Train' from Waterloo to railway-owned Southampton Docks continued to be operated by the Southern Railway (SR) from 1923. Alternating with a similar service which was operated by the Great Western Railway between Paddington and Weymouth Quay (see page 66), the heavy SR train was normally hauled by an 'N15' ('King Arthur') Class 4-6-0 on the 80-mile journey via Basingstoke, Winchester and Eastleigh. The train was suspended on the outbreak of the Second World War and reintroduced in 1946. It continued to be operated by the newly-formed Southern Region of British Railways from 1948 (see page 223).

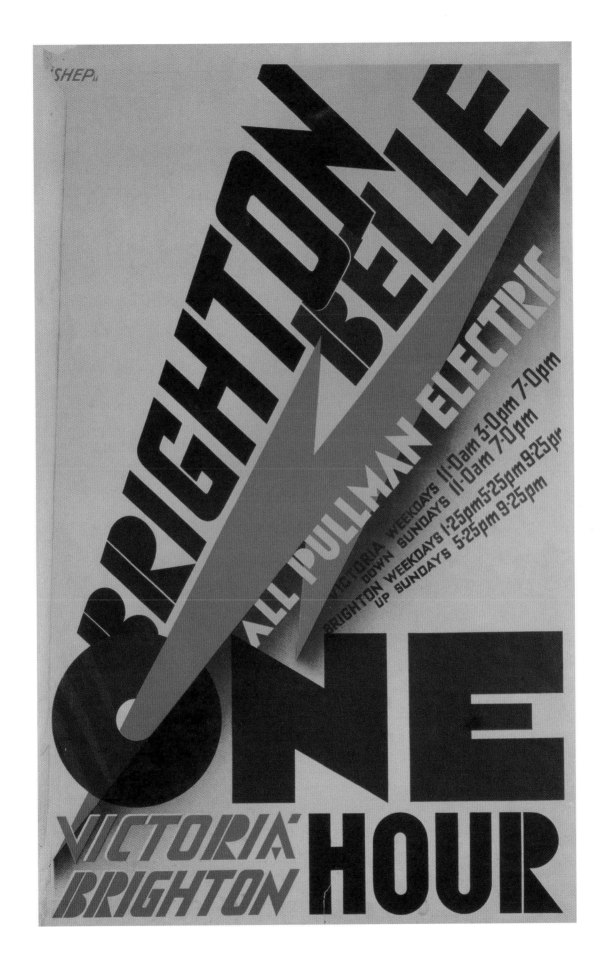

The Devon Belle

Waterloo to Ilfracombe/Plymouth

Unlike the 'Bournemouth Belle' (see page 113) and the all-electric 'Brighton Belle' (see page 116), the summer-only 'The Devon Belle' had an extremely short existence. Hauled by the latest Bulleid 'Merchant Navy' Class 4-6-2s as far as Exeter Central, this all-Pullman train was introduced by the Southern Railway in June 1947. Departing from Waterloo at 12 noon the 12- or 14-coach train was officially non-stop to Sidmouth Junction but, in fact, engines were changed out of sight at Wilton to the west of Salisbury – the only train booked to run non-stop through Salisbury since an accident there in 1906. At Exeter the train was split with one portion going on to Ilfracombe and the other to Plymouth. Bulleid's new Light Pacifics were ideal locomotives for this second leg of the journey although banking assistance was always needed up the steep Braunton Bank and on the return trip past the Slade Reservoirs out of Ilfracombe.

Unusually the Ilfracombe portion of the train carried an observation car at the rear. This was not the first time such cars had been used in Britain – the short-lived 'Coronation' (see page 116) run by the London & North Eastern Railway before the war carried an observation car and after the war these were used on Highland tourist routes in Scotland. Paying a supplement, observation car passengers on 'The Devon Belle' must have had a wonderful close-up view of the banking engine as the train struggled up the 1-in-36 Braunton Bank between Barnstaple and Ilfracombe. Naturally the observation car had to be turned on a turntable at the end of each journey. The train continued to be operated by the Southern Region of British Railways until 1954 (see pages 224–225).

BELOW: *This Southern Railway poster of 1947 promoted the newly-introduced 'The Devon Belle' all-Pullman train that operated during the summer months between Waterloo and Ilfracombe/Plymouth. Original artwork by Marc Fernand Severin.*

The
DEVON
BELLE

Fridays, Saturdays, Sundays and Mondays in each direction

dep 12.0 noon	Waterloo	arr 5.20 p.m
arr 3.16 p.m	Sidmouth Jct.	dep 2.3 p.m
arr 3.36 p.m	Exeter Ctl.	dep 1.40 p.m
arr 5.32 pm	Ilfracombe	dep 12.0 noon
arr 5.36 pm	Plymouth Friary	dep 11.30 a.m

NEW!

ALL-PULLMAN TRAIN TO THE WEST OF ENGLAND

Golden Arrow

Victoria to Paris Gare du Nord

The London, Brighton & South Coast Railway had included Pullman cars in its boat trains to Dover since 1906 (see page 41). However, soon after the formation of the Southern Railway in the 1923 'Big Four Grouping' an all-Pullman boat train was introduced between Victoria and Dover Marine from where passengers crossed the English Channel by ferry to Calais. This train was officially named the 'Golden Arrow' in 1929 – on the French side of the Channel the corresponding train between Calais and Paris was called 'Flèche d'Or'. In 1936 the SR built a luxury ferry, the *Canterbury*, for the sole use of its 1st Class passengers on the London to Paris route. The ship was also fitted with rails on the cargo deck which carried through coaches of the luxury 'Night Ferry' sleeper train (see pages 121 and 230–231) between the two capitals.

The 'Golden Arrow' was usually hauled between Victoria and Dover by 'N15' ('King Arthur') Class 4-6-0s until the introduction of the more powerful 'LN' ('Lord Nelson') Class 4-6-0s in 1926. These were then the mainstay of motive power on this heavily-loaded train until the outbreak of the Second World War.

The outbreak of war brought an end to the service, only returning again in April 1946 and this time hauled by Oliver Bulleid's air-smoothed Pacific locomotives. On Nationalization of the railways in 1948 the 'Golden Arrow' continued to be operated by the Southern Region of British Railways (see pages 226–227).

OVERLEAF: *Poster produced for the SR in 1936 promoting the improved 'Golden Arrow' service to Paris when the new luxury cross-Channel ferry, the Canterbury, was introduced between Dover and Calais.*

BELOW: *The 'Golden Arrow' all-Pullman train, hauled by SR air-smoothed 'West Country' Class 4-6-2 No 21C119 (later named Bideford), enters Dover Marine station in 1947.*

THE *NEW*
"GOLDEN
ARROW"
PULLMAN

WITH SPECIAL
BOAT SERVICE
FROM MAY 15

SOUTHERN RAILWAY

LONDON
VICTORIA
DEPART 11 a.m
PARIS
NORD
ARRIVE 5·35 p.m
20 MINUTES QUICKER

PARIS
NORD
DEPART 12 noon
LONDON
VICTORIA
ARRIVE 6·35 pm
40 MINUTES QUICKER

Night Ferry

Victoria to Paris Gare du Nord/Brussels-Zuid

The 'Night Ferry' ('Ferry de Nuit') was inaugurated by the Belgian International Sleeping Car Company (Compagnie Internationale des Wagon-Lits) in 1936 after the completion of new train ferry terminals at Dover and Dunkerque. Between Dover Marine and Victoria it was operated by the Southern Railway. Providing a 1st Class overnight sleeping car service between London and Paris/Brussels, the train was one of the heaviest to be operated on Britain's railways with up to 19 coaches being hauled between Victoria and Dover. Double heading by steam locomotives was the order of the day until the train was withdrawn on the outbreak of the Second World War. The 'Night Ferry' was reinstated by the Southern Railway in 1947 and continued to be operated by the newly-formed Southern Region of British Railways from 1948 (see pages 230–231).

BELOW: *The 'Night Ferry' train bound for Paris and Brussels via Dover and Dunkerque waits to depart from Victoria behind lead engine SR 'Battle of Britain' Class 4-6-2 No 21C156* Croydon *on 15 December 1947.*

Ocean Liner Expresses

Waterloo to Southampton Docks

Boat trains between Waterloo and Southampton Docks were run for many years by the London & South Western Railway (see page 39) and, from 1923, by the Southern Railway. Southampton Docks was then owned by the Southern Railway and in the 1930s the company invested heavily in these facilities providing modern rail-connected shipping terminals for ocean-going liners – by then Southampton had overtaken Liverpool as the main port for trans-Atlantic passenger liners. These boat trains often included Pullman cars for the use of 1st Class passengers and were run as required but the outbreak of the Second World War in 1939 soon put an end to all this. The 'Ocean Liner Expresses' were reinstated in 1946 and continued to be operated by the Southern Region of British Railways from 1948 (see pages 232–233).

RIGHT: *With original artwork by Charles 'Shep' Shepherd, this colourful and stylish poster of 1947 promotes the four all-Pullman trains then in service on the Southern Railway.*

BELOW: *Featuring the new Cunard RMS Queen Mary and the French Line's SS Normandie off Spithead, 'The World's Greatest Liners use Southampton Docks' poster was produced for the Southern Railway in 1936. Original artwork by Leslie Carr.*

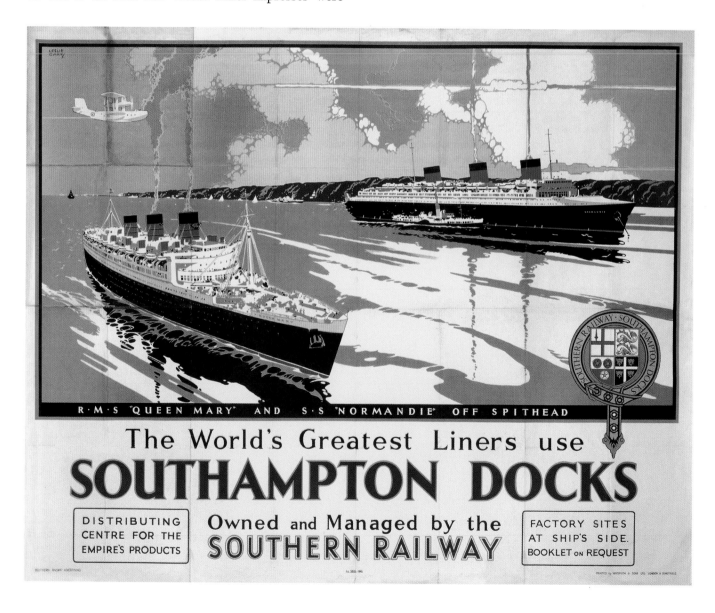

R·M·S "QUEEN MARY" AND S·S "NORMANDIE" OFF SPITHEAD

The World's Greatest Liners use
SOUTHAMPTON DOCKS

DISTRIBUTING CENTRE FOR THE EMPIRE'S PRODUCTS

Owned and Managed by the
SOUTHERN RAILWAY

FACTORY SITES AT SHIP'S SIDE. BOOKLET on REQUEST

Southern Belle

Victoria to Brighton

First introduced by the London, Brighton & South Coast Railway (LBSCR) in 1908 (see page 116), this Pullman train continued to be operated by the newly-formed Southern Railway from 1923. Ex-LBSCR motive power was soon replaced by newer 'N15' ('King Arthur') Class 4-6-0s but this was not to last long as electrification of the Victoria to Brighton route was completed at the end of 1932. On 31 December the very last steam-hauled 'Southern Belle' ran from Victoria behind ex-LBSCR Baltic tank locomotive No 2333 *Remembrance* and the very next day it was replaced by the new all-electric 'Brighton Belle' Pullman train (see page 116).

Thanet Belle

Victoria to Ramsgate/Canterbury

A luxury all-Pullman train was first introduced by the South Eastern & Chatham Railway between Victoria and Kent in 1921 (see page 56). Known as the 'Thanet Belle' the train ran non-stop between London and Margate, ending or starting its journey at Ramsgate Harbour. The train was continued by the Southern Railway from 1923 but by 1931 the Pullman content of the train had dwindled to just one coach. The train was suspended during the Second World War but was reintroduced by the Southern Region of British Railways in 1948 (see page 228).

1948 to 1994
BRITISH RAILWAYS

Government control of Britain's railways during the Second World War had been in the hands of the Railway Executive Committee – this control actually lasted for over eight years from 30 August 1939 until 31 December 1947. The war had left Britain's virtually bankrupt railways in very poor shape with infrastructure, track, locomotives and rolling stock all suffering from wartime damage and lack of investment and maintenance. While Nationalization of the railways had been on the cards following the First World War the problem then was solved by grouping 120 railway companies into just four – the 'Big Four Grouping' of 1923 (see pages 62–63) saw the newly enlarged GWR, LMS, LNER and SR take over a similarly rundown system and by the 1930s Britain's railways were among the best in the world.

However the concept of Nationalization was not rejected following the end of the Second World War. Once the dust had settled on a war-ravaged country Clement Attlee's Labour Government enacted the Transport Act 1947 which was given royal assent on 6 August that year. Under the Act railways (including their shipping interests), canals, ports, harbours, bus companies and long-distance road haulage were acquired by the state and put under the control of the newly-formed British Transport Commission (BTC) – each form of transport had its own executive committee with the new British Railways being the commercial name of the Railway Executive. This ambitious plan was admirable, bringing together all forms of land transport to form an integrated system, but in reality nothing much changed.

And so on 1 January 1948 British Railways was born. It was divided into six geographical regions: Southern, Western, London Midland, Eastern, North Eastern and Scottish. While well-intentioned, Nationalization did not stop inter-regional rivalry with the likes of the Western Region more-or-less continuing in the same autonomous fashion from Swindon as had its predecessor, the GWR.

The new British Railways (BR) not only inherited a motley collection of thousands of non-standard steam locomotives, some dating back to the 1870s, along with some very ancient wooden rolling stock but also a dense network of around 20,000 route miles of railway. Many lines competed with each other, a throwback to the pre-Grouping years of the late 19th century, while several thousand miles of loss-making and antiquated rural branch lines were a serious drain on BR's finances.

The British Transport Commission dealt with the latter problem by setting up the Branch Lines Committee which oversaw the closure of over 230 routes totalling around 3,000 route miles between 1948 and 1962 – a national coal shortage during the harsh winter of 1947 had already seen a suspension of services on some of them. On the plus side the BTC grasped the nettle in 1951 and approved the construction of 11 new classes of standard steam locomotives to replace the existing ageing fleet – using domestically mined coal to fuel them was then still viewed favourably by the Government instead of importing foreign oil to run new diesel locomotives.

Over the coming years there were also changes, not necessarily for the good, to BR's regional boundaries. The most notorious examples were in the West Country where all routes west of Salisbury and the northern half of the Somerset & Dorset Joint Railway were transferred from the Southern Region to the Western Region, leading to downgrading to secondary routes or inevitable closures. The transfer of the former Great Central Railway mainline from Sheffield to Marylebone from the Eastern Region to the London Midland Region in 1958 also led to its subsequent closure. The North Eastern Region was merged with the Eastern Region in 1967.

Despite all of the optimism generated in 1948 the following years saw BR's financial position gradually deteriorate and union-organized national rail strikes in the 1950s just compounded the problem. Freight traffic was being lost at an alarming rate to road transport and by 1955 BR recorded its first operating loss, the same year that BR published its *Modernisation Plan* which spelt the end for steam. Drastic surgery was required for the ailing railways of Britain. Along came Dr Richard Beeching and his 1963 Report (*The Reshaping of British Railways*) which eventually led to the closure of 4,000 miles of railway, 2,500 stations and the loss of over 65,000 railway jobs. British Railways was rebranded British Rail in 1965 and the highly successful Inter-City brand was introduced a year later. The end of standard-gauge steam on British Railways came in 1968 with some locomotives being condemned to the scrap heap although they were only a few years old. New air-conditioned Mk 3 coaches entered service between 1975 and 1988 and their introduction was widely applauded by the travelling public. The HST 125s were introduced in 1976, also making an excellent impression on the travelling public, and journey times on their

routes were slashed. The regions of British Rail were replaced by business sectors in 1982 but the railways were soon losing nearly one billion pounds a year. Major change was once again looming for Britain's railways and on 1 April 1994 they were privatized. RIP British Railways/British Rail.

OVERLEAF: *On Nationalization in 1948 the British Railways network was divided into six operational regions. There were changes to these boundaries over the following years and the North Eastern Region was absorbed by the Eastern Region in 1967.*

Motorail

Carrying both passengers and their cars, the Motorail services as we knew them started in 1955 with the introduction by the Eastern Region of BR of an overnight London to Perth service. A daytime service between London Holloway and Edinburgh was introduced in 1960 and within a few years the network had expanded to include destinations from London such as Stirling, Inverness, Fishguard and St Austell. Outside of London there were services between Manchester and Dover, Sutton Coldfield and Inverness, Newcastle and Exeter, Newcastle and Dover, York and Inverness. The majority of the trains ran overnight and were made up of sleeping cars attached to either flat car transporter wagons or converted end-loading GUV covered wagons. Cars were loaded on and off the train via an end-loading dock at a

station. The only purpose-built Motorail terminal opened at Kensington Olympia in London in 1961, remaining in use until 1981.

Motorail services peaked in the late 1970s with around 30 destinations served but the opening of new motorways and the increasing reliability of cars led to a gradual decline in routes. The last Motorail service ran in 1995 but in 1999 First Great Western re-introduced a Motorail service which was attached to its overnight 'Night Riviera' sleeping car train between Paddington and Penzance. It last ran with a Motorail van in 2005.

BELOW: *Cars loaded on double-deck rail transporters wait to depart on a Motorail service from Kensington Olympia, 24 May 1966.*

Eastern and North Eastern Regions

Formed on 1 January 1948 the Eastern and North Eastern regions of the newly nationalized British Railways took over all the routes of the former London & North Eastern Railway south of the Scottish border. Between them they operated passenger services, including the all-important Anglo-Scottish trains, along the East Coast Main Line between King's Cross and Berwick-upon-Tweed.

The Eastern Region's main London termini were at King's Cross and Liverpool Street – the former serving the East Coast Main Line and the latter serving East Anglia. In 1949 the Eastern Region gained Fenchurch Street station and routes to Tilbury and Southend from the London Midland Region. Marylebone station, served by trains on the former Great Central Railway mainline from Sheffield, was also an Eastern Region London terminal until 1958 when this route was transferred to the London Midland Region.

The Eastern Region stretched northwards from London to Sheffield and Doncaster and eastwards to Lincolnshire, Cambridgeshire, Norfolk, Suffolk and Essex. The North Eastern Region covered the area stretching from Doncaster northwards to Leeds, Kirkby Stephen, Carlisle and Berwick-upon-Tweed and eastwards to Newcastle Sunderland, York and Hull. The North Eastern Region was absorbed by the Eastern Region in 1967. After this merger the headquarters of the enlarged Eastern Region was established at York.

Construction of mainline steam locomotives continued for some years at both Doncaster and Darlington Works. At Doncaster 14 of Peppercorn Class 'A2' Pacifics were built in 1948 and 26 of Peppercorn Class 'A1' Pacifics between 1948 and 1949. Twenty-three of the latter class were also built at Darlington along with 60 of the Thompson Class 'B1' 4-6-0s – Darlington Works ceased building steam locomotives in November 1956 and it closed in 1966. Introduced in 1942, the versatile Thompson 'B1' Class 4-6-0s continued to be built with 290 being constructed by the North British Locomotive Company of Glasgow up to April 1952. Doncaster also built 42 of the BR Standard Class 5 4-6-0s between August 1955 and May 1957, when steam locomotive construction

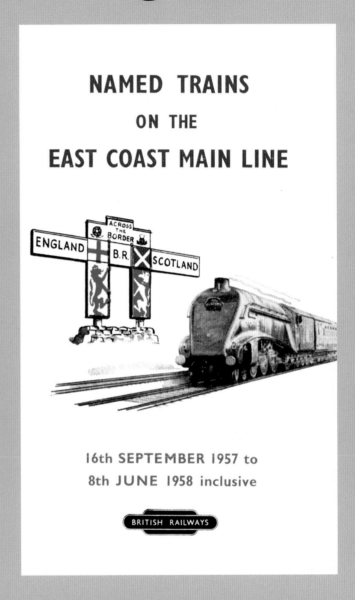

NAMED TRAINS ON THE EAST COAST MAIN LINE

16th SEPTEMBER 1957 to 8th JUNE 1958 inclusive

BRITISH RAILWAYS

ceased. Between 1961 and 1966 the works, known as 'The Plant', built 40 Class 85 and 40 Class 86 25 kv electric locomotives. In 1969 it became part of British Rail Engineering Limited and went on to build 85 Class 56 and 50 Class 58 diesel-electric locomotives by 1987.

Two other railway works are also worth mentioning. Although locomotive construction at Stratford Works in East London had ended in 1924, this facility continued to be used for the maintenance of locomotives, latterly diesels, until 1991. At the former Great Central Railway works at Gorton, near Manchester, steam locomotive construction ceased in 1951 with the delivery of the last of 10 Thompson Class 'B1' 4-6-0s. Gorton also built 57 of Class 76 (1950–53) and seven Class 77 (1953–4) electric locomotives for the Manchester to Sheffield via Woodhead line. The works closed in 1963.

Boat trains were operated from Liverpool Street to Harwich and from King's Cross to Tyne Commission Quay, near Newcastle, while sleeping car trains were run between King's Cross and Newcastle and Scottish destinations.

Old rivalries surfaced when the former Great Central Railway mainline between Sheffield Victoria and Marylebone was transferred from the Eastern Region to the London Midland Region in 1958 and from that date the line was living on borrowed time with express services between the two cities withdrawn or rerouted and other services placed in the hands of worn-out steam locomotives – closure in 1966 was inevitable.

Both regions suffered considerably from rail closures in the 1950s and 1960s, the latter a result of Dr Beeching's 'axe'. Notable among the pre-Beeching closures were the Midland & Great Northern Joint Railway's route across Cambridgeshire and Norfolk, which bit the dust on 28 February 1959, and the trans-Pennine Barnard Castle to Penrith line, which closed on 22 January 1962. In Eastern England there were many Beeching closures of rural railways in Lincolnshire, Cambridgeshire, Norfolk and Suffolk although the East Suffolk Line between Ipswich and Lowestoft was fortunately reprieved. In the North East the four lines radiating out from Market Weighton, the Hornsea and Withernsea branches and two routes serving Whitby were all major victims of Dr Beeching's 'axe'.

Electrification of the former Great Central Railway route across the Pennines between Manchester and Sheffield via Woodhead was completed in 1954 but by then its 1,500 V DC overhead system was already obsolete and it closed to passengers in 1969 and to freight in 1981. Electrification of Eastern Region routes gathered pace from the 1950s onwards with lines from Liverpool Street and Fenchurch Street to Shenfield completed in 1949 and extended to Southend in 1956, Colchester and Clacton in 1959 and finally to Norwich in 1986. The King's Cross to Royston line was electrified in 1978 and extended to Cambridge in 1988 and King's Lynn in 1992. The East Coast Main Line out of King's Cross was electrified in stages between 1976 and 1991.

Following sectorisation of Britain's railways the Eastern Region ceased to be an operating unit in the 1980s and the new Anglia Region took over responsibility for the routes radiating out from Liverpool Street to Cambridgeshire, Norfolk, Suffolk and Essex. As a prelude to privatisation the ER was disbanded in 1992.

On a visit from Gloucester I spent about 5 hours trainspotting at King's Cross station on 14 April 1962. Although the 'Deltic' diesels had started to appear there was still plenty of steam action to be seen in the shape of three 'A1' Class, five 'A3' Class and five 'A4' Class Pacifics, two 'V2' Class 2-6-2 and two BR Standard Class 7 'Britannia' Pacifics. An interesting haul for a young lad from the west!

A visit to Stratford shed (30A) in East London on 4 September 1962 revealed an amazing variety of steam and diesel locomotives where a total of 118 locomotives were recorded. On the steam side there were representatives of Classes B1, J15, J17, J19, J66, J69, L1, N7 and BR Standard Class 2 2-6-0 and BR Standard Class 4 2-6-4T, without doubt all heading for a one-way trip to the scrapyard very soon. Diesels didn't interest me so much but of note were five of the unreliable 'Baby Deltics' (D5902, D5903, D5908, D5904, D5909) which were in store pending a decision on their future.

I had a wonderful trainspotting trip to the Eastern Region in the summer of 1965, taking in many lines that were subsequently closed – King's Lynn to Hunstanton, King's Lynn to Wymondham via Swaffham and Dereham, Magdalen Road to March via Wisbech, Cambridge to March via St Ives, Grimsby to Boston via Louth. Sadly steam traction on these routes there was none by then but I did find time to travel up the East Coast Main Line on 13 August from Peterborough to Doncaster behind D1551 and thence to Grimsby via Frodingham & Scunthorpe. At Doncaster there was still plenty of steam activity, albeit by then only on freight services – in a short space of time there and on the subsequent trip to Grimsby I recorded 25 steam locomotives represented by ex-WD 2-8-0s, BR Standard Class '9F' 2-10-0s, 'B1' Class 4-6-0s and even two 'K1' 2-6-0s and a solitary 'O4/8' Class 2-8-0. Happy days!

The Aberdonian

King's Cross to Aberdeen

Introduced by the London & North Eastern Railway between King's Cross and Aberdeen in 1927 (see page 90), 'The Aberdonian' sleeping car train continued to run through the Second World War and from 1948 it became the responsibility of the Eastern, North Eastern and Scottish regions of British Railways. There was only a slow improvement in the schedules after the war and by 1960 the down train left King's Cross at 7.30 p.m. and arrived in Aberdeen at 7.19 a.m. the next morning – the up train fared slightly better with an 8.20 p.m. departure from Aberdeen arriving at King's Cross at 7.47 a.m. the next morning. Steam haulage ended with the introduction of the powerful 'Deltic' diesels in 1961 when there was a marked improvement with nearly an hour soon being shaved off journey times. In the early 1970s the late evening departures from King's Cross and Aberdeen were renamed the 'Night Aberdonian' and the title 'The Aberdonian' bestowed on a daytime service between the two cities. While the title 'Night Aberdonian' was dropped in the Autumn of 1982 the introduction of HST 125s in 1978 saw a rapid acceleration of the daytime service – in 1982 taking over the 10 a.m. departure slot from King's Cross held for years by the 'Flying Scotsman' (see pages 15, 96–98 and 140–141) with a journey time of

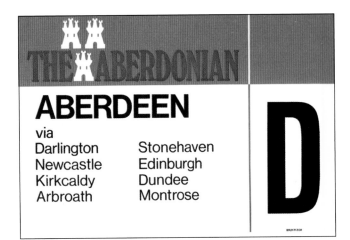

ABOVE: *A coach window sticker for the daytime 'The Aberdonian' in the latter days of diesel haulage.*

BELOW: *Peppercorn Class 'A1' 4-6-2 No 60123 H. A. Ivatt roars through Hadley Wood station with the down 'The Aberdonian' in the 1950s.*

just under 7½ hours for both the up and down services. The title 'The Aberdonian' was discontinued in 1987. Today, the 'Caledonian Sleeper' offers an overnight Anglo-Scottish sleeping car service although the London terminus of the train is now Euston.

The Broadsman

Liverpool Street to Sheringham

'The Broadsman' was one of several short-lived named trains introduced by the newly-formed Eastern Region of British Railways in the early years following Nationalization of the railways. Already served in the summer by through coaches conveyed on 'The Norfolkman' (see page 149) between Liverpool Street and Cromer, the seaside resort of Sheringham saw its own named train when 'The Broadsman' was introduced in 1950 – the difference between these two trains was that 'The Norfolkman' had an early morning departure from Liverpool Street while 'The Broadsman' had a similarly timed departure from Sheringham. A restaurant car was conveyed between London and Cromer – here, Cromer High station closed in 1954 and trains were rerouted to Cromer Beach where the Sheringham coaches were detached or attached.

The introduction of the new BR Standard Class 7 'Britannia' Class 4-6-2s between Liverpool Street and Norwich in 1951 brought a massive improvement to services with overall journey times being slashed by 26 minutes. Over the following two years the service was speeded up again and, despite stops at Diss, Stowmarket and Ipswich, the down train was covering the 115 miles from Liverpool Street to Norwich in only 2 hours. The summer 1955 timetable shows the down train taking 73 minutes for the 68¾ miles to Ipswich where there was a 3-minute wait then only 44 minutes for the 46¼ miles from there to Norwich. Sadly this steam spectacular did not last long as new English Electric Type 4 diesels were introduced in 1958 and the 'Britannias' were soon dispersed to other parts of BR. By the autumn of 1960, with diesel haulage, the up train was leaving Sheringham at 7.33 a.m. and arriving at Liverpool Street at 10.55 a.m., while the down train was leaving London at 3.30 p.m. and arriving at Sheringham at 7.05 p.m. The train was withdrawn in June 1962.

RIGHT: The summer 1961 timetable for 'The Broadsman'.

BELOW: 'The Broadsman' approaches Norwich Thorpe behind BR Standard Class 7 'Britannia' 4-6-2 No 70007 Coeur-de-Lion in September 1952. The locomotive was then just 18 months old.

THE BROADSMAN

SHERINGHAM, CROMER, NORWICH, IPSWICH
AND
LONDON (Liverpool Street)

WEEKDAYS

	am			pm
Sheringham .. ..dep	7 33	London (Liverpool Street).. ..dep		3 30
West Runton.. .. .. .. „	7 38	Ipswich .. ..arr		4 51
Cromer (Beach) .. .. .. „	7 52	„ .. ..dep		4 54
North Walsham (Main).. .. „	8 12	Norwich (Thorpe) .. .. ..arr		5 40
Wroxham .. .. „	8 24	Salhouse .. .. „		6 0
Norwich (Thorpe).. .. .. „	8 45	Wroxham .. .. „		6 7
Ipswich .. ..arr	9 30	Worstead .. .. „		6 16
„ .. ..dep	9 32	North Walsham (Main) .. .. „		6 23
London (Liverpool Street) arr	10 55	Gunton.. .. .. „		6 34
		Cromer (Beach) .. .. „		6 48
		West Runton .. .. „		7 1
		Sheringham .. .. „		7 5

Restaurant Car available between Cromer and London (Liverpool Street).

Passengers travelling from Liverpool Street, Sheringham and Cromer (Beach) also from Norwich to Ipswich and Liverpool Street and Ipswich to Liverpool Street, by this service, can reserve seats in advance on payment of a fee of 2s. 0d. per seat.

Butlins Express

King's Cross to Skegness | Liverpool Street to Clacton-on-Sea

Billy Butlin's holiday camps had opened at Skegness and Clacton-on-Sea before the Second World War but had closed for the duration when they were used as army camps. After the war they were speedily reopened and soon gained popularity with the British public. Special stations were also opened for the more inaccessible locations – Filey Holiday Camp station in East Yorkshire, Penychain station in North Wales and Heads of Ayr station in Scotland all opened in 1947 – Heads of Ayr closed in 1968, Filey in 1977 but Penychain is still open serving a holiday and caravan park.

Special named trains were also introduced on the Eastern Region of British Railways to carry hordes of happy campers from London to Butlin's Holiday Camps at Skegness and Clacton-on-Sea – usually hauled by a 'B1' Class 4-6-0, these trains even carried the headboard 'Butlins Express' on the front of the locomotive. The first King's Cross to Skegness train ran in June 1958 and was hauled by King's Cross shed's 'B1' 4-6-0 No 61331. To mark this auspicious occasion the train also conveyed British Railway executives who were given a guided tour of the camp in the afternoon by Billy Butlin. These trains continued to run into the 1960s but changing holiday habits brought about by cheap holidays in the Mediterranean sun soon put an end to all this.

BELOW: *Hi-de-Hi! Class 'B1' 4-6-0 No 61406 of Immingham shed calls at Peterborough North with the 'Butlins Express' from Skegness on 18 July 1959.*

Cambridge Buffet Expresses

King's Cross to Cambridge

ntroduced by the London & North Eastern Railway in 1932 (see page 90), four of the popular 'Cambridge Buffet Expresses' between King's Cross and Cambridge were reintroduced by the Eastern Region of British Railways in 1950. Motive power by then was provided by either 'B17' Class 4-6-0s or the newer 'B1' Class 4-6-0s until the advent of new Brush Type 2 diesels in the late 1950s. Although slower than their pre-war predecessors, all trains still included an open buffet car which proved extremely popular with homeward-bound commuters as the author can verify being a regular user in the early 1970s – shoulder-to-shoulder standing room in the smoke-filled Gresley buffet car as the train rattled northwards in the evening rush hour! The trains sadly ceased running following electrification of the route from King's Cross to Royston in 1978.

BELOW: *Class 'B2' 4-6-0 No 61644* Earlham Hall *makes a spirited start from Cambridge station with a 'Cambridge Buffet Express' in 1959. Built in 1935, this loco was soon destined for the scrap heap.*

Capitals Limited
King's Cross to Edinburgh and Aberdeen

By 1939 (and thanks to corridor tenders allowing crew members to change over without stopping) the 'Flying Scotsman' express (see page 96) had become the longest regular non-stop run in the world covering the 393 miles between King's Cross and Edinburgh in just 7 hours. The outbreak of the Second World War stopped this golden age of high-speed travel, which was only resumed in 1949 when the new 'Capitals Limited' was inaugurated by the Eastern, North Eastern and Scottish regions of British Railways as the new non-stop express between the two capitals – by then the 'Flying Scotsman' had already been downgraded with an intermediate stop at Newcastle. Running only during the summer months with a 9.30 a.m. departure from King's Cross and a 9.45 a.m. departure from Edinburgh, the new train also carried through coaches to and from Aberdeen. Hauled between King's Cross and Edinburgh by an 'A4' Pacific fitted with a corridor tender, the train was very heavy consisting of 13 coaches including a kitchen car, buffet car, two restaurant cars and a ladies' restroom but strangely had only a limited number of 1st Class seats. By 1952 the train had been speeded up to nearly match the 'Flying Scotsman's' pre-war schedules and in 1953 it was renamed as 'The Elizabethan' in honour of the coronation of Queen Elizabeth II (see page 137).

BOTTOM LEFT: *The driver of Class 'A4' 4-6-2 No 60017* Silver Fox *being interviewed by the press at King's Cross station prior to departing with the 'Capitals Limited', 30 June 1952.*

BELOW: *This BR poster of 1950 promotes the 'Capitals Limited' express. Original artwork by A. N. Wolstenholme.*

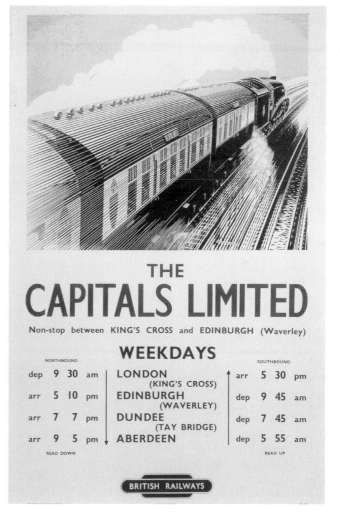

THE
CAPITALS LIMITED
Non-stop between KING'S CROSS and EDINBURGH (Waverley)

WEEKDAYS

NORTHBOUND				SOUTHBOUND		
dep	9 30 am	LONDON (KING'S CROSS)		arr	5 30 pm
arr	5 10 pm	EDINBURGH (WAVERLEY)		dep	9 45 am
arr	7 7 pm	DUNDEE (TAY BRIDGE)		dep	7 45 am
arr	9 5 pm	ABERDEEN		dep	5 55 am
READ DOWN					READ UP	

BRITISH RAILWAYS

The Day Continental

Liverpool Street to Harwich Parkeston Quay

The London & North Eastern Railway brought in 'The Day Continental' restaurant car express in 1947 (see page 94). This express connected with cross-channel ferries to and from the Hook of Holland and Esbjerg at Parkeston Quay in Harwich and was continued by the Eastern Region of British Railways from 1948. In its early years this express was hauled by 'B1' Class 4-6-0s but with the introduction of new BR Standard Class 7 'Britannias' 4-6-2s at Stratford Depot in 1951 its schedule was speeded up considerably. In the autumn of 1960 the 'The Day Continental' left Liverpool Street at 9.15 a.m. and arrived at Parkeston Quay at 10.55 a.m. while the up train left Parkeston Quay at 7 p.m. and arrived back in London at 8.36 p.m. This may not seem fast but much of the journey was over some of the busiest commuter lines in the world. By this date the 'Britannias' had been replaced by English Electric Type 4 (Class 40) diesels followed by Type 3 (Class 37) and finally Brush Type 4 (Class 47) locos. The train lost its name in 1987.

BELOW: *Class 'B1' 4-6-0 No 61004 Oryx of Parkeston shed waits to depart from Liverpool Street with the down 'The Day Continental' on 8 July 1958.*

The East Anglian

Liverpool Street to Norwich

ntroduced by the London & North Eastern Railway in 1937 (see page 94) 'The East Anglian' restaurant car express was suspended during the Second World War but reinstated in 1946. From 1948 it was operated by the Eastern Region of British Railways and was usually hauled by a Class 'B17' or 'B1' 4-6-0 until the arrival of the new BR Standard Class 7 'Britannia' 4-6-2s, fresh out of Crewe Works, in 1951. These magnificent locomotives soon transformed express services out of Liverpool Street and cut journey times considerably and their high-speed performances on the route to Norwich have gone down in the annals of post-war railway history. Sadly this was all too short lived and by 1960 English Electric Type 4 diesels had taken over – the up train still left Norwich at 11.45 a.m. and, with one stop at Ipswich, reached London at 2.05 p.m. (on Saturdays it arrived 10 minutes earlier). The down train left Liverpool Street at 6.30 p.m. and arrived back at Norwich (again with a stop at Ipswich) at 8.40 p.m. The train lost its title in 1962.

BELOW: *BR Standard Class 7 'Britannia' 4-6-2 No 70036* Boadicea *of Stratford shed passes through Stratford station in East London with 'The East Anglian' in August 1955.*

The Easterling

Liverpool Street to Lowestoft Central/Yarmouth South Town

A short-lived refreshment car train which ran during the summer months, this train travelled non-stop from London via Ipswich and the East Suffolk Line to Beccles where the two portions – one for Lowestoft Central and the other for Yarmouth South Town – were divided. These two portions were joined together at Beccles on the return journey. In its early years motive power was provided by a 'B17' 4-6-0 but new 'Britannia' Class 7 Pacifics soon replaced these ex-LNER workhorses. The 1955 summer timetable shows the train leaving Liverpool Street at 11.03 a.m. (10.33 a.m. on Saturdays) and arriving at Beccles at 1.16 p.m. (12.52 p.m. Saturdays), thence Yarmouth South Town was reached at 1.38 p.m. (1.14 p.m. Saturdays) and Lowestoft Central was reached at 1.43 p.m. (1.19 p.m. Saturdays). The return working (Monday–Saturday) arrived back at Liverpool Street at 10 p.m. The train was withdrawn at the end of the 1958 summer season and the line between Beccles and Yarmouth South Town closed on 2 November 1959.

BELOW: *The summer 1955 timetables for four named trains, including 'The Easterling', serving East Anglia from Liverpool Street.*

THE NORFOLKMAN
WEEKDAYS 13th JUNE TO 17th SEPTEMBER inclusive

		E	S			E	S
		a.m.	a.m.			p.m.	p.m.
London (Liverpool Street)	...dep.	9 30	9 30	Sheringham ...dep.	4 26	4 26
Ipswich { arr.	10 46	10 53	West Runton ... „	4 30	4 30
Ipswich { dep.	10 49	10 56	Cromer (Beach) ... „	4 42	4 42
Norwich (Thorpe) ...arr.	11 40	11 51	North Walsham (Main) „	5 5	5 5
		p.m.	p.m.	Wroxham ... „	5 20	5 20
Wroxham ... „	12 10	12 20	Norwich (Thorpe) ... „	5 45	5 45
North Walsham (Main)	„	12 22	12 35	Ipswich ... { arr.	6 36	6 38
Gunton ... „	12 33	...	Ipswich ... { dep.	6 38	6 41
Cromer (Beach) ... „	12 47	...	London (Liverpool Street) ...arr.	7 55	8 6
West Runton ... „	1 2	1 17				
Sheringham ... „	1 6	1 21				

E—Saturdays excepted   S—Saturdays only

Seats can be reserved in advance at a fee of 1/- per seat at the seat reservation offices, Liverpool Street or any other London terminus, station booking offices Sheringham and Cromer, seat reservation office, Norwich (for journeys to Ipswich and London), or through the usual agencies.

THE EASTERLING
WEEKDAYS 27th JUNE TO 10th SEPTEMBER inclusive

		S	E			p.m.
		a.m.	a.m.			
London (Liverpool Street)	...dep.	10 33	11 3	Yarmouth (South Town) ...dep.	7 15
		p.m.	p.m.			
Beccles ... ▲...arr.	12 52	1 16	Lowestoft (Central) ... „	7 16
Lowestoft (Central) ... „	1 19	1 43	Beccles ... ... „	7 42
Yarmouth (South Town) ... „	1 14	1 38	London (Liverpool Street) arr.	10 0

E—Saturdays excepted.   S—Saturdays only

Seats can be reserved in advance at a fee of 1/- per seat at the seat reservation offices, Liverpool Street or any other London terminus, station booking offices Lowestoft (Central) and Yarmouth (South Town), or through the usual agencies.

THE BROADSMAN
WEEKDAYS 13th JUNE TO 17th SEPTEMBER inclusive

		a.m.			E	S
					p.m.	p.m.
Sheringham ...	...dep.	6 23	London (Liverpool Street) dep.	3 30	3 30
West Runton ...	... „	6 27	Ipswich ... { arr.	4 43	4 53
Cromer (Beach) ...	... „	6 39	Ipswich ... { dep.	4 46	4 56
Gunton... ...	... „	6 54	Norwich (Thorpe) ...arr.	5 30	5 35
North Walsham (Main)	... „	7 2	Salhouse ... ... „	5 56	—
Worstead ...	... „	7 8	Wroxham ... „	6 3	6 16
Wroxham ...	... „	7 16	Worstead ... „	6 12	—
Salhouse ...	... „	7 24	North Walsham (Main) „	6 19	6 28
Norwich (Thorpe) ...	... „	7 45	Gunton ... „	6 30	6 39
Diss ...	... „	8 11	Cromer (Beach) ... „	6 44	6 53
Stowmarket ...	... „	8 29	West Runton ... „	6 58	7 6
Ipswich ...	{ arr.	8 42	Sheringham ... „	7 2	7 10
Ipswich ...	{ dep.	8 45			
London (Liverpool Street)	arr.	10 0			

E—Saturdays excepted   S—Saturdays only

Seats can be reserved in advance at a fee of 1/- per seat at the seat reservation offices, Liverpool Street or any other London terminus, station booking offices Sheringham and Cromer, seat reservation office, Norwich (for journeys to London and intermediate stations), or through the usual agencies.

THE EAST ANGLIAN
WEEKDAYS 13th JUNE TO 17th SEPTEMBER inclusive

		a.m.			p.m.
Norwich (Thorpe)	...dep.	11 45	London (Liverpool Street) dep.	6 30
Ipswich	{ arr.	12 D36	Ipswich ... { arr.	7 C45
Ipswich	{ dep.	12 D38	Ipswich ... { dep.	7 C49
London (Liverpool Street) arr.	1 D55	Norwich (Thorpe) ...arr.	8 C40

C—On Fridays arrives Ipswich 7.53, departs 7.56 and arrives Norwich (Thorpe) 8.51 p.m.

D—On Fridays and Saturdays arrives Ipswich 12.38, departs 12.41 and arrives Liverpool Street 2.6 p.m.

Seats can be reserved in advance at a fee of 1/- per seat at the seat reservation offices, Liverpool Street or any other London terminus, station booking office Ipswich, seat reservation office, Norwich (Thorpe), or through the usual agencies.

REFRESHMENT CAR TRAINS

The Elizabethan

King's Cross to Edinburgh Waverley/Aberdeen

The outbreak of the Second World War stopped the golden age of high-speed travel on the East Coast Main Line. It was only resumed in 1949 when the new 'Capitals Limited' (see page 133) was inaugurated by the Eastern, North Eastern and Scottish Regions of British Railways as the new non-stop express between King's Cross and Edinburgh. By 1952 the train had been speeded up to nearly match the pre-war schedules and in 1953 it was renamed 'The Elizabethan' in honour of Queen Elizabeth II's coronation. Hauled northbound by 'A4' Pacific No 60028 *Walter K. Whigham*, the introduction of this train on 29 June that year saw journey times cut to 6¾ hours in both directions and a year later it was cut to 6½ hours or just about a mile-a-minute for the 393-mile journey. Running only during the summer months, the heavily-loaded train, weighing in at around 420 tons, was probably the most demanding ever seen in Britain but Gresley's 'A4' Pacifics were certainly up to the job. Locomotives used on this run were fitted with corridor tenders allowing crews to change over without a stop, making this the longest scheduled non-stop railway journey in the world.

To celebrate this achievement British Transport Films made a highly regarded 20-minute documentary film of the train in 1954 – *Elizabethan Express* starred 'A4' Class Pacific No 60017 *Silver Fox* and featured a journey between the two capitals accompanied by music written by Clifton Parker.

The last steam-hauled 'The Elizabethan', hauled northbound by 'A4' Pacific No 60022 *Mallard*, ran on 8 September 1961 to be replaced by the new English Electric 3,300 hp 'Deltic' diesels. The train ran for the 1962 and 1963 summer seasons behind these new machines but as they did not have a corridor connection a stop was made at Newcastle for a crew change – so much for progress! The train ceased to run in September 1963.

BOTTOM LEFT: *The 1956 menu cover from 'The Elizabethan' restaurant car.*

BELOW: *The inaugural run of 'The Elizabethan' on 29 June 1953. The non-stop express from King's Cross to Edinburgh is headed by Class 'A4' 4-6-2 No 60028* Walter K. Whigham.

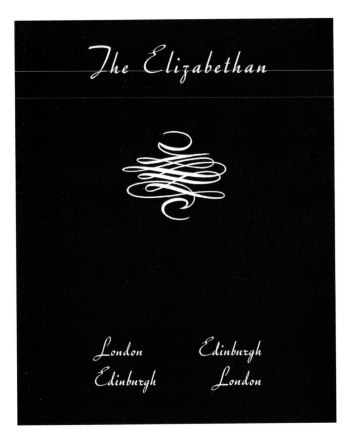

The Fair Maid

King's Cross to Perth

Following in the footsteps of the pre-war 'Coronation' (see pages 91–93), the introduction of 'The Talisman' (see pages 160–161) between King's Cross and Edinburgh in 1956 was hailed such a success that an additional morning working was inaugurated in 1957. The start of the winter timetable in that year saw this morning service renamed 'The Fair Maid' with the northern terminus extended to Perth. The new train was named after Sir Walter Scott's novel *The Fair Maid of Perth*, which is about the 14th century Battle of North Inch. With intermediate stops at Darlington, Newcastle, Berwick and Edinburgh, the down train took 8 hrs 28 min to complete its journey while the up train took 8 hrs 50 min. The new extended working was not successful and a year later the train lost its name and reverted back to the morning 'The Talisman' service between King's Cross and Edinburgh.

RIGHT: *The 1957 menu cover from 'The Fair Maid' restaurant car.*

BELOW: *Driver attaching the headboard to Class 'A4' 4-6-2 No 60015* Quicksilver *in readiness for the inaugural run of the 'The Fair Maid'. King's Cross shed, 3 September 1957.*

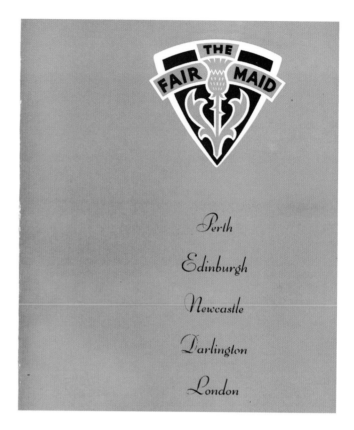

Perth

Edinburgh

Newcastle

Darlington

London

The Fenman

Liverpool Street to Hunstanton/Bury St Edmunds

Working express trains out of Liverpool Street along some of the busiest commuter lines in the world was no mean feat. Needless to say journey times between the capital and Cambridge via Broxbourne were fairly lethargic and it was into this scene that the Eastern Region's new named buffet car train, 'The Fenman', was introduced between Liverpool Street and the Norfolk seaside resort of Hunstanton in the summer of 1949. Running Mondays to Fridays, departure for the up train from Hunstanton was at 6.45 a.m. then all stations to King's Lynn where the train reversed direction. There were then intermediate stops at Downham, Ely and Cambridge where a portion from Bury St Edmunds was attached before reaching Liverpool Street at 10.04 a.m. The down train left the capital at 4.30 p.m. and with the same stops arrived at Hunstanton at 8.05 p.m. The train was speeded up in 1953, losing the Bury St Edmunds portion but adding one for March and Wisbech which was attached or detached at Ely. For some obscure reason the train ran on Saturdays but was unnamed and minus the buffet car. Until the advent of diesel haulage in 1959, the train was normally hauled by a 'B17' Class or 'B1' Class 4-6-0. The rot had set in by 1960 with the March and Wisbech portion dropped and the train starting or terminating its journey at King's Lynn – passengers to or from Hunstanton then had to travel in a separate diesel multiple unit.

I was fortunate to travel on 'The Fenman' from King's Lynn to Liverpool Street behind English Electric Type 3 (Class 37) diesel D6710 on 16 August 1965. The train lost its name in 1968 and the Hunstanton branch was closed on 5 May 1969, much to the anger of local residents and Poet Laureate John Betjeman.

BOTTOM LEFT: *The summer 1950 leaflet for 'The Fenman'.*

BELOW: *Class 'B1' 4-6-0 No 61392 arrives at Audley End station with 'The Fenman', 22 August 1956. The 112-mile journey from Hunstanton to Liverpool Street took over 3 hours, at an average speed of 35 mph.*

The Flying Scotsman

King's Cross to Edinburgh Waverley

The successor to the 'Special Scotch Express' (see page 15), 'The Flying Scotsman' restaurant car express between King's Cross and Edinburgh Waverley was introduced by the London & North Eastern Railway in 1924 (see pages 96–97). With the help of corridor tenders it became a non-stop service between King's Cross and Edinburgh in 1928. It continued to operate through the Second World War and continued to be run by the Eastern, North Eastern and Scottish regions of British Railways from 1948.

In the summer of 1949 the new 'Capitals Limited' express (see page 133) took over the non-stop service and 'The Flying Scotsman' consequently lost this honour with stops en route at Grantham and Newcastle Central. In 1955 the train was once again accelerated running non-stop between King's Cross and Newcastle Central, cutting the London to Edinburgh journey time to 7 hours. Gresley's 'A4' Pacifics were replaced in 1962 by new 3,300 hp 'Deltic' diesels – these powerful locomotives, assisted by newly-introduced long stretches of 100 mph running along the East Coast Main Line, soon cut the 393-mile journey time, including the Newcastle stop, to a record-breaking 6 hours.

In turn, the 'Deltics' were replaced by HST 125 sets between 1976 and 1981 and the opening of the Selby diversion improved matters further. Electrification of the East Coast Main Line was completed in 1990 and since then InterCity 225 sets with a maximum permissible speed of 125 mph have provided an even faster service. Since privatisation the train has continued to run with a speeded-up service complete with special 'Flying Scotsman' livery being introduced in 2011 – the up train now takes 4 hrs 39 min between the two capitals. Strangely the 10 a.m. down working from King's Cross which takes 4 hrs 21 min does not carry the name in the timetable.

BOTTOM LEFT: *The down 'The Flying Scotsman' passes non-stop through York behind Peppercorn Class 'A1' 4-6-2 No 60156 Great Central on 10 April 1954.*

BELOW: *Original watercolour produced in 1962 for a poster promoting travel on 'The Flying Scotsman' behind one of the new 'Deltic' 3,300 hp diesel locos.*

In this atmospheric 1950s photograph by Eric Treacy, 'The Flying Scotsman' departs from King's Cross behind Class 'A4' 4-6-2 No 60014 Silver Link.

The Harrogate Sunday Pullman

King's Cross to Leeds/Bradford/Harrogate

'The Yorkshire Pullman' (see page 109) had been introduced by the London & North Eastern Railway in 1935, replacing the 'West Riding Pullman' (see page 99) which had been introduced in 1923. On Sundays this set of Pullman coaches was used for the 'The Harrogate Sunday Pullman' but this train was withdrawn on the outbreak of war in 1939. It was reinstated by the Eastern and North Eastern regions of British Railways in June 1950 as a Sundays-only service which ran non-stop between King's Cross and Leeds. Here the train divided – one portion travelling to and from Bradford and other to and from Harrogate. In the 1950s and early 1960s the train was usually hauled by one of Leeds Copley Hill

shed's Peppercorn 'A1' Class Pacifics but these were replaced by new 'Deltic' diesels in 1962. The train was withdrawn in March 1967.

RIGHT: *Class 'A2/3' 4-6-2 No 60500* Edward Thompson *approaches Stoke Summit with 'The Heart of Midlothian' express on 18 July 1959.*

BOTTOM RIGHT: *The 1951 linear route map of 'The Heart of Midlothian'.*

BELOW: *'The Harrogate Sunday Pullman' in all its glory passes Beeston Junction south of Leeds pulled by Peppercorn Class 'A1' 4-6-2 No 60148* Aboyeur, *c.1960.*

The Heart of Midlothian

King's Cross to Edinburgh

For many years the two early afternoon departures (2 p.m.) from Edinburgh and King's Cross remained nameless but in 1951 British Railways bestowed the name of 'The Heart of Midlothian' on these trains to commemorate the Festival of Britain. Consisting of 12 brand-new all-steel BR standard (Mk 1) coaches, each train also included the largest kitchen car ever put into service in Britain – cooking was carried out using a flexible source from either anthracite or electricity. At its inception both up and down trains departed at 2 p.m. and with stops at Peterborough, York, Darlington and Newcastle the down train arrived in Edinburgh at 9.55 p.m. Carriages for Morpeth, Alnmouth and Berwick were removed at Newcastle and followed on as a slower train. Conveying through coaches from Aberdeen, the up train called at Berwick, Newcastle, Darlington, York and Grantham and arrived at King's Cross at 10.02 p.m. Motive power was provided by a variety of ex-LNER Pacifics until 'Deltic' diesels took over in 1962, when timings were slashed to give a 6½-hour journey for the up train and 6¾ hours for the down service. The train lost its name in 1968.

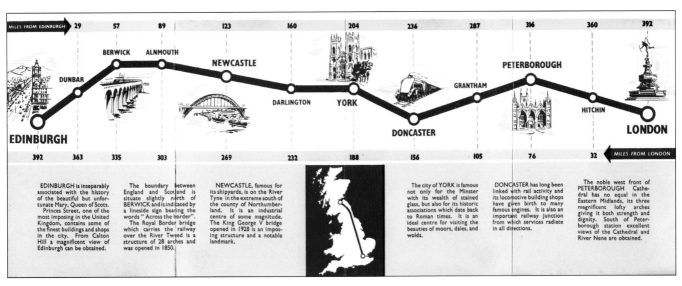

EDINBURGH is inseparably associated with the history of the beautiful but unfortunate Mary, Queen of Scots. Princes Street, one of the most imposing in the United Kingdom, contains some of the finest buildings and shops in the city. From Calton Hill a magnificent view of Edinburgh can be obtained.

The boundary between England and Scotland is situate slightly north of BERWICK and is indicated by a lineside sign bearing the words "Across the border". The Royal Border bridge which carries the railway over the River Tweed is a structure of 28 arches and was opened in 1850.

NEWCASTLE, famous for its shipyards, is on the River Tyne in the extreme south of the county of Northumberland. It is an industrial centre of some magnitude. The King George V bridge opened in 1928 is an imposing structure and a notable landmark.

The city of YORK is famous not only for the Minster with its wealth of stained glass, but also for its historic associations which date back to Roman times. It is an ideal centre for visiting the beauties of moors, dales, and wolds.

DONCASTER has long been linked with rail activity and its locomotive building shops have given birth to many famous engines. It is also an important railway junction from which services radiate in all directions.

The noble west front of PETERBOROUGH Cathedral has no equal in the Eastern Midlands, its three magnificent lofty arches giving it both strength and dignity. South of Peterborough station excellent views of the Cathedral and River Nene are obtained.

The Hook Continental

Liverpool Street to Harwich Parkeston Quay

'The Hook Continental' restaurant car express was introduced by the London & North Eastern Railway in 1927 (see page 101). The service was suspended during the Second World War but reintroduced in late 1945. It continued to be operated by the Eastern Region of British Railways from 1948. Motive power was then provided by 'B17' or 'B1' 4-6-0s but the introduction of new BR Standard Class 7 4-6-2 'Britannias' to Stratford shed in 1951 brought a marked improvement to the service and the down journey time to Parkeston Quay was slashed to only 1 hr 30 min. The 'Britannias' were replaced by English Electric Type 4 diesels in 1958, further speeding up the train by 10 minutes, followed by Class 37 and Class 47 haulage until electrification of the route in 1986. With the introduction of electric multiple units the train lost its name in 1987.

RIGHT: *Waiter serving 1st Class passengers on 'The Hook Continental', 20 June 1961.*

BELOW: *Stratford shed's brand new BR Standard Class 7 'Britannia' No 70001* Lord Hurcomb *prepares to haul 'The Hook Continental' in the summer of 1951.*

The Hull Pullman

King's Cross to Hull

Replacing previous Pullman services to Leeds, Bradford and Harrogate, 'The Yorkshire Pullman' (see pages 109 and 170–171) received its name in 1935 and conveyed Pullman carriages to or from Hull that were detached from or attached to the main train at Doncaster. Although withdrawn for the duration of the Second World War, the train returned in 1946 and continued to run with the Hull portion until March 1967 when a new luxury Pullman train, 'The Hull Pullman', was introduced. Initially hauled by a Class 47 diesel, the seven-coach up train put in a spirited performance with the 10.35 a.m. departure from Hull reaching King's Cross in 189 minutes. Departing from King's Cross in the early

evening the down train took 195 minutes – both trains called at Doncaster, Goole and Brough. 'Deltic' haulage was introduced in the early 1970s when the train was lengthened and continued to run in this guise until 1978 when it was replaced by the non-Pullman 'The Hull Executive'. Usually hauled by a 'Deltic' diesel, the latter train ceased to run in this form in early 1981 when it was replaced by HST 125s.

BELOW: *'Deltic' Class 55 diesel No 55017* The Durham Light Infantry *leaves Doncaster with the up 'The Hull Pullman' on 22 June 1977.*

The Master Cutler

Marylebone/King's Cross to Sheffield Victoria

Introduced between Marylebone and Sheffield Victoria by the London & Eastern Railway in 1947 (see page 101), 'The Master Cutler' restaurant car express continued to be operated by the newly-formed Eastern Region of British Railways from 1948. That year saw the train leave Sheffield Victoria at 7.40 a.m. and, after stops at Nottingham Victoria, Leicester Central and Rugby Central, arrived at Marylebone at 11.15 a.m. The down train left Marylebone at 6.15 p.m. and with the same stops arrived back at Sheffield at 10.02 p.m. The downgrading of the former Great Central Railway route saw 'The Master Cutler' transferred to King's Cross in 1958. Up to then the train had firstly been hauled by 'B1' 4-6-0s, then 'A3' Pacifics and latterly by BR Standard Class 5 4-6-0s. From 15 September 1958, with new English Electric Type 4 diesels at the head of the train, the new route from King's Cross provided a much faster service for Sheffield businessmen, getting them into the capital at 10.15 a.m.

with a 7.20 p.m. departure for the return service. The only intermediate stop in both directions was at Retford. Pullman cars were introduced in September 1960 and these were also used for the 'Sheffield Pullman' (see page 157) express between King's Cross and Sheffield, but with more stops, that ran during the day. The Pullman cars were replaced by standard coaching stock in April 1966 and 'The Master Cutler' was discontinued in 1968. Sheffield Victoria station closed on 5 January 1970.

LEFT: *Headed by Class 'B1' 4-6-0 No 61376, 'The Master Cutler' is seen at full speed on the Great Central mainline near Rugby, c.1953.*

BELOW: *This hand-coloured photograph shows 'The Master Cutler' hauled by English Electric Type 4 Class 40 diesel D209 on its new route from Sheffield to King's Cross in the autumn of 1960.*

The Night Scotsman

King's Cross to Edinburgh Waverley

Operated by the London & North Eastern Railway since 1923 (see page 102), 'The Night Scotsman' continued to be operated by the Eastern, North Eastern and Scottish regions of British Railways from 1948, but by then this sleeping car train only operated between King's Cross and Waverley. By the 1950s, often with new Peppercorn 'A1' Class Pacifics at the head, the train had been speeded up with one stop at Newcastle Central in both directions. The winter 1960 timetable shows that the official Newcastle stop had been dropped (although there would have been a crew change here), the steam-hauled train by then only conveying sleeping car passengers. The down train left King's Cross at 11.35 p.m. (Monday–Friday and Sunday/10.15 p.m. Saturday) and arrived at Edinburgh at 7.26 a.m. (5.55 a.m. on Sundays). The up train left Edinburgh at 10.50 p.m. daily and arrived at King's Cross at 6.43 a.m. New 3,300 hp 'Deltic' diesels were introduced at the head of this train in the summer of 1963 and schedules were immediately slashed to just under 7 hours including a crew change at Newcastle. The train continued to operate until 1988 when it was withdrawn. Today the 'Caledonian Sleeper' operates two overnight sleeping car trains between Euston and various destinations in Scotland.

BELOW: *Peppercorn Class 'A1' 4-6-2 No 60155* Borderer *is being prepared to haul 'The Night Scotsman' at King's Cross shed in front of BBC television cameras filming a Richard Dimbleby documentary about the train, 20 August 1952.*

The Norfolkman

Liverpool Street to Norwich/Cromer

Post-war successor (during the summer months) to the famous 'The Norfolk Coast Express' (see page 22) which was introduced by the Great Eastern Railway in 1907 but discontinued on the outbreak of the First World War, 'The Norfolkman' restaurant car express was introduced by the Eastern Region of British Railways in 1948. Running between Liverpool Street and Norwich Thorpe during the winter months, the train was extended to run to and from Cromer and Sheringham during the summer. Prior to the introduction of the new BR Standard Class 7 'Britannia' Pacifics in 1951 motive power was provided by 'B17' or 'B1' 4-6-0s and the down train left Liverpool Street at 10 a.m. and, after a 3-minute stop at Ipswich, arrived in Norwich Thorpe at 12.20 p.m. – in the summer it continued on, reversing direction out of Thorpe station behind a 'B1'

Class 4-6-0, stopping at Wroxham, North Walsham, Cromer High, West Runton and Sheringham (1.38 p.m.) – the train was slower on Saturdays. Cromer High station closed on 20 September 1954, after which the train was diverted to run to Cromer Beach. In the reverse direction the train left Sheringham at 3.35 p.m. and arrived back at Liverpool Street at 7.20 p.m. The 'Britannia' Pacifics managed to lop a full 10 minutes off the Liverpool Street to Norwich run and these timings continued with English Electric Type 4 diesel haulage introduced in 1959. Sadly, the train lost its name in June 1962.

BELOW: *Brand new BR Standard Class 7 'Britannia' No 70000 Britannia about to depart from Liverpool Street with 'The Norfolkman' on 2 February 1951.*

The Norseman

King's Cross to Tyne Commission Quay

For some years before the Second World War the London & North Eastern Railway ran a boat train to and from King's Cross that connected with a steamer service to and from Norway at Tyne Commission Quay, near Newcastle. Reintroduced as 'The Norseman' by British Railways in 1950, the down train had, by 1961, various departure times on Mondays, Wednesdays, Thursdays and Saturdays (9.20 a.m./9.30 a.m./9.40 a.m.) from King's Cross and called at York before arriving at Newcastle Central at 2.24 p.m./2.45 p.m. The ex-LNER Pacific, or on occasions a 'V2' 2-6-2, locomotive was taken off here and the heavy train was hauled for the rest of its journey to Tyne Commission Quay usually by a 'V3' 2-6-2 tank locomotive. Another boat train left King's Cross at 10.40 a.m. on summer Saturdays to connect with a steamer sailing to Stavanger (for Oslo Vest). In the opposite direction 'The Norseman' had an 11 a.m. departure from Tyne Commission Quay on Sundays and Fridays and a 7 a.m. departure on Mondays and Thursdays. An oddity of the North Eastern Region timetable of summer 1961 was that only the up train was named 'The Norseman'. Diesels in the shape of English Electric Type 4s and 'Deltics' had usurped steam haulage of the train by 1962. The train was withdrawn in 1966.

BELOW: *Rebuilt from a Class 'P2' 2-8-2 in 1944, Class 'A2/2' 4-6-2 No 60502* Earl Marischal *is seen here at the head of 'The Norseman', c.1960.*

The North Briton

Leeds City to Edinburgh Waverley and Glasgow Queen Street

An express restaurant car service had operated between Leeds City and Edinburgh Waverley since the early 20th century. The service had been extended to Glasgow Queen Street by 1914. By the outbreak of the Second World War and despite heavier loadings the schedule had seen vast improvements with nearly an hour lopped off the timings.

Reintroduced and named in 1949, 'The North Briton' became the first post-war service to include a mile-a-minute schedule (between Darlington and York). Haulage was usually behind ex-LNER 'A3' Pacifics or (from c.1950)

new Peppercorn 'A1' Class Pacifics from Leeds Neville Hill shed until they were replaced by Brush Type 4 (Class 47) diesels in the 1960s. The summer 1961 timetable saw the train leaving Leeds City at 9.15 a.m. on weekdays and after calling at York, Darlington, Newcastle and Dunbar arrived at Edinburgh Waverley at 1.53 p.m. (1.44 p.m. on Saturdays). Glasgow Queen Street was reached at 3.14 p.m. In the opposite direction Glasgow was left at 4 p.m. and with the same stops reached Leeds at 10.08 p.m. The train lost its name in 1968.

BELOW: *The first of its class, Class 'A3' 4-6-2 No 60036 Colombo makes a spectacular start from Leeds City station with 'The North Briton', c.1952.*

The Northumbrian

King's Cross to Newcastle-upon-Tyne

Receiving its name in 1949, 'The Northumbrian' restaurant car express was effectively a relief train to the overcrowded 1 p.m. departure from King's Cross to Edinburgh which during the Second World War had grown to over 20 coaches in length. During the last year of steam haulage in the summer of 1961 the down restaurant car train left King's Cross at 12.30 p.m. and after calling at Grantham, York, Darlington and Durham arrived at Newcastle at 5.48 p.m. (5.49 p.m. on Saturdays).

This train also conveyed through carriages for Scarborough which were detached at York and, on certain days, for Tyne Commission Quay detached at Newcastle. The up train left Newcastle at 12.50 p.m. (11.55 a.m. on Saturdays) and with the same stops plus Peterborough arrived at King's Cross at 6.07 p.m. The Saturday service omitted the Peterborough stop and arrived in the capital at 5.48 p.m. Following a couple of years of diesel haulage the train lost its name in 1964.

BELOW: *Class 'A3' 4-6-2 No 60105* Victor Wild *pauses at Grantham station with 'The Northumbrian' on 4 July 1956.*

The Queen of Scots

King's Cross to Glasgow Queen Street via Leeds and Harrogate

Introduced by the London & North Eastern Railway in 1928 (see page 104) and discontinued during the Second World War, 'The Queen of Scots' Pullman train was reintroduced by the Eastern, North Eastern and Scottish regions of British Railways in 1948. By then 'A3' Pacifics were hauling the train until new Peppercorn 'A1' Class Pacifics were introduced in the summer of 1950. Their introduction led to a speeding-up of the train which was then leaving King's Cross at 11.45 a.m. and arriving at Glasgow Queen Street at 9.20 p.m. – in the opposite direction departure from Glasgow was at 10.30 a.m. with arrival in London at 8.10 a.m. Steam haulage was replaced by English Electric Type 4 and 'Deltic' diesels in the early 1960s.

With the new 'Deltic' diesels in charge, by the summer of 1961 the train's schedule had been accelerated – the down train leaving King's Cross at 11.50 a.m. and after running non-stop to Leeds followed by stops at Harrogate, Darlington, Newcastle, Edinburgh Waverley and Falkirk High arrived at Glasgow Queen Street at 8.55 p.m. Without the Falkirk stop the up train left Glasgow at 11 a.m. and arrived at King's Cross at 8.09 p.m. (8.20 p.m. on Saturdays). After withdrawal of the train in 1964, the Pullman car sets were then transferred to a King's Cross to Harrogate express, 'The White Rose' (see pages 168–169).

BELOW: *Hauled by Peppercorn Class 'A1' 4-6-2 No 60127 Wilson Worsdell, 'The Queen of Scots' Pullman train crosses the Royal Border Bridge at Berwick-upon-Tweed, c.1950.*

THE QUEEN OF SCOTS

PULLMAN - EACH WEEKDAY

(KING'S CROSS) LONDON and GLASGOW (QUEEN STREET)

calling in each direction at

LEEDS HARROGATE DARLINGTON NEWCASTLE EDINBURGH

BRITISH RAILWAYS

PUBLISHED BY THE RAILWAY EXECUTIVE (EASTERN REGION) (AR 1006)   PRINTED IN GREAT BRITAIN   JORDISON & CO., LTD., PRINTERS, LONDON & MIDDLESBROUGH

LEFT: *1950s' BR poster promoting travel on 'The Queen of Scots'
Pullman train. Original artwork by Reginald Mayes.*

BELOW: *Hauled by a Class 'A3' 4-6-2, the luxury 'The Queen of Scots'
Pullman train nears the end of its long journey from Glasgow Queen Street
as it approaches King's Cross station, c.1948.*

The Scarborough Flyer

King's Cross to Scarborough Central/Whitby Town

This summer-only restaurant car express was introduced by the London & North Eastern Railway as the 'Scarborough Flier' [sic] in 1927, and was reintroduced by the Eastern and North Eastern regions of British Railways in 1950 (see page 105). The new schedule never lived up to the pre-war timings and by the summer of 1961 the down train was scheduled to leave King's Cross at 11.28 a.m. (Saturdays only, also Fridays 21 July to 18 August) and after calling at Grantham arrived at York at 3.11 p.m. (2.58 p.m. on Fridays). Here the Whitby portion was detached and after calling at Malton arrived at Scarborough Central at 4.11 p.m. (3.58 p.m. on Fridays). The Whitby portion arrived at its destination after travelling via Malton and Pickering at 5.21 p.m. The up service was unusual with a 10.42 a.m. departure from Scarborough on Saturdays only arriving back in the capital with the Whitby portion at 3.42 p.m. – on Sundays there was a 10.35 a.m. departure from Scarborough but

this time with no Whitby portion and it arrived in London at 3.56 p.m. Locomotive haulage between London and York was usually provided by an 'A3' Pacific or 'V2' 2-6-2 and from York to Scarborough by a 'B1' 4-6-0. The train lost its name at the end of the 1963 summer timetable. A victim of Dr Beeching's 'axe', the scenic line from Malton to Grosmont via Pickering was closed on 8 March 1965 but reopened north of Pickering in 1973 as the North Yorkshire Moors Railway – this is now one of the most popular heritage railways in Britain.

RIGHT: *Two views of the 'Sheffield Pullman'. No doubt caused by a diesel failure, the steam-hauled train is seen at Wymondley on 16 June 1961 headed by Class 'V2' 2-6-2 No 60817. The lower photo shows English Electric Type 3 (Class 37) D6749 at Corby Glen on 29 August 1962.*

BELOW: *King's Cross shed's Class 'A4' 4-6-2 No 60014 Silver Link heads through New Southgate station with 'The Scarborough Flyer' on 3 August 1957.*

Sheffield Pullman

King's Cross to Sheffield Victoria/Midland

The 'Sheffield Pullman' was introduced by the Eastern Region of British Railways in 1958. The train used the same Pullman coaches as the newly-diverted 'The Master Cutler' (see pages 146–147) thus making use of stock that would have otherwise lain idle during the off-peak period. Diesel-hauled from the beginning (although occasionally it would see steam haulage in its early years), the express was upgraded with new Pullman coaches in 1960 by which time the down train was leaving King's Cross at 11.20 a.m. and after calling at Peterborough, Grantham and Retford arrived at Sheffield Victoria at 2.24 p.m. Here there was a quick turnaround and the up train left at 3.20 p.m. and with the same stops arrived back in the capital at 6.25 p.m. – using the same coaching stock the down 'The Master Cutler' departed for Sheffield only 55 minutes later. The service was diverted to and from Sheffield Midland station in 1965 and was withdrawn in 1968.

The South Yorkshireman

Marylebone to Bradford Exchange

One of only two named trains that operated over the former Great Central mainline out of Marylebone – see also 'The Master Cutler', (pages 146–147) – 'The South Yorkshireman' was introduced by the Eastern Region of British Railways on 31 May 1948. In its first year of service the up train left Bradford Exchange at 10 a.m. and after stops at Huddersfield, Sheffield Victoria, Nottingham Victoria, Loughborough Central, Rugby Central and Aylesbury arrived at Marylebone at 3.15 p.m. (3.27 p.m. on Saturdays). The down train left Marylebone at 4.50 p.m. and, with the same stops except that Rugby was omitted and Penistone included, arrived back at Bradford at 10.20 p.m. The train was normally hauled by a 'B1' 4-6-0 or 'A3' Pacific between London and Sheffield and from there to Bradford by an ex-LMS Class '5MT' 4-6-0. The final train, on 2 January 1960, arrived back at Marylebone behind BR Standard Class 5 4-6-0 No 73066. By this date the Great Central route had been handed over to the London Midland Region and it was then served only by a few stopping trains between Marylebone and Nottingham until closure of this as a through route in 1966.

RIGHT: *The summer 1948 leaflet for 'The South Yorkshireman' showing its route from London to Bradford.*

BOTTOM RIGHT: *The up 'The South Yorkshireman' is seen here at Bradley Junction just to the east of Huddersfield behind Class 'B1' 4-6-0 No 61020 Gemsbok, 26 September 1959.*

BELOW: *Headed by Stanier Class 5 4-6-0 No M5101, 'The South Yorkshireman' departs from Bradford Exchange on its 5¼-hour journey to Marylebone, c.1948.*

BRITISH RAILWAYS

THE
SOUTH
YORKSHIREMAN

LONDON (MARYLEBONE)
RUGBY LEICESTER NOTTINGHAM
SHEFFIELD HUDDERSFIELD BRADFORD

MAY 31st to
SEPTEMBER 25th inclusive
1948

Published by the Railway Executive (Eastern Region).   P4/34/47.   W. & S. Ltd.

The Talisman

King's Cross to Edinburgh Waverley

Introduced in 1956, 'The Talisman' was the successor to the pre-war streamlined 'Coronation' express (see pages 91–93) that ran between King's Cross and Edinburgh. Hauled once again by Gresley's 'A4' Pacifics, the restaurant car express train included the luxurious 1st Class articulated coaches used by its predecessor although the beaver tail observation car had gone to pastures new in the Highlands of Scotland. The new train was a resounding success and the following year British Railways launched an additional morning service in both directions. The inaugural run of the down morning express on 17 June 1957 was hauled by King's Cross shed's immaculate 'A4' 4-6-2 No 60025 *Falcon*. An experiment to extend this new train (renamed 'The Fair Maid', see page 138) to Perth in the autumn of 1957 was not a commercial success and it was withdrawn the following year. By the autumn of 1960 the down morning 'The

Talisman' was departing from King's Cross at 8.05 a.m. and after stops at Darlington, Newcastle, and Berwick arrived at Edinburgh at 3.06 p.m. The up morning service left Edinburgh at 8.30 a.m. and after the same stops arrived at King's Cross at 3.35 p.m. The afternoon 'The Talisman' was much quicker with only one stop at Newcastle in both directions – the up train took 6 hrs 49 min while the down train took 2 minutes longer. Steam gave way to the new 'Deltic' diesels in 1961/62 and this soon led to an acceleration of the trains. An extension to Glasgow Queen Street for the morning train in 1962 also bit the dust in a fairly short time. The use of older Pullman cars in the make-up of the train was also a short-lived experiment. Such was the immense power of the 'Deltics' that by 1967 both the up the down afternoon trains were completing the 393-mile journey in just under 6 hours.

The train was withdrawn in 1968 but reinstated three years later to one service in each direction. HST 125's took over from the 'Deltics' in 1978 but the train had lost its name by 1991 by which time the East Coast Main Line had been electrified.

I witnessed D9019 *Royal Highland Fusilier* in a bit of bother when hauling the up morning 'The Talisman' at Peterborough on 12 August 1965 – unfortunately the locomotive had failed and was being assisted by D5056.

LEFT: *Hauled by 'A4' Class 4-6-2 No 60028* Walter K. Whigham, *'The Talisman' sets off on its journey from King's Cross to Edinburgh Waverley on 18 September 1956.*

RIGHT: *The front cover of the menu for the new 'The Talisman' express restaurant car, 1956.*

BELOW: *'Deltic' diesel-electric D9016* Gordon Highlander *calls at Newcastle Central for a crew change while hauling 'The Talisman', c.1963. Withdrawn in 1981, this powerful loco has since been preserved.*

The Tees-Thames

King's Cross to Saltburn

'The Tees-Thames' was a short-lived restaurant car express that operated between King's Cross and Saltburn via York. Inaugurated on 2 November 1959, the up train left Saltburn at 7.05 a.m., calling at Redcar East, Redcar Central, Middlesbrough, Thornaby and Eaglescliffe before arriving at York at 8.40 a.m. where locomotives were changed and extra coaches added. Haulage from Saltburn to York was usually behind a 'B1' 4-6-0 or 'V2' 2-6-2. The train departed from York at 8.48 a.m. and ran non-stop to Welwyn Garden City before arriving at King's Cross at 12.28 p.m. Haulage between York and London was usually behind an 'A1', 'A3' or 'A4' Pacific until the advent of English Electric Type 4 diesels in the winter of 1960/61. The return down train left King's Cross at 2 p.m. and after stopping at Peterborough, and Grantham arrived at York at 5.46 p.m. Here locomotives were changed for the final run to Saltburn, arriving at 7.34 p.m. 'The Tees-Thames' was withdrawn in September 1961 after less than two years in service.

RIGHT: *The final summer 1961 timetable for the short-lived 'The Tees-Thames' express.*

BELOW: *Class 'A3' 4-6-2 No 60103 Flying Scotsman passes the 'Deltic' diesel-electric prototype at Peterborough while hauling the down 'The Tees-Thames' express, 1960.*

THE TEES-THAMES
RESTAURANT CAR EXPRESS

SALTBURN, REDCAR, MIDDLESBROUGH, THORNABY, YORK and LONDON (King's Cross)

WEEKDAYS

			SO am 6 5	SX am 7 5					SX pm	SO pm
SALTBURN	..	.. dep	6 5	7 5	LONDON (King's Cross)	..	dep		2 0	4 20
Redcar East	..	.. ,,	6 12	7 12	Peterborough (North)	..	.. ,,		3 26	5 54
Redcar (Central)	..	.. ,,	6 17	7 17	Grantham	..	.. ,,		4 5	6 38
Middlesbrough	{ arr		6 31	7 35	Doncaster..	..	.. ,,		..	7 45
	{ dep		6 34	7 40				arr	..	8 11
Thornaby	..	.. ,,	6 41	7 47	Selby	..	.. {	dep	..	8 13
West Hartlepool	..	.. ,,	..	7A10				arr	5 37	8 33
Eaglescliffe	..	.. ,,	6 48	7 54	York	..	.. {	dep	5 44	8 43
York	..	.. { arr	7 35	8 40	Eaglescliffe	..	.. arr		6 33	9 33
	{ dep		7 43	8 48	West Hartlepool	..	.. ,,		7A18	10T15
Selby	..	.. { arr	8 1	..	Thornaby..	..	.. ,,		6 41	9 42
	{ dep		8 3	..	Middlesbrough	{ arr			6 47	9 48
Doncaster	..	.. arr	8 28	..		{ dep			6 51	9 53
Retford	..	.. ,,	9 5	..	Redcar (Central)	..	.. arr		7 9	10 11
Grantham	..	.. ,,	9 47	..	Redcar East	..	.. ,,		7 12	10 14
Peterborough (North)	..	,,	10 27	..	SALTBURN	..	.. ,,		7 23	10 24
Welwyn Garden City	..	,,	..	11 51						
LONDON (King's Cross)		,,	11 59	pm 12 20						

A—Change at Eaglescliffe.   SO—Saturdays only.   SX—Saturdays excepted.
T—Change at Thornaby.

Seats are reservable in advance for passengers travelling from London (King's Cross) and from Saltburn, Redcar (Central) and Middlesbrough daily and York (Mondays to Fridays) to London (King's Cross) on payment of a fee of 2s. 0d. per seat.

Tees-Tyne Pullman

King's Cross to Newcastle Central

Seen by British Railways as a successor to the 'Silver Jubilee' (see pages 106–108), the all-Pullman 'Tees-Tyne Pullman' entered service in 1948. Sadly, apart from using the same route and calling at Darlington, this new train was a shadow of the pre-war high-speed streamliner initially taking an hour longer to complete the same journey. By 1949 the up train was leaving Newcastle at 9.15 a.m. and arriving at King's Cross at 2.15 p.m., while the down train left London at 4.45 p.m. and arrived back at Newcastle at 9.45 p.m. – this allowed only 2½ hours in the capital for business meetings. Motive power for the nine-coach train was usually provided by an 'A4' Pacific until these were replaced by English Electric Type 4s in the late 1950s. By 1960 timings had improved but they were still nowhere near their pre-war levels – however passengers could while away their time in the popular Hadrian Bar car! In the autumn of that year the up train left Newcastle at 9.25 a.m. and after stopping at Darlington reached King's Cross at 2.14 p.m. The down service left the capital at 4.50 p.m. and after stopping at York and Darlington reached Newcastle at 9.41 p.m. The introduction of 'Deltic' diesels in the early 1960s saw a marked improvement with the up train reaching an average speed of just over 80 mph between Darlington and York – a first in Britain for a scheduled service. By 1975, 40 years after the introduction of the 4-hour 'Silver Jubilee', the down train was reaching Newcastle in 3 hrs 45 min. Despite this, the train was withdrawn in 1976. However, the name was later bestowed on the record-breaking HST service of 1985.

RIGHT: *The route map of the 'Tees-Tyne Pullman', April 1949.*

FAR RIGHT: *Silver service on board the record-breaking HST 'The Tees-Tyne Pullman' of 1985.*

BELOW: *'A4' Class 4-6-2 No 60006* Sir Ralph Wedgwood *is seen here hauling the 'Tees-Tyne Pullman' at Ganwick Curve, between Hadley North and Potters Bar, 2 September 1952.*

THE ROUTE OF THE TEES-TYNE PULLMAN

NEWCASTLE
Sunderland
R. Tyne
Durham
R. Tees
R. Wear
DARLINGTON
Middlesbrough
NORTH
SEA
York
Hull
R. Ouse
Doncaster
R. Don
R. Trent
The Wash
N
Grantham
Peterborough
R. Ouse
Norwich
Yarmouth
Cambridge
Harwich
KING'S CROSS
LONDON
R. Thames

Published by the Railway Executive (N.E. Region) 4/49 Printed in Gt. Britain   B.J. & Co. York

Tees Tyne Pullman
Bill of Fare
Prices include 15% VAT, service not included.

Two course meal

This comprises main dish, with sweet, savoury or cheese board.
Coffee is included. The price is governed by the choice of main dish.
Additional items may be selected from the à la carte list.

Steak "Pullman" £10·95
*Sirloin Steak in a White Wine Sauce
with Tomatoes, Mushrooms and Onions*

Fillet of Sole Maître d'Hôtel £8·95

Smoked Ham and Roast Chicken with Mixed Salad £7·95

Celery Hearts, Garden Peas

Sauté and Parsley Potatoes

Raspberry Charlotte Russe

Selection of Fresh Fruit

Selection from the Cheese Board with Salad and Biscuits

Sardines on Toast

Coffee Service

If you prefer, select any of the following dishes:—

A la carte

Asparagus Soup with Fresh Cream	95p	Prawn Salad	£3·25
Choice of Chilled Fruit Juices	60p	Raspberry Charlotte Russe	£1·25
Grilled Grapefruit with Honey	£1·15	Selection of Fresh Fruit	£1·00
Avocado Vinaigrette	£1·65	Cheese Board, Salad and Biscuits	£1·20
Avocado with Prawns	£2·35	Sardines on Toast	£1·20
Smoked Salmon Pâté	£1·70	Buttered Toasted Teacake	
Ardennes Pâté	£1·35	with Preserves or Honey	95p
Sandwich Selection: *Three half*		Fresh Danish Pastry	75p
rounds chosen from Prawns,		Biscuits	16p
Cheese, Ham, Tongue	£1·60	Coffee Service	75p
Wholemeal Asparagus Flan		Pot of Freshly Brewed Tea	75p
with Mixed Salad	£2·95		

TRAVELLERS FARE

PI 7/85

Trans-Pennine

Liverpool Lime Street to Hull

Six sets of diesel multiple units (later Class 124) built at Swindon Works made up the innovative 'Trans-Pennine' series of express trains linking Liverpool to Hull (introduced 1960). The stylish six-car trains included a buffet and grill car serving hot meals. With rapid acceleration the lightweight trains made easy going of the former London & North Western Railway's heavily-graded route across the Pennines with the majority of the six return services each weekday taking just under 3 hours for their journey. Two extra services were run on weekdays between Liverpool and Leeds. In their early years the multiple units had the logo 'Trans-Pennine' emblazoned below the panoramic wrap-round windows at each end with the name also carried on roof boards attached to the sides of each coach.

In 1979 the 'Trans-Pennine' service was reorganized with locomotive haulage serving the main artery between Liverpool and York. From then onwards the original 'Trans-Pennine' diesel multiple units combined with reallocated Western Region (Class 123) Inter-City cousins were used for a Leeds to Hull service until they were replaced by locomotive hauled stock in 1984.

RIGHT: *Poster produced by BR in the early 1960s to promote travel on the 'Trans-Pennine' service.*

BELOW: *Within a year of introduction the distinctive 'Trans-Pennine' headboards had gone. Here a 'Trans-Pennine' diesel multiple unit speeds through Copley Hill at Leeds with a Hull to Liverpool express on 3 May 1961.*

The Tynesider

King's Cross to Newcastle Central

This sleeping car express was put into service by the Eastern and North Eastern regions of British Railways in 1950. In its first year of operation the down train was leaving King's Cross at 11.45 p.m. and after numerous stops en route arrived at Newcastle at 6.08 a.m. – these are Monday–Friday timings, although the train ran to slightly different schedules at weekends. The up train left Newcastle at 10.35 p.m. and, with stops at Durham, Darlington, York and Grantham, arrived at King's Cross at 4.45 a.m. Either way it could hardly be called an express! The train was steam-hauled until the early 1960s when diesels took over – the 1960/61 winter timetable shows the down train also conveying through sleeping cars for Edinburgh Waverley. The train was withdrawn in 1967.

The West Riding

King's Cross to Leeds Central/Bradford Exchange

Introduced by the Eastern and North Eastern regions of British Railways in 1949, 'The West Riding' was the successor to the London & North Eastern Railway's pre-war streamlined high-speed 'The West Riding Limited' (see pages 109) which was suspended, never to return, on the outbreak of the Second World War. Some of the luxurious twin-articulated coaches from the pre-war train were initially incorporated in this new restaurant car express which was usually hauled between King's Cross and Leeds by one of the new Peppercorn 'A1' Class Pacifics from Copley Hill shed – between Wakefield Westgate and Bradford Exchange the 'express' was ignominiously hauled by two ex-LNER 'N2' 0-6-2 tank engines in its early years! By the autumn of 1960 the routine had changed with the down train leaving King's Cross at 7.45 a.m. and after calling at Hitchin, Retford, Doncaster and Wakefield (where the Bradford portion was detached for its journey via Morley Top) arrived at Leeds at 11.38 a.m. The up train left Leeds at 7.30 a.m. (Bradford 7.05 a.m.) and arrived in King's Cross at 11.15 a.m. Brand new 'Deltic' diesels took over a year later but the train lost its name in 1967.

BOTTOM LEFT: *Hauling the 'The West Riding', Class 'A4' 4-6-2 No 60029 Woodcock at speed on Werrington Troughs, north of Peterborough, on 18 July 1959.*

BELOW: *Route map for the newly-introduced 'The West Riding', 1949.*

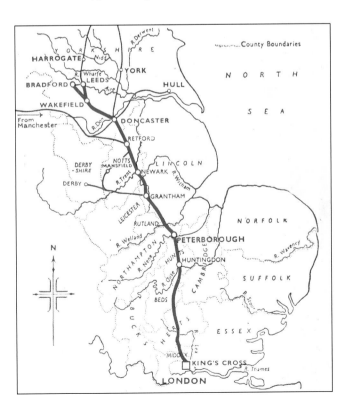

The White Rose

King's Cross to Leeds Central/Bradford Exchange

An unnamed service had operated between the West Riding of Yorkshire and London since the early 20th century and 'The White Rose' was its post-war successor, introduced by British Railways on 23 May 1949. The new train conveyed through coaches to and from Bradford and was in the capable hands of 'A1', 'A3' or 'A4' Pacifics between Leeds and London until 'Deltic' diesels appeared at the end of 1961. The inaugural timetable shows the up train leaving King's Cross at 9.15 a.m. and, after stops at Doncaster and Wakefield, arriving at Leeds Central at 1.16 p.m. At Wakefield the Bradford portion was detached and, after stopping at Morley Top, arrived at 1.38 p.m. In the opposite direction the Bradford portion left at 4.50 p.m. with stops at Batley and Dewsbury, while the main train left Leeds at 5.15 p.m., arrival of the combined train in London was at 9.55 p.m.

Gradually replacing steam from the autumn of 1961, the new 'Deltics' at the front of the train soon brought a rapid acceleration to its schedule. However when 'The Queen of Scots' all-Pullman' train (see pages 153–155) was withdrawn in 1964 the coaches from that train were transferred to 'The White Rose' service which was then extended to run to and from Harrogate. The train was withdrawn in 1967.

RIGHT: *Photographed by Eric Treacy, 'A3' Class 4-6-2 No 60046 Diamond Jubilee waits to depart from Leeds Central station with the up 'The White Rose', c.1955.*

BELOW: *The summer 1949 leaflet for 'The White Rose'.*

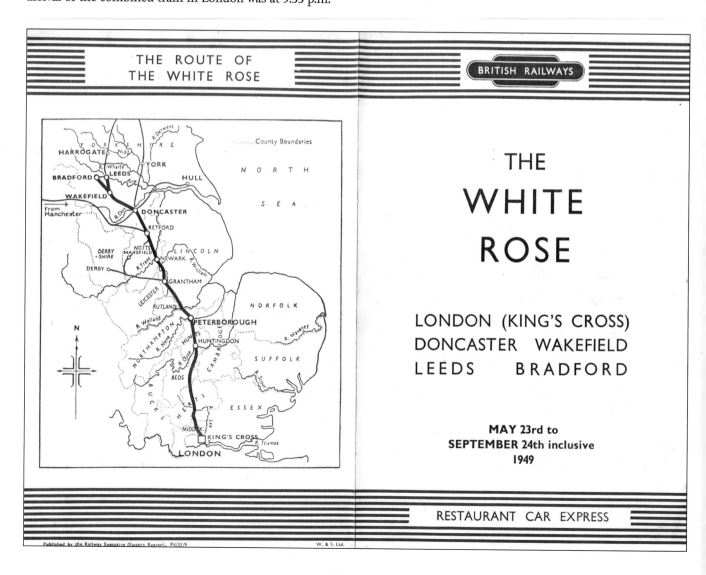

THE ROUTE OF
THE WHITE ROSE

BRITISH RAILWAYS

THE

WHITE

ROSE

LONDON (KING'S CROSS)
DONCASTER   WAKEFIELD
LEEDS   BRADFORD

MAY 23rd to
SEPTEMBER 24th inclusive
1949

RESTAURANT CAR EXPRESS

Published by the Railway Executive (Eastern Region). P4/55/9   W. & S. Ltd.

Yorkshire Pullman

King's Cross to Hull/Leeds/Bradford/Harrogate

ntroduced by the London & North Eastern Railway in 1935 (see page 109), the 'Yorkshire Pullman' was suspended during the Second World War and reinstated in 1946. From 1948 it was operated by the Eastern and North Eastern regions of the newly-formed British Railways. The heavy 11-coach Pullman express with portions for Hull (detached at Doncaster) and Bradford (detached at Leeds) was usually hauled between King's Cross and Leeds by an 'A3' Pacific until the new Peppercorn 'A1' Class Pacifics entered service in 1948–9. By the winter of 1960/61, less than 12 months before the arrival of 'Deltic' diesels, the steam-hauled up train was leaving Harrogate at 10.07 a.m. and after collecting the Bradford portion at Leeds and the Hull portion at Doncaster arrived at King's Cross at 2.45 p.m. The down train left King's Cross at 5.20 p.m. and arrived at Harrogate at 10.02 p.m.

The arrival of the 'Deltics' and new Metropolitan-Cammell Pullman cars in the autumn of 1961 brought a rapid acceleration to the down train with 38 minutes being slashed off the King's Cross–Leeds schedule. The up train saw a similar acceleration a year later. The Hull portion became the separate 'The Hull Pullman' (see page 145) in 1967 and consequently the stop at Doncaster was omitted and the schedule further speeded up with the down train taking only 181 minutes between King's Cross and Leeds. The train was withdrawn in 1978.

RIGHT: *King's Cross shed's immaculate Class A3 4-6-2 No 60062 Minoru about to depart from King's Cross station on the down 'Yorkshire Pullman', April 1961.*

BELOW: *The summer 1948 leaflet for the 'Yorkshire Pullman'.*

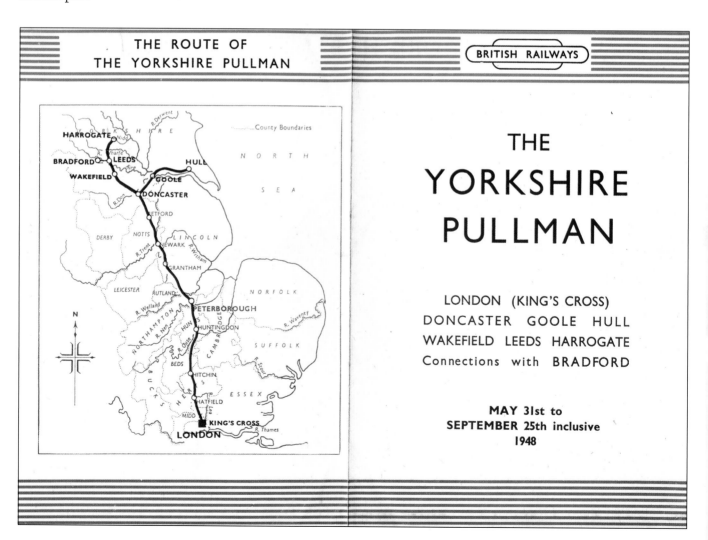

THE ROUTE OF THE YORKSHIRE PULLMAN

BRITISH RAILWAYS

THE

YORKSHIRE

PULLMAN

LONDON (KING'S CROSS)
DONCASTER GOOLE HULL
WAKEFIELD LEEDS HARROGATE
Connections with BRADFORD

MAY 31st to
SEPTEMBER 25th inclusive
1948

London Midland Region

When formed on 1 January 1948 the newly nationalized London Midland Region (LMR) of British Railways (BR) took over the network of the London Midland & Scottish Railway south of the Anglo-Scottish border. From its main London termini of Euston and St Pancras the LMR continued to operate restaurant car expresses to the Midlands, North Wales and the northwest as well as Anglo-Scottish services via the West Coast Main Line and the Settle–Carlisle Line. In addition to the inter-regional services operated jointly with the Scottish Region (see page 209), the LMR also ran two inter-regional named trains: the 'Pines Express' (see page 195) between Manchester and Bournemouth jointly with Southern Region and 'The Devonian' (see page 179) between Bradford and Paignton jointly with the Western Region. The LMR also operated sleeping car services between London and Barrow-in-Furness, Carlisle, Glasgow, Edinburgh, Inverness, Leeds, Liverpool, Manchester, Oban and Stranraer and also inter-regional sleeper services between Bristol and Newcastle, Plymouth and Manchester, Liverpool and Glasgow and Manchester and Glasgow. The LMR operated boat trains between Euston and Holyhead (for Dun Laoghaire), Liverpool (for Dublin,

BELOW: *Poster produced in 1961 for the London Midland Region to celebrate the first phase of West Coast Main Line electrification on completion of the routes between Crewe and Manchester and Crewe and Liverpool.*

An artist's impression of an electrically hauled express passing a local electric train between Liverpool and Crewe

LONDON MIDLAND ELECTRIFICATION

MANCHESTER · LIVERPOOL · BIRMINGHAM · LONDON

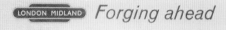 *Forging ahead*

Electric trains are now running between Liverpool and Crewe, completing the second stage of this vast scheme. The first stage, between Manchester and Crewe, was completed in 1960.

Belfast and Isle of Man), Heysham (for Belfast/Isle of Man) and Stranraer (for Larne) and also between Manchester and Heysham (for Belfast).

Mainline locomotive construction continued apace at Crewe Works and Derby Works. At Crewe the very last 'Coronation' Class Pacific was completed in 1948 while further Stanier Class 5MT 4-6-0s were also built here until 1949 along with examples that were built at Horwich Works until 1951. Crewe went on to build 55 BR Class 7 'Britannia' 4-6-0s from 1951 to 1954 and the unique Class 8 4-6-2 No 71000 *Duke of Gloucester* in 1954. The last steam locomotive built at Crewe was BR Standard Class 9F 2-10-0 No 92250 which was completed at the end of 1958. Derby Works built 130 of the BR Standard Class 5 4-6-0s between 1951 and 1957. Both Derby and Crewe then switched to building mainline diesel-electric locomotives with Derby producing 10 Class 44 (1959–60) and 56 Class 46 (1961–3) and between them they also built 127 of Class 45 (1960–62). Crewe also built 202 of Class 47 diesel-electric locomotives in the 1960s, 44 of the Class 52 diesel-hydraulics for the Western Region (1962–3) and 197 Class 43 diesel-electric power cars (1975–82) for the InterCity 125 HST. Crewe also built 36 of the Class 87 (1973–5), 50 Class 90 (1987–90), and 31 Class 91 (1988–91) mainline electric locomotives after which locomotive building by British Rail Engineering ceased.

The 'Beeching Report' of 1963 brought many route closures within the LMR. Notable among these was the line from Bangor to Afonwen which closed in stages between 1964 and 1970; the former Great Central Railway mainline which closed as a through route on 5 September 1966; the line across the Lake District between Penrith and Workington which closed in stages between 1966 and 1972. However many routes were reprieved, notable among them being the Settle–Carlisle Line, the Cumbrian Coast Line and the Sheffield to Manchester route via the Hope Valley – the electrified Sheffield to Manchester via Woodhead line was closed instead.

The LMR was the last region of BR to use steam haulage and this ended in August 1968. The principal route electrified by the LMR was the West Coast Main Line which was completed in stages: Crewe to Manchester in 1960, Crewe to Liverpool in 1962, Euston to Crewe in 1966, the Birmingham loop in 1967 and Weaver Junction (north of Crewe) to Carlisle and beyond to Glasgow in 1974.

Major regional boundary changes occurred in 1958 when LMR lines southwest of Birmingham and in South Wales were transferred to the Western Region and lines in Lincolnshire and Yorkshire were transferred to the Eastern and North Eastern Regions. At the same time the LMR gained the Great Central (Marylebone to Sheffield) route from the Eastern Region. A further boundary change came in 1963 when the region gained all lines west of Birmingham from the Western Region. The final change came in 1974 when the Chiltern Line from Marylebone to Birmingham was also gained from the Western Region.

The LMR ceased to be an operating unit following sectorisation in the 1980s and ceased to exist in 1992.

On a visit to Camden shed (1B) on 4 September 1962 I was lucky enough to spot some iconic ex-LMS Pacifics not long before they were withdrawn. 'Princess Royal' Class: 46206 (withdrawn 20/10/62); 'Coronation' Class: 46227 (w/d 12/62), 46229 (w/d 02/64 + preserved), 46236 (w/d 03/64), 46239 (w/d 10/64), 46240 (w/d 10/64). Other than two 'Jubilee' Class 4-6-0s (45631 and 45736) all the rest in the shed were a total of 18 English Electric Type 4 diesels.

While on a trainspotting trip to Carlisle on 29 July 1964 I was fortunate enough to visit both Kingmoor (12A) and Upperby (12B) engine sheds. Despite the fact that steam haulage was to end on BR in just over four years' time, these two engine sheds were still the equivalent of trainspotters' heaven. At Kingmoor I recorded no less than 86 steam locomotives, including eight BR Standard Class 7 'Britannia' 4-6-2s, three 'Coronation's Class 4-6-2s, four 'Royal Scot' 4-6-0s, one 'Rebuilt Patriot' Class 4-6-0 and four 'Jubilee' Class 4-6-0s. At Upperby I recorded 40 steam locomotives including one 'Princesss Royal' Class 4-6-2 (albeit withdrawn), four 'Coronation' Class 4-6-2s, two 'Royal Scot' Class 4-6-0s, five 'Rebuilt Patriot' Class 4-6-0s and four 'Jubilee' Class 4-6-0s. Time was also spent at Carlisle station on this trip and another on 1 August – apart from recording a handful of English Electric Type 4 and 'Peak' diesels, I was in steam paradise, an experience never to be forgotten, but sadly soon to end.

Belfast Boat Express

Manchester Victoria to Heysham Harbour

Originally introduced by the London Midland & Scottish Railway, the 'Belfast Boat Express' had the dubious honour of being the last steam-hauled named train on British Railways. Connecting with steamers to and from Belfast at Heysham Harbour, the last down steam-hauled train left Manchester Victoria at 8.55 p.m. on 4 May 1968 behind Carnforth shed's Stanier 'Black 5' 4-6-0 No 45342 – the next day the last steam-hauled up train left Heysham Harbour at 6.15 a.m. behind sister engine No 45025. Apart from the period 1968 to 1970 when the port facilities were being rebuilt, the train continued to run with diesel haulage until 5 April 1975 when the ferry services to Belfast were withdrawn. The Heysham Harbour branch was closed on 6 October 1975 but reopened on 11 May 1987 when ferry sailings to the Isle of Man were introduced.

BELOW: *The very last steam-hauled named train in Britain, the 'Belfast Boat Express', makes its last departure from Manchester Victoria to Heysham Harbour behind Stanier Class 5 4-6-0 No 45342 on 4 May 1968.*

The Caledonian

Euston to Glasgow Central

The London Midland and Scottish regions of British Railways introduced 'The Caledonian' in 1957 as the successor to the pre-war 'Coronation Scot' streamlined train (see page 75) between Euston and Glasgow Central. With one intermediate stop at Carlisle the up train left Glasgow at 8.30 a.m. and the down train left Euston at 4.15 p.m. Hauled by Stanier's ex-LMS de-streamlined 'Coronation' Class Pacifics, the train was 10 minutes slower than the 'Coronation Scot' even though it had one less coach. The average speed between Euston and Carlisle was just over 60 mph and between Carlisle and Glasgow just under. An up test run in September 1957 saw the train arrive 37 minutes ahead of time at Euston but, despite this amazing performance, there was no change to the schedule. The train was one of very few to not only carry its name on a front headboard attached to the locomotive but also at the rear of the last coach.

An additional 'The Caledonian' was introduced in 1958, this time leaving Euston at 7.45 a.m. and from Glasgow at 4 p.m. – these were known as the 'Morning Caledonian' and the 'Afternoon Caledonian' respectively but they were withdrawn less than a year later. With electrification of the West Coast Main Line gathering pace the train's schedule was slowed in 1962 and by the following year, with English Electric Type 4 diesels now in control, had three more stops added – in addition to Carlisle it now called at Stafford, Crewe and Wigan. The train was withdrawn at the end of the summer timetable in September 1964.

BELOW: 'Coronation' Class 4-6-2 No 46240 City of Coventry *waits to depart from Glasgow Central with the up 'The Caledonian' for Euston on 21 July 1959.*

OVERLEAF TOP: *Hauled by 'Coronation' Class 4-6-2 No 46236* City of Bradford, *'The Caledonian' makes a fine sight as it exits Northchurch Tunnel, Berkhamsted, on 21 September 1960.*

OVERLEAF BOTTOM: *The stylish cover of the restaurant car tariff for 'The Caledonian' issued by BR in 1957.*

The Caledonian

You are sitting in *The Caledonian*, the latest named train on the West Coast Route between England and Scotland.

With *The Royal Scot* and *The Mid-day Scot* this train provides the limited stop daytime service between London Euston and Glasgow Central Stations, a distance of 401¼ miles.

Few journeys can in so short time give so varied a picture of Britain. Look out in particular for the wild beauty of the upper Lune Gorge south of Tebay and the upper reaches of the Clyde north of Beattock.

Do not miss the crossing of the Border by Gretna, just north of Carlisle, and your only view of the sea between London and Carlisle at Hest Bank near Lancaster. You get three more glimpses of the sea between Carlisle and Lockerbie and if the weather be clear you will see Skiddaw in the Lake District too.

Spare a glance, even, for the Manchester Ship Canal by Warrington no less than for the Lake hills west of Penrith. All these, and more, you can see in comfort from your seat in *The Caledonian*.

If you enjoy the comfort of *The Caledonian*, and are travelling again, we would remind you that all seats are reservable, and should be booked in advance, as the accommodation is limited.

THE CALEDONIAN

Tariff

The Comet

Euston to Manchester London Road/Piccadilly

ntroduced by the London Midland & Scottish Railway in 1932 (see page 74), and suspended during the Second World War, 'The Comet' was once one of the fastest services between Manchester and London. The restaurant car express was reintroduced by the London Midland Region of British Railways in 1949 and, until the introduction of English Electric Type 4 diesels in its latter years, it was usually hauled by a 'Royal Scot' 4-6-0 or a BR Standard 'Britannia' Class 4-6-2. In 1954 the train was considerably speeded-up with a 3½-hour journey time between London and Manchester. However, by 1962, with West Coast Main Line electrification underway, the train's schedule had slowed considerably – the down train was leaving London Euston at 9.50 a.m. (Monday–Friday) and with stops at Stoke-on-Trent, Macclesfield and Stockport Edgeley arrived at Manchester Piccadilly at 1.51 p.m. The up train left Manchester Piccadilly at 5.55 p.m. (Monday–Friday), calling at Stockport Edgeley and Watford Junction before arriving at Euston at 9.35 p.m. Following modernization, Manchester London Road was renamed Manchester Piccadilly in 1960. With electrification of the West Coast Main Line gathering pace, 'The Comet' was withdrawn at the end of the summer season in 1962.

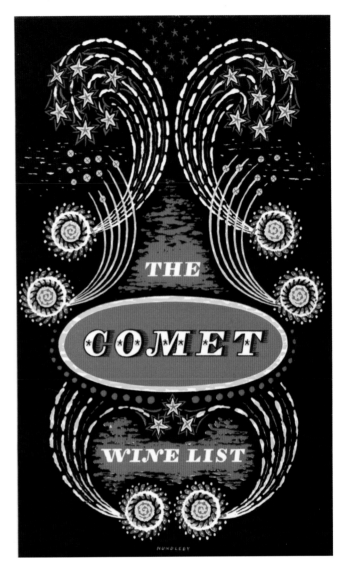

RIGHT: *The eye-catching wine tariff from 'The Comet' with original artwork by 'Hundleby'.*

BELOW: *Experimentally fitted with Westinghouse air-pumps, BR Standard Class 7 'Britannia' 4-6-2 No 70043 is seen hauling 'The Comet' in 1954. The loco was later fitted with smoke deflectors and named Lord Kitchener.*

Bristol Barrow Road shed's 'Jubilee' Class 4-6-0 No 45699 Galatea being prepared before hauling 'The Devonian' as far as Bristol, c.1960. After withdrawal in 1964, this locomotive was stored at Barry Scrapyard for 15 years before being preserved.

The Devonian

Bradford Forster Square/Exchange to Paignton/Kingswear

Established by the London Midland & Scottish Railway in 1927 (see page 76), suspended during the Second World War and reinstated in 1946, 'The Devonian' restaurant car train continued to be operated between Bradford Forster Square and Paignton and Kingswear by the London Midland and Western regions of British Railways from 1948. During the winter months it ran nameless between Bradford and Bristol only. Until the advent of 'Peak' Class 45 diesels in 1961 the weekday train was normally hauled between Leeds City and Bristol Temple Meads by an ex-LMS Holbeck (55A) 'Jubilee' Class 4-6-0. At Bristol this locomotive was exchanged for an ex-GWR 'Castle' Class 4-6-0 for the run to Paignton. Probably the last year that saw some steam haulage was the summer of 1962 when the Saturdays-only main train left Bradford Forster Square at 9.05 a.m., reversed direction at Leeds City and arrived at Paignton at 6.00 p.m. – the normal weekday stops (Monday–Friday) at Sheffield Midland, Derby, Birmingham New Street and

Gloucester were all omitted. Strangely the timetable for this year does not show the train continuing on to Kingswear. In the reverse direction the Saturday train departed from Kingswear at 9.00 a.m. and Paignton at 9.30 a.m. and arrived at Bradford at 6.57 p.m. but this time omitted the usual stops at Bristol, Cheltenham and Birmingham – locomotives were still changed at Bristol and the motive power between Kingswear and Paignton was often provided by a humble ex-GWR '5700' Class 0-6-0PT complete with headboard and express passenger train headcode! Despite the advent of the 'Peak' diesels in the early 1960s, journey times saw little improvement, Exchange station in Bradford replaced Forster Square as the northerly starting station in 1967 and the train lost its name in 1975.

BELOW: *'Castle' Class 4-6-0 No 7000* Viscount Portal *is seen here approaching Whiteball Tunnel, near Wellington in Somerset, with 'The Devonian' on 17 June 1958.*

The Emerald Isle Express

Euston to Holyhead

Passengers wishing to travel overnight to Ireland via Holyhead had for years used the trusted 8.45 p.m. departure from Euston – known as 'The Irish Mail' (see pages 37, 77–78 and 181–182), its arrival at Holyhead in the early hours left a lot to be desired for those wishing to put their head down on the ferry. To cater for travellers wanting a good night's sleep on the ferry an earlier train left Euston at 5.35 p.m. – introduced after the Second World War this restaurant car train was given the name of 'The Emerald Isle Express' in 1954. With intermediate stops at Stafford, Crewe, Chester and Llandudno Junction the train arrived at Holyhead at 10.55 p.m. for the ferry crossing to Dun Laoghaire. Connecting with the ferry from Ireland, the up service left Holyhead at 7.30 a.m. and arrived back at Euston at 1.18 p.m. Motive power was usually provided by BR Standard 'Britannia' or 'Coronation' Class Pacifics until these were replaced by new English Electric Type 4 diesels in the early 1960s. By then, with West Coast Main Line electrification gathering pace, the arrival time at Holyhead for the down train had slid to 11.13 p.m. with the arrival of the up train at Euston put back to 1.30 p.m. (Sunday–Thursday)/1.40 p.m. (Friday and Saturday). From April 1966 the train was diverted with electric haulage between Euston and Coventry and then diesel haulage to and from Holyhead via Birmingham New Street – the result was that the train became even slower. Matters improved once electrification was completed between Euston and Crewe in 1967 with no less than 90 minutes shaved off the schedule of the up train – strangely the down train was still diverted via Birmingham New Street but with nearly half an hour cut off the journey time. The train lost its title in May 1975.

BOTTOM LEFT: *Holyhead shed's BR Standard Class 7 'Britannia' 4-6-2 No 70048 (later named* The Territorial Army 1908–1958*) approaches Headstone Lane near Harrow with the up 'The Emerald Isle Express' on 15 April 1957.*

BELOW: *The stylish menu cover for 'The Emerald Isle Express', late 1950s.*

THE EMERALD ISLE EXPRESS

The Irish Mail

Euston to Holyhead

A mail train had operated between Euston and Holyhead since 1848 (see page 37) but it was only named 'The Irish Mail' by the London Midland & Scottish Railway in 1927 (see pages 77–78). The train continued to be operated by the London Midland Region of British Railways from 1948. By the early 1950s it was being hauled by new 'BR Standard 'Britannia' 4-6-2s and even the 'Coronation' Class 4-6-2s for a short while after their demotion from West Coast Main Line duties in the late 1950s and early 1960s. By this time the down night train (8.40 p.m. out of Euston) was booked to run non-stop between Euston and Holyhead (arrival 2 a.m.). The up train was slower with stops at Chester, Crewe and Rugby. Such was the demand for seats on the night service that relief trains to both up and down trains were also run. Steam had been replaced by English Electric Type 4 diesels by the early 1960s and in 1966 the switch-on of the electrified West Coast Main Line between Euston and Crewe introduced the first ever change of locos for the train at the latter junction station. With the demise of mail being carried by rail, the onset of cheap air travel and faster ferry crossings 'The Irish Mail' was discontinued in 1985.

OVERLEAF: *The BR 1955 summer timetable and explanatory leaflet for 'The Irish Mail'.*

BELOW: *Stanier Class 5 4-6-0 No 45056 and an unidentified 'Coronation' Class 4-6-2 rest at Euston station after arriving with the heavily loaded up 'The Irish Mail', 8 April 1960.*

BELOW (INSET): *This early BR luggage label celebrates the centenary of the world's oldest named train, 'The Irish Mail', 1848–1948.*

THE IRISH MAIL

DAY SERVICE between LONDON AND DUBLIN

BRITISH RAILWAYS

THE IRISH MAIL

The successful debut of railways operated by locomotives in 1830, the introduction of the penny post in 1840, and a demand for a faster mail service between London and Dublin were sequences in a cycle of events which led directly to the construction of the Chester and Holyhead Railway (1844-1850) and the establishment of the first all-railway owned route to Ireland. The Chester and Holyhead Company built four ships for the new service; two of their names are perpetuated by the present 5,000 ton motor ships *Cambria* and *Hibernia*.

The Irish Mail made its inaugural run in August 1848. Robert Stephenson's masterpiece, the famous Britannia Tubular Bridge, was not then finished and rails reached only to Bangor, then from Llanfair to Holyhead. Passengers and mail were conveyed by coach over Telford's Suspension Bridge between the railheads.

The Britannia Bridge was opened in 1850 and so was forged the final link in the chain of railway communication between London and Holyhead and the creation of the route of *The Irish Mail* as it is today.

Tinlings, Liverpool

BRITISH RAILWAYS

BR 35109/23

THE IRISH MAIL
DAY SERVICE
1st July to 17th September 1955

TO IRELAND—WEEKDAYS

LONDON Euston	dep.	8 15 am
HOLYHEAD	dep.	2 30 pm
DUN LAOGHAIRE	arr.	5 45 pm
DUBLIN		
Westland Row	arr.	6 43 pm

FROM IRELAND
MONDAYS TO FRIDAYS

DUBLIN		
Westland Row	dep.	8 00 am
DUN LAOGHAIRE	dep.	9 15 am
HOLYHEAD	arr.	12 35 pm
LONDON Euston	arr.	6 40 pm

SATURDAYS

DUBLIN		
Westland Row	dep.	10 00 am
DUN LAOGHAIRE	dep.	11 35 am
HOLYHEAD	arr.	2 50 pm
LONDON Euston	arr.	9 10 pm

The *Irish Mail* overnight service runs throughout the year in both directions.

RESERVATION OF SEATS

Seats on the trains to and from Holyhead can be reserved in advance, fee 1/- each seat. For journeys from London reservations can be made at Euston and other London terminal stations, or official railway agents.

Passengers travelling from Ireland should apply to the General Agent, British Railways, 15 Westmoreland Street, Dublin.

STEAMER RESERVATION TICKETS

Steamer reservation tickets, issued free of charge, will be required for sailings to and from Ireland on certain days during the holiday season. A folder containing full information can be had on request to the addresses shown above.

MEALS

Breakfast, Morning Coffee, Luncheon, Afternoon Tea and Dinner as appropriate according to the direction of travel are served in the refreshment car. Light refreshments and a corridor service are made available whenever practicable.

The Lakes Express

Euston to Windermere/Workington

The year 1927 saw the introduction of 'The Lakes Express' by the London Midland & Scottish Railway (see page 79). The service was suspended during the Second World War and then reinstated by the London Midland Region of British Railways in the summer of 1950.

By the early 1960s the weekday (Monday–Saturday) restaurant car train had lost its Blackpool and Barrow/Whitehaven portions – in 1962 the down train left Euston at 11.35 a.m. and arrived at Workington at 7.53 p.m. while the up train left Workington at 8.40 a.m. and arrived at Euston at 5.10 p.m. There was also a portion for Windermere which was detached from the train at Oxenholme. The main portion continued to Penrith where there was a change of locomotive – newly-introduced Ivatt Class 2 2-6-0s would then haul the train

through the Lake District to Keswick and Workington. The train survived in this form until 1965 after which the Penrith to Workington line – a victim of Dr Beeching's 'axe' – was closed in two stages: Keswick to Workington closed in 1966 and Penrith to Keswick in 1972. Windermere continued to be served by a nameless train from Euston for a few more years but completion of West Coast Main Line electrification in 1974 saw an end to this service.

BELOW: *Hauled by former Cardiff Canton locomotive BR Standard Class 'Britannia' No 70019* Lightning, *'The Lakes Express' is seen here passing Winwick Quay signal box, Warrington, in the early 1960s.*

The Lancastrian

Euston to Manchester London Road/Piccadilly

Introduced by the London Midland & Scottish Railway in 1928 (see page 79), 'The Lancastrian' restaurant car express between Euston and Manchester London Road was suspended on the outbreak of the Second World War and not named by the London Midland Region of British Railways until 1957. The pre-war through coaches carried on the down train to Colne and Rochdale had already been withdrawn in 1952 and one peculiarity of the train was that the up and down services took different routes – between Mondays and Fridays (departure from Euston at 7.45 a.m.) the down train travelled via Crewe and Stockport arriving in Manchester Piccadilly at 11.38 a.m. However the up service (departure from Manchester at 4.05 p.m.) travelled via the more difficult Macclesfield and Stoke-on-Trent route before reaching Euston at 8.05 p.m. (Monday–Friday). On Saturdays both up and down trains travelled via Stoke. (All times courtesy of the LMR summer 1962 timetable.) The train's sister, 'The Mancunian' (see pages 79 and 185) also took both routes but in the opposite directions. The train was discontinued at the end of the summer timetable in 1962 when most expresses between London and Manchester were retimetabled to run via the Midland route to and from St Pancras to make way for the electrification of the West Coast Main Line.

LONDON EUSTON and MANCHESTER PICCADILLY					
WEEKDAYS					
	Mons. to Fris.	Sats.		Mons. to Fris.	Sats.
	am	am		pm	pm
London Euston ....dep	7 45	8 30	Manchester Piccadilly ....dep	4 5	4 10
Watford Junction .. .. .. ,,	8‡10	8‡58			
Rugby Midland .... ,,	....	10 28	Stockport Edgeley .. .. .. ,,	4 17	4 24
Nuneaton Trent Valley .. .. ,,	..	10 44			
Stoke-on-Trent .... ,,	....	11 57	Macclesfield .... ,,	4 36	4 43
Macclesfield .. .. ,,	pm 12 28		Stoke-on-Trent.. .. .. .. ,,	5 9	5 13
Crewe.................... ,,	10 59	....			
Stockport Edgeley .. .. ..arr	11 27	12 48	Watford Junction ....arr	7‡29	7‡43
Manchester Piccadilly .... ,,	11 38	1 3	London Euston.. .. .. .. ,,	8 5	8 15

ABOVE: *The summer 1962 timetable for 'The Lancastrian'.*

The Manchester Pullman/The Liverpool Pullman

Euston to Manchester Piccadilly/Liverpool Lime Street

Following completion of West Coast Main Line (WCML) electrification between Euston and Manchester in 1966, the diesel 'The Midland Pullman' service (see pages 190–191) between St Pancras and Manchester Central ended and the trains were transferred to the Western Region. They were replaced by electric locomotive haulage along the WCML with a new eight-coach all-Pullman train running two return journeys each weekday. By 1967 the schedule had been cut to 2½ hours between the two cities. A similar service was provided between Liverpool and Euston but in this case the train consisted of only four Pullman cars plus four normal second class coaches. The latter service ended in 1975 but 'The Manchester Pullman' (from 1985 onwards the Pullman coaches were replaced by new BR Mk 3 coaches) continued in operation until 1997, making it the last surviving Pullman service in Britain.

ABOVE: *The up 'Manchester Pullman' leaves Manchester Piccadilly behind Class 86/2 electric loco No 86228 on 8 June 1984.*

The Mancunian

Euston to Manchester London Road/Piccadilly

In 1927 the London Midland & Scottish Railway (see page 79) introduced 'The Mancunian' restaurant car express. It was discontinued during the Second World War but revived by the London Midland Region of British Railways in 1949. As in the pre-war years the up and down trains took different routes, travelling up via Crewe and Wilmslow and down via Stoke-on-Trent – the exact opposite of 'The Lancastrian' (see pages 79 and 184). The through coaches from Colne and Rochdale, which were attached to the up train at Wilmslow, were withdrawn in 1952 and by the summer of 1962, with electrification of the West Coast Main Line already underway, the weekday train was making slow progress with the 9.40 a.m. departure from Manchester running non-stop to Euston in 3 hrs 40 min – the down train took 3 hrs 55 min with a stop at Wilmslow. The Saturday down service was even slower with additional stops at Cheadle Hulme and Stockport Edgeley. By the very early 1960s steam haulage in the shape of rebuilt 'Royal Scot' 4-6-0s or 'Britannia' Pacifics had given way to diesel haulage in the shape of English Electric Type 4s. In the autumn of 1962 almost all services to and from Manchester were diverted to run via the Midland route to and from St Pancras because of electrification work on the West Coast Main Line – 'The Mancunian' was the only exception, continuing to run to and from Euston until April 1966 when it was withdrawn.

BELOW: 'Royal Scot' Class 4-6-0 No 46111 Royal Fusilier *and English Electric Type 4 diesel (Class 40) D215* Aquitania *stand at Euston after arriving with the up 'The Mancunian' and the up 'The Merseyside Express' respectively on 21 October 1959.*

The Manxman

Euston to Liverpool Lime Street

Providing connections with steamers to and from the Isle of Man, 'The Manxman' restaurant car express was introduced by the London Midland & Scottish Railway in 1927 (see page 80). The train was discontinued on the outbreak of the Second World War but reintroduced as a summer-only service by the London Midland Region of British Railways in 1951. Running Mondays to Saturdays in the summer months the 1962 down service left Euston at 10.20 a.m. (10.25 a.m. on Saturdays) and with an intermediate stop at Crewe arrived at Lime Street at 2.20 p.m. (2.35 p.m. on Saturdays). The up train left Lime Street at 2.05 p.m. (2.10 p.m. on Saturdays) and after a stop at Rugby arrived at Euston at 5.50 p.m. (6.20 p.m. on Saturdays). Until English Electric Type 4 diesels took over in the early 1960s the heavily loaded train was often hauled by ex-LMS 'Princess Royal' Pacifics from Liverpool Edge Hill shed. Electrification of the West Coast Main Line saw the train discontinued at the end of the 1965 summer timetable.

RIGHT: *Poster produced for BR in 1955 promoting 'The Manxman' boat express. Original artwork featuring a 'Royal Scot' loco by A. N. Wolstenholme.*

BELOW : *'Princess' Class 4-6-2 No 46203* Princess Margaret Rose *passes Winsford while hauling 'The Manxman' in August 1959.*

The Merseyside Express

Euston to Liverpool Lime Street

Introduced between Euston and Liverpool Lime Street by the London Midland & Scottish Railway in 1927 (see page 80), 'The Merseyside Express' lost its name on the outbreak of the Second World War but was revived in 1946. From 1948 it continued to be operated by the London Midland Region of British Railways. Loading up to 15 coaches, including two restaurant cars, the heavy train was normally hauled by a Liverpool Edge Hill 'Princess Royal' Pacific and, for a while, also carried through coaches to and from Southport Chapel Street. By the summer of 1962 steam had given way to English Electric Type 4 haulage with the up service leaving Liverpool at 10.10 a.m. and travelling non-stop to Euston where it arrived at 1.55 p.m. (15 minutes later on a Saturday). The down service left Euston at 6.10 p.m. (6.05 p.m. on Saturdays) and made an intermediate stop on the outskirts of Liverpool at Mossley Hill before reaching Lime Street at 10.10 p.m. The train lost its name following the completion of electrification of the West Coast Main Line between Euston and Manchester in 1966.

RIGHT: *The cover of the wine list for 'The Merseyside Express', c.1955.*

BELOW: *A sign of things to come as the 'Deltic' prototype diesel-electric loco, complete with speed whiskers, heads 'The Merseyside Express' past Edge Hill, Liverpool, c.1956.*

The Mid-Day Scot

Euston to Glasgow Central

The London Midland & Scottish Railway, introduced 'The Mid-Day Scot' in 1927 (see page 81) and it continued to operate throughout the Second World War and thence from 1948 by the newly-formed London Midland and Scottish regions of British Railways. The Aberdeen and Edinburgh portions had already ended in 1939 and by now the train only operated between Euston and Glasgow Central. During the years of steam haulage motive power for this heavy train was usually supplied by an ex-LMS Stanier Pacific although the unique BR Standard Class 8 4-6-2 No 71000 *Duke of Gloucester* was also a regular performer from 1954 onwards. By the summer of 1962, with diesel haulage in the shape of English Electric Type 4s, the up weekday train was departing from Glasgow at 1.30 p.m. and with stops at Carlisle, Wigan and Crewe arrived at Euston at 8.55 p.m.

The down weekday train left Euston at 1 p.m. and with stops at Crewe, Carlisle and Carstairs arrived at Glasgow at 8.30 p.m. The Saturday service was slower but the Sunday service was painfully slow – the down service taking just over 9 hours and the up service taking 9½ hours to complete their journeys – all due to electrification work on the West Coast Main Line. The train lost its name in 1966.

LEFT: *Edge Hill shed's 'Rebuilt Patriot' Class 4-6-0 No 45525* Colwyn Bay *storms up through Edge Hill Cutting with up 'The Merseyside Express, in the early 1950s.*

BELOW: *Hauled by 'Coronation' Class 4-6-2 No 46221* Queen Elizabeth, *'The Mid-Day Scot' passes through Low Gill station, Cumbria, 1959.*

The Midland Pullman

St Pancras to Manchester Central

The British Transport Commission took over the British Pullman Car Company in 1954 and a year later the British Railways Modernisation Programme was published – one of its main objectives was the replacement of steam by diesel power. A committee was soon set up to look into the introduction of diesel-hauled express passenger trains and in 1957 it was announced that the Metropolitan-Cammell Carriage & Wagon Company of Birmingham would build five high-speed diesel multiple-unit Pullman sets to be introduced in 1958 on the London Midland Region (LMR) between St Pancras and Manchester Central and on the Western Region (WR) between Paddington and Bristol and Birmingham.

Finished in two-tone Nanking blue and white with a grey roof, the coaches were fitted with double glazing, air conditioning and sumptuous seating with passengers being served at their tables by staff dressed in matching blue uniforms. The streamlined power cars at each end of the train were each fitted with a 1,000 hp NBL/MAN diesel engine driving electric transmission with a top speed of 90 mph. The two LMR sets were six-car formation (this included the two non-accommodating power cars) providing 132 1st Class seats while the three WR sets were eight-car formation (see 'Blue Pullmans, pages 237–238).

Following delays the first 'Blue Pullmans' finally entered service on the LMR between St Pancras and

The New MIDLAND PULLMAN

First Class de luxe travel — Supplementary fares

8.50 am	Manchester Central ↑	9.21 pm	Mondays to Fridays from 4th July	12.45 pm	St. Pancras ↑	4.00 pm
9.04 am	Cheadle Heath	9.07 pm			Leicester	
12.03 pm ↓	St. Pancras	6.10 pm		2.10 pm ↓	London Road	2.33 pm

 The last word in rail comfort. Limited accommodation, book in advance

Manchester on 4 July 1960. With West Coast Main Line electrification now underway they were to provide the fastest journey time ever between Manchester and London until this major project was completed. Running only from Mondays to Fridays, the up train left Manchester Central at 8.50 a.m. and with one stop at Cheadle Heath arrived at St Pancras at 12.03 p.m. (by 1962 the departure had been brought forward to 7.45 a.m. with an 11 a.m. arrival in the capital). The down train left St Pancras at 6.10 p.m. and with one stop at Cheadle Heath arrived back in Manchester at 9.21 p.m. (9.20 p.m. in 1962). In between these two services the 'Blue Pullman' sets managed a trip from St Pancras to Leicester and back (in 1962 extended to Nottingham). The trains were withdrawn in April 1966 on completion of electrification between Euston and Manchester Piccadilly and transferred to the Western Region (see page 238).

LEFT: *Stylish BR Poster and timetable produced for the inaugural 'The Midland Pullman' on 4 July 1960. Original artwork by A. N. Wolstenholme.*

RIGHT: *BR poster of 1962 promoting 'The Midland Pullman' service between St Pancras and Manchester Central and the new extended midday service to Nottingham Midland.*

BELOW: *'The Manchester Pullman' waits to depart from St Pancras station in the 1960s.*

The Midlander

Euston to Wolverhampton High Level

Receiving its name in 1950, 'The Midlander' was the successor to the pre-war 2-hour expresses that were operated by the London Midland & Scottish Railway between Euston and Birmingham New Street. Competing with the GWR's similar service between Paddington, Birmingham Snow Hill and Wolverhampton Low Level the LMS trains started or ended their journeys at Wolverhampton High Level. Running only from Mondays to Fridays, the restaurant car express was normally hauled by 'Jubilee' Class 4-6-0s until diesel haulage took over in the very early 1960s. However it failed to match the pre-war 2-hour schedule and by 1962 the 11.30 a.m. from New Street with a stop at Coventry was arriving at Euston at 1.40 p.m. The down service left Euston at 5.40 p.m. and after stopping at Coventry arrived back at New Street at 7.47 p.m. The train was withdrawn in 1963 when all express services between Euston and Birmingham were transferred onto the former GWR line from Paddington via Leamington to make way for electrification of the West Coast Main Line. With the latter completed a new Euston to Birmingham New Street service was introduced in 1967. One of the peak hour return services was named 'The Executive', giving a fast journey time between Euston and Birmingham of just over 90 minutes each way. This name was dropped in 1970.

BELOW: *'Jubilee' class 4-6-0 No 45734* Meteor *speeds through Bletchley with 'The Midlander', 1 September 1958.*

The Northern Irishman

Euston to Stranraer Harbour

Originally nicknamed 'The Paddy', this overnight sleeper train between London and Stranraer was introduced by the Midland Railway (see page 46) in the early years of the 20th century and continued to be operated by the London Midland & Scottish Railway through to 1947 (see page 82). From 1948, under the new management of the London Midland and Scottish regions of British Railways, the train continued to run, receiving its official name, 'The Northern Irishman', in 1952. With a locomotive change in the wee small hours at Carlisle, the newly-introduced BR Standard Class 6 'Clan' 4-6-2s locomotives were then in charge over the gruelling, mainly single-track, section through the wilds of Galloway between Dumfries and Stranraer. The summer 1962 timetable saw the train leave Euston at 7.20 p.m. (Monday–Friday)/7.15 p.m. (Sunday only) and, after calling at Bletchley, Rugby and Nuneaton detached a restaurant car at Crewe. Thereafter it called at Wigan before the locomotive change at Carlisle. Stranraer Harbour was reached at 5.28 a.m. the next day where a connection was made with a ferry service to Larne in Northern Ireland. In the reverse direction the train left Stranraer Harbour at 10 p.m. and arrived back at Euston at 8.15 a.m. (8.45 a.m. on Saturdays) the next day.

The closure of the 'Port Road' between Dumfries and Challoch Junction on 14 June 1965 (steam-hauled until the end) saw 'The Northern Irishman' diverted via Girvan, Ayr and Mauchline adding another 60 miles to the journey. The train remained steam-hauled between Stranraer Harbour and Carlisle with trains being double-headed to cope with the severe gradients of this route south of Girvan. The train lost its name in 1966 although there remained an unnamed diesel-hauled Euston to Stranraer service until the 1980s.

BELOW: *Having been hauled from Euston to Carlisle by English Electric Type 4 (Class 40) diesel-electric D267, 'The Northern Irishman' waits to depart behind replacement BR Standard Class 6 'Clan' 4-6-2 No 72005 Clan Macgregor for Stranraer Harbour, early 1960s.*

The Palatine

St Pancras to Manchester Central

ntroduced by the London Midland & Scottish Railway in 1938, 'The Palatine' restaurant car express between St Pancras and Manchester Central was discontinued on the outbreak of the Second World War. It was later revived by the London Midland Region of British Railways in 1957 and, until the advent of new 'Peak' Class diesels in 1960, was normally hauled by a 'Jubilee' or 'Royal Scot' 4-6-0. By the summer of 1962, with the diesels in charge, the restaurant train was departing from St Pancras at 7.55 a.m. and after stopping at Luton, Wellingborough, Leicester, Derby, Matlock and Miller's Dale arrived at Manchester Central at 11.54 a.m. The return service left Manchester at 2.25 p.m. and with stops at Chinley, Miller's Dale, Matlock, Derby and Leicester arrived back in the capital at 6.20 p.m. The train was rerouted via Nottingham from the autumn of 1962 and it was not uncommon for it to load up to 14 coaches. 'The Palatine' express lost its name in 1964 and the former Midland Railway route through the Peak District between Matlock and Chinley closed in 1968.

'Royal Scot' Class 4-6-0 No 46110 Grenadier Guardsman arrives at Manchester Central station with the down 'The Palatine' from St Pancras, 31 May 1958.

Pines Express

Manchester London Road/Mayfield to Bournemouth West

Operated by the London Midland & Scottish Railway (LMS) since 1927 (see page 83), the 'Pines Express' between Manchester and Bournemouth via the Somerset & Dorset Joint Railway (S&DJR) was discontinued on the outbreak of the Second World War. It was reintroduced in 1946 by the LMS and was then continued by the London Midland and Southern regions of British Railways. By then the restaurant car train also included through coaches to and from Sheffield, except on summer Saturdays when this became a separate train. However, the journey time of 7 hrs 7 min by 1958 hardly meant that the train was an 'express' and was significantly slower than the same journey 36 years before. The virtual takeover of the steeply-graded S&DJR route across the Mendip Hills by the Western Region in 1958 spelt the end for through workings over the line and the last 'Pines Express' over this route ran on 8 September 1962 and was appropriately hauled single-handedly by BR Standard

Class '9F' 2-10-0 No 92220 *Evening Star* – the last steam locomotive to be built by British Railways. After that date the train was rerouted to run via Oxford and Basingstoke – the weekday train now taking 7 hrs 11 min between Bournemouth West and Manchester Piccadilly with it being hauled between Oxford and Bournemouth via Basingstoke by Southern Region Bulleid Pacifics until the bitter end. Bournemouth West closed in 1965 and the last ever 'Pines Express' over this route to Bournemouth Central ran on 4 March 1967.

After the Second World War the 'Pines' was normally hauled by 'Jubilee' or 'Black Five' 4-6-0s between Manchester and Bath (Green Park – formerly Queen Square). These were replaced by BR Sulzer Type 4s in the early 1960s but the route south from Bath was a different kettle of fish. The steeply-graded line over the Mendips necessitated double-heading of the train until the introduction of BR Standard Class '9F' 2-10-0s in 1960

BR Standard Class '9F' 2-10-0 No 92220 Evening Star *pauses at Evercreech Junction to take on water while hauling the last 'Pines Express' to travel over the Somerset & Dorset Joint Railway on 8 September 1962.*

and locomotive combinations on a summer Saturday were unique anywhere on BR. Pairings of ex-LMS Class '2P' 4-4-0s, S&DJR Class '7F' 2-8-0s, Stanier 'Black 5' 4-6-0s, SR 'West Country' and 'Battle of Britain' 4-6-2s, elderly ex-Midland Railway Johnson Class '3F' 0-6-0s, ex-LMS Fowler '4F' 0-6-0s and BR Standard Class '5MT' 4-6-0s were a common sight between Bath Green Park and Evercreech Junction. While the '9Fs' were the first locomotives able to haul heavy passenger trains over the Mendips without assistance their arrival on the scene came too late to save the line from closure.

Rebuilt 'West Country' Class 4-6-2 No 34047 Callington approaches Tilehurst with the southbound rerouted 'Pines Express' on 30 January 1965.

The Red Rose

Euston to Liverpool Lime Street

'The Red Rose' was one of three restaurant car expresses running between Euston and Liverpool that were named in the Festival of Britain year of 1951. This train was usually in the capable hands of a 'Princess Royal' Class 4-6-2s or 'Royal Scot' Class 4-6-0s from Liverpool Edge Hill depot until the early 1960s when English Electric Type 4 diesels took over hauling the train. In steam days the down train was running non-stop between Euston and Lime Street, with a journey time of just 3½ hours, while the up train stopped at Crewe and still reached Euston 5 minutes quicker (both Monday–Friday schedules in 1955). With diesel haulage and electrification of the West Coast Main Line underway, by 1962 the train had become slower – the summer timetable for that year shows the down service leaving Euston at 12.15 p.m. and arriving at Liverpool at 4.10 p.m. (Saturdays 4.20 p.m.) while the up train left Liverpool at 5.30 p.m. and after stopping at Crewe arrived at Euston at 9.10 p.m. (9.20 p.m. on Saturdays). The train lost its name following completion of the West Coast Main Line electrification between Euston and Liverpool in 1966.

RIGHT: *The 1955 leaflet produced by BR for 'The Red Rose' express.*

BELOW: *English Electric Type 4 (Class 40) diesel-electric loco D287 is seen here passing through Nuneaton with 'The Red Rose' on 25 April 1964.*

THE RED ROSE

each weekday between
LONDON AND
LIVERPOOL

BRITISH RAILWAYS

The Robin Hood

St Pancras to Nottingham Midland

By 1959 an unnamed express giving Nottingham businessmen a day in London had been operating between that city and St Pancras for over 60 years. In that year the London Midland Region bestowed the appropriate name of 'The Robin Hood' on this train which was initially usually hauled by 'Royal Scot' 4-6-0s until 'Peak' diesels took over in the early 1960s. Travelling via Manton and Melton Mowbray the restaurant car express left Nottingham Midland at 8.15 a.m. and after stopping only at Manton arrived at St Pancras at 10.30 a.m. The return service left the capital at 5.25 p.m. but this time stopped at Bedford, Wellingborough, Kettering and Manton before arriving back at Nottingham at 8.04 p.m. (both summer 1962 timetable). The introduction of diesel haulage soon saw the schedule of the up train cut to 2 hours exactly but the train's name was dropped as early as 1962. The Nottingham to Kettering route via Melton Mowbray was closed to passenger trains on 1 May 1967 but the southern section from Glendon Junction to Wymondham Junction was reopened to passenger traffic in 2009. Part of the route north of Melton Mowbray is now used by the 13½-mile-long Old Dalby Test Track.

RIGHT: *The summer 1962 timetable for the short-lived 'The Robin Hood'.*

BELOW : *Kentish Town shed's 'Royal Scot' Class 4-6-0 No 46133*
The Green Howards *prepares to depart from St Pancras with the down 'The Robin Hood' in 1961.*

The Robin Hood

Restaurant Car Express

NOTTINGHAM MIDLAND and LONDON ST. PANCRAS

MONDAYS TO FRIDAYS

		am				pm
Nottingham Midland	.. .. dep	8*15	London St. Pancras	.. .. dep	5*25
			Bedford Midland Road	.. .. „	6 25
Manton	.. „	8‡53	Wellingborough Midland Road .. „		6 47
			Kettering	.. „	7 1
			Manton	.. „	7 24
London St. Pancras	.. arr	10 30	Nottingham Midland	.. arr	8 4

The Royal Highlander

Euston to Aberdeen/Inverness/Fort William

Having been introduced by the London Midland & Scottish Railway in 1927 (see page 84), the Anglo-Scottish 'The Royal Highlander' sleeping car train lost its name on the outbreak of the Second World War. It continued to run nameless through the war and then through to Nationalization in 1948. From then onwards it was operated by the London Midland and Scottish regions with the name being reintroduced in 1957. For a few years it was still steam-hauled but by then the Aberdeen portion had been dropped and the advent of English Electric Type 4 diesel power soon saw further improvements to the schedule – by the summer of 1962 the heavily loaded down train was departing from Euston at 6.40 p.m. (Monday–Friday)/7 p.m. (Sunday) and after stops at Crewe and Perth arrived at Inverness at 8.39 a.m. (Tuesday-Saturday)/8.46 a.m. (Monday). The up train left Inverness at 5.40 p.m. (Monday–Saturday) and made stops at Perth, Carlisle,

Crewe, Nuneaton, Rugby and Bletchley before arriving at Euston at 8.25 a.m. (Tuesday–Saturday)/9 a.m. (Sunday). In later years the train also conveyed sleeping cars to and from Fort William which travelled via the West Highland Line and Glasgow Queen Street. Although the train lost its name in 1985 this service is now provided by the 'Caledonian Sleeper' – one of only two overnight sleeping car trains left running on Britain's rail network, the other being the 'Night Riviera' between Paddington and Penzance.

BOTTOM LEFT: *Stanier Class 5 4-6-0 No 45365 is the lead locomotive at Inverness shed on 29 July 1959 before hauling 'The Royal Highlander' to Perth where they would be replaced by a Stanier 'Pacific' for the journey south to Carlisle and London.*

BELOW: *The summer 1962 timetable for 'The Royal Highlander' sleeping car train.*

The Royal Highlander

LONDON EUSTON and INVERNESS

First and second class sleeping accommodation is available between London and Inverness

	Mon. to Fri. nights	Sun. nights		Mon. to Fri. nights	Sat. nights
	pm	pm		pm	pm
London Euston ....dep	6 40	7 0	Inverness ....dep	5†40	5†40
			Perth .. .. ,,	9†50	9†50
				am	am
Crewe .. .. ,,	10 13	10 38	Carlisle .... ,,	1 39	1 39
			Crewe .. ..arr	4 37	4 41
	am	am	Nuneaton .... ,,	5 51	6 6
Perth ....arr	4 33	4 49	Rugby Midland .. .. ,,	6 20	6 35
			Bletchley .... ,,	....	7†40
Inverness .. .. ,,	8 39	8 46	London Euston .. .. ,,	8 25	9 0

⊢—Stops when required to set down sleeping car passengers only on notice being given to the attendant before arrival at Rugby.

Restaurant Car facilities are available London to Crewe and Perth to Inverness on the Northbound service and Inverness to Perth on the Southbound service.

†—A Breakfast Tray Service is available for sleeping car passengers on this train. Orders will be accepted by the sleeping car attendant from passengers on joining the train up to and including Perth.

This train stops at most stations Pitlochry to Inverness.

Seats may be reserved in advance for passengers travelling from London and Inverness on payment of a fee of 2s. 0d. per seat.

Royal Scot

Euston to Glasgow Central

Introduced by the London & North Western Railway and the Caledonian Railway in 1862 (see page 60), the 'Royal Scot' continued to be operated by the London Midland & Scottish Railway from 1923 to 1947 (see page 85) and by the London Midland and Scottish regions of British Railways from 1948. From 1950 the two prototype diesel-electric locomotives – Nos 10000 and 10001 – were a regular feature hauling this famous Anglo-Scottish train and in 1952 a new set of BR coaches replaced the pre-war coaching stock. At the same time journey times improved so that both up and down journeys between Euston and Glasgow Central were completed in 8 hours – despite an unscheduled stop at Carlisle for crew changing. Further improvements came in the autumn of 1959 when the Carlisle stop was advertised in the new timetable and the journey times reduced to 7 hrs 15 min – this was made possible by reducing the number of coaches used.

By 1962, with electrification of the West Coast Main Line now underway, the train was usually hauled by an English Electric Type 4 diesel but the departure from Euston had been retimed to 9.30 a.m. and with a stop at Carlisle the train reached Glasgow at 4.50 p.m. (Monday–Friday). The Saturday working took 40 minutes longer and on Sundays the train was virtually reduced to stopping-train status with stops at Rugby, Crewe, Carlisle, Beattock and Motherwell, arriving at Glasgow at 7.20 p.m.

Following electrification of the WCML to Glasgow in 1974 the 'Royal Scot' continued to run until 2003 when the name was dropped. Today the fastest Pendolino Class 390 trains from Euston to Glasgow now take only 4 hrs 31 min to complete the journey.

'Coronation' Class 4-6-2 No 46241 City of Edinburgh makes a stirring sight as it passes Scout Green signal box on the climb up Shap Fell with the down 'Royal Scot', late 1950s.

While on a trainspotting trip to Carlisle on Saturday 1 August 1964, I had the good fortune to travel on the down 'Royal Scot' to Glasgow Central behind a steam locomotive. An English Electric Type 4 diesel arrived at Carlisle hauling the train but this locomotive failed and (oh joy!) was replaced by BR Standard 'Britannia' Class 4-6-2 No 70002 *Geoffrey Chaucer*. The train eventually left at 4.32 p.m. (25 minutes late) and despite a slow start the grimy locomotive passed through Lockerbie at 63 mph. After stopping at Beattock for a banking engine, the train topped Beattock Summit at 6.01 p.m. at a speed of just 30 mph. Then matters improved with speed increasing until 72 mph was reached through Crawford and Abington. After slowing for Carstairs the train accelerated to reach 65 mph through Carluke and arrived at Glasgow Central station at exactly 7 p.m. Despite being an hour late into Glasgow I was enthralled by this unexpected steam bonanza, having spent most of the journey with my head out of the coach window!

The Shamrock

Euston to Liverpool Lime Street

British Railways introduced this service in 1954. 'The Shamrock' connected with steamers to and from Belfast and Dublin at Liverpool and the heavily loaded restaurant car express was normally in the hands of Edge Hill or Camden 'Princess Royal' Pacifics until they were replaced by English Electric Type 4s around 1960. Connecting with overnight ferries from Ireland the up train left Liverpool at 8.15 a.m. (Monday–Friday)/8.30 a.m. (Saturday) and after calling at Mossley Hill, Crewe and Bletchley arrived at Euston at 12.15 p.m. (Monday–Friday)/12.35 p.m. (Saturday). The down service left Euston at 4.55 p.m. and ran non-stop to Liverpool arriving at 8.50 p.m. (Monday–Friday). On Saturdays this train left the capital at 4.30 p.m. and after calling at Rugby and Crewe arrived at Liverpool at 8.45 p.m. As with most named trains on the West Coast Main Line 'The Shamrock' lost its name following completion of electrification between Euston and Liverpool in 1966.

BELOW: *Rugby shed's Stanier Class 5 4-6-0 No 44866 pilots an unidentified 'Royal Scot' Class 4-6-0 through Bletchley with the up 'The Shamrock' on 3 April 1960.*

The Thames-Clyde Express

St Pancras to Glasgow St Enoch

ntroduced by the London Midland & Scottish Railway in 1927 (see page 87), 'The Thames-Clyde Express' restaurant car train was suspended on the outbreak of the Second World War and restored by the London Midland and Scottish Regions of British Railways in 1949. It was a difficult route to work – coal mining subsidence south of Leeds brought speed restrictions and diversions while the heavily graded and gruelling 72-mile Settle–Carlisle Line with its 13 tunnels and 23 viaducts taxed the crews of steam locomotives to their limit. During this post-war period the train was usually headed by Holbeck's 'Jubilee' or 'Royal Scot' 4-6-0s and even ex-LNER 'A3' Class 4-6-2s until these were replaced by BR Sulzer Type 4 diesels in the early 1960s. Despite this, journey times remained poor – the summer 1962 timetable showed the Monday–Friday train departing St Pancras at 10.10 a.m. and after calling at

Leicester, Chesterfield, Sheffield, Leeds, Carlisle, Annan, Dumfries and Kilmarnock it arrived at Glasgow St Enoch at 7.50 p.m. – a journey time of 9 hrs 40 min and 2 hrs 20 min slower than the rival 'Royal Scot' between Euston and Glasgow Central. In the reverse direction the Monday–Friday service took 9 hrs 45 min to complete the 426¼-mile journey, which was fine if you enjoyed superb scenery and were a rail enthusiast! This couldn't go on much longer and, with the completion of West Coast Main Line electrification in 1974, the train, by then diverted to run to and from Glasgow Central, lost its title.

BELOW: *Watched by a young trainspotter, Leeds Holbeck shed's Class 'A3' 4-6-2 No 60080 Dick Turpin gets ready to leave Leeds City station with the down 'The Thames-Clyde Express' on a wet day in July 1960.*

The Ulster Express

Euston to Heysham Harbour

London Midland & Scottish Railway introduced this service in 1927 (see page 88) and suspended it during the Second World War. 'The Ulster Express' was reintroduced by the London Midland Region of British Railways in 1949. Connecting with steamer services to and from Belfast at Heysham Harbour, the often heavily-loaded train to and from Euston was hauled by either ex-LMS 'Princess Royal'/'Coronation' Class Pacifics or 'Royal Scot' Class 4-6-0s.

By the summer of 1962 steam haulage had been replaced by English Electric Type 4s and the down train was departing from Euston at 5.40 p.m. (Monday–Thursday)/5.45 p.m. (Friday) and after stopping at Crewe arrived at Heysham Harbour at 11.05 p.m. (11.12 p.m. on Fridays) to connect with the overnight steamer to Donegal Quay in Belfast. On Saturdays the train left Euston at 6.40 p.m. and after calling at Crewe and Preston arrived at Heysham at midnight. There was also a much slower service on Sunday nights. The up train left Heysham at 6.55 a.m. seven days a week with an arrival at Euston at 11.50 a.m. (1 p.m. on Sundays). Both up and down services conveyed both restaurant and buffet cars.

Following electrification of the West Coast Main Line 'The Ulster Express' continued to operate with a combination of electric and diesel locomotive haulage until the Heysham to Belfast steamer service was withdrawn in 1975. The Heysham branch was closed 4 October 1975 but reopened in 1987 to connect with sailings to and from the Isle of Man.

BELOW: *Camden shed's 'Coronation' Class 4-6-2 No 46229* Duchess of Hamilton *at rest at Euston after arriving with the up 'The Ulster Express' on 14 August 1959. This fine loco has since been preserved with its original streamlined casing.*

The Waverley

St Pancras to Edinburgh Waverley

Introduced as the 'Thames-Forth Express' in 1923 (see page 88), this restaurant car train between St Pancras and Edinburgh via the Settle–Carlisle Line and the Waverley Route was discontinued on the outbreak of the Second World War. It was reinstated without its name in 1945. From 1948 it continued to be operated by the newly-formed London Midland and Scottish regions of British Railways. The year 1957 saw an acceleration of this service, which was also named 'The Waverley', at the same time haulage between London and Leeds City – where there was an engine change – and Leeds and Carlisle was usually provided by a 'Jubilee' or 'Royal Scot' 4-6-0 and between Carlisle and Edinburgh by an ex-LNER 'A3' Pacific. The latter locomotives also put in appearances on the Settle & Carlisle section for a few years before 'Peak' diesels took over in the early 1960s – by then the train had been reduced to a summer-only working.

The summer 1962 timetable shows the down train leaving St Pancras at 9.10 a.m. (Monday–Saturday) and arriving at Edinburgh at 6.55 p.m. (7.17 p.m. on Saturdays). The up train left Edinburgh at 10.05 a.m. (Monday–Saturday) and arrived at St Pancras at 8.10 p.m. (8.30 p.m. on Saturdays). With 14 intermediate stops for the down train and 15 for the up train this was hardly an express and could not compete with the much faster journey times on the West Coast and East Coast routes. With dwindling patronage and the closure of the Waverley Route imminent the train was withdrawn in 1968. The Waverley Route closed on 6 January 1969.

After visiting Kingmoor and Upperby sheds in Carlisle on a trainspotting trip, I was lucky enough to travel on the down 'The Waverley' between the border city and Edinburgh Waverley on 29 July 1964. The train engine was Class 45 'Peak' diesel No D24 and the scenic journey over the lonely Waverley Route was enthralling, including a sighting of ex-LNER 'A3' Pacific No 60052 *Prince Palatine* en route. Outside Hawick engine shed (64G) I spotted BR Standard Class 2 2-6-0 Nos 78047 and 78048. The day ended at Edinburgh with a quick visit to St Margarets shed (64A) where there were still plenty of ex-LNER steam locomotives to be seen followed by a visit to Haymarket shed (64B) which was by that time 100 per cent diesel. Those were the days!

OVERLEAF: *BR Standard Class 5 4-6-0 No 73166 struggles manfully with the northbound 'The Waverley' near Keighley in the summer of 1962. This widely travelled locomotive was then reallocated to Royston, Patricroft, Exmouth Junction and Yeovil Town sheds before finally ending its days at Oxford in 1965.*

BELOW: *Leeds Holbeck Shed's BR Standard Class 7 'Britannia' No 70044 Earl Haig departs from Leeds City station with the down 'The Waverley', c.1960.*

The Welsh Dragon

Llandudno to Rhyl

The only named train to be operated in a push-pull mode by a steam locomotive, 'The Welsh Dragon' was introduced by the London Midland Region of British railways in the 1950s. Usually powered by an Ivatt Class 2 2-6-2T carrying a headboard, the train connected the two resorts via Colwyn Bay and Abergele during the summer months only. From the mid-1950s the steam train was occasionally replaced by diesel multiple units but this service seems to have been discontinued in the early 1960s.

BELOW: 'The Welsh Dragon' prepares to leave for Llandudno behind Ivatt Class 2 2-6-2T No 41320, late 1950s.

The Welshman

Euston to Llandudno/Porthmadog/Pwllheli

In 1927 the LMS (see page 88) introduced 'The Welshman' as a summer-only restaurant car express that linked Euston with the seaside resorts of North Wales. Suspended during the Second World War, it was revived by the London Midland Region of British Railways in 1950 with through coaches to and from Llandudno, Porthmadog and Pwllheli. The summer 1962 timetable shows the Monday to Friday down service (on Saturdays it ran as two separate trains) leaving Euston at 11.20 a.m. and, after calling at Rugby and Crewe, arriving in Chester at 3.26 p.m. where the train was divided – the Llandudno portion calling at resorts along the North Wales coast before arriving at its destination at 5.03 p.m. The second portion continued non-stop to Penmaenmawr and then called at Llanfairfechan and Bangor where engines were changed – a Fairburn 2-6-4 tank from Bangor shed taking over for the rest of the

journey. From Bangor the train headed south to Caernarfon and then along the single-track line to Afon Wen on the Cambrian Coast line where the Pwllheli coaches were detached. Porthmadog was reached at 6.33 p.m. The up train left Porthmadog at 11 a.m. (Monday–Friday)/Llandudno at 1.05 p.m. and reached Euston at 6.35 p.m. – some journey! On Saturdays the Llandudno portion ran as a separate train in both directions. This service was discontinued at the end of the 1964 summer season and the Caernarfon to Afon Wen line was closed soon after.

BELOW: *Bangor shed's Fairburn 2-6-4T No 42075 arrives at Caernarfon with the Pwllheli/Porthmadog portions of the down 'The Welshman' from Euston, July 1963.*

Scottish Region

Formed on 1 January 1948, the Scottish Region of British Railways took over the former routes of the LMS and LNER in Scotland. In addition to the Anglo-Scottish passenger services via the East Coast Main Line, the West Coast Main Line and the Waverley route the region operated trains from Glasgow and Edinburgh to the following principal destinations in Scotland: Inverness, Kyle of Lochalsh and the Far North; Perth, Dundee and Aberdeen; Oban, Fort William and Mallaig; Ayr and Stranraer. Apart from Anglo-Scottish services, the region did not operate any additional sleeper trains within its borders. Ocean liner boat trains were also operated between Glasgow St Enoch and Greenock Prince's Pier until these ended in November 1965.

Glasgow's main railway termini were at Central, St Enoch, Queen Street and Buchanan Street. Edinburgh's main railway stations were at Princes Street terminus and Waverley (through station). Railway works at Cowlairs and St Rollox continued to carry out maintenance and overhaul work on steam locomotives but the days of locomotive building were long gone – Cowlairs Works closed in 1968. Progress was made on electrification of the Glasgow suburban lines in the 1960s, steam haulage was eradicated in 1967 and closures of lines continued apace during this period following the publication of the 'Beeching Report' – the most notorious of these was the closure of the Waverley Route in January 1969 and the very last was the line to Kilmacolm which closed in January 1983. Edinburgh Princes Street terminus closed in September 1965, Glasgow St Enoch terminus closed in June 1966 and Glasgow Buchanan Street in November 1966. Fortunately the closures of the Far North lines, the Kyle of Lochalsh

route and that to Stranraer didn't go ahead, saved by public and political pressure.

Electrification of the West Coast Main Line to Glasgow was completed in 1974, from Glasgow to Ayr in 1986 and the East Coast Main Line to Edinburgh was completed in 1991. The Scottish Region was renamed ScotRail in 1983 and this brand name continued to be used through privatization in 1997 and then by the various franchises to the present day.

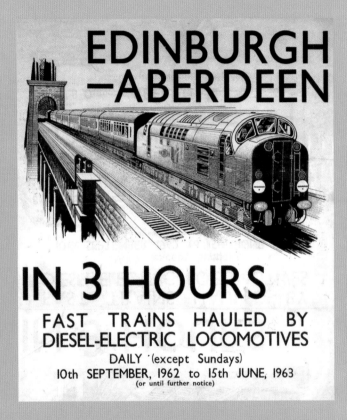

ABOVE: *1962 poster promoting the new 3-hour expresses between Glasgow and Aberdeen. The diesels were often replaced by steam locomotives.*

I was lucky enough to visit 10 engine sheds in the Glasgow and Edinburgh area on 29 March 1964. I, and about 400 other trainspotters, travelled overnight from Birmingham courtesy of the Warwickshire Railway Society behind ex-LMS 'Coronation' Class 4-6-2 No 46256 *Sir William A. Stanier*, F.R.S. and arrived at Glasgow Central at 6.20 a.m. Transported in a convoy of coaches to the various engine sheds, I spotted no less than 675 locomotives of which more than half were steam. What a brilliant day! On another trip I visited Aberdeen Ferryhill shed (61B) on 31 July of that year and was lucky enough to record seven 'A4' Class Pacifics (Nos 60004, 60006, 60010, 60012, 60016, 60023, 60026) along with No 60007 stored at Kittybrewster shed (61A). To end the day I travelled back to Glasgow behind No 60019. An 'A4' heaven!

Bon Accord

Glasgow Buchanan Street/Queen Street to Aberdeen

Introduced in 1937 by the London Midland & Scottish Railway, the 'Bon Accord' was suspended during the Second World War but reinstated in 1949 with an early morning departure from Aberdeen and an early afternoon return from Glasgow. As with all of the Glasgow to Aberdeen 3-hour expresses the 'Bon Accord' saw Gresley 'A4' Pacific haulage from 1962 until 1966 following the displacement of those famous streamlined locomotives from the East Coast Main Line by 'Deltic' diesels. The 'A4' swansong ended on 3 September 1966 and Buchanan Street station closed on 7 November of that year, after which the train was diverted to run to and from Queen Street. Diesels had already taken over hauling the train but after the closure of the route from Stanley Junction to Kinnaber Junction via Forfar on 4 September 1967 it was diverted to run via Perth, Dundee and Montrose. The train lost its title in May 1968.

BELOW: *'A4' Class 4-6-2 No 60004* William Whitelaw *hauls the 'Bon Accord' express near Bridge of Allan, north of Stirling, September 1964.*

Fife Coast Express

Glasgow Queen Street/Buchanan Street to St Andrews

The 'Fife Coast Express', a summer-only train for holidaymakers between Glasgow and East of Fife coastal line, had been operated by the London & North Eastern Railway since 1924 (see page 95) but was suspended on the outbreak of the Second World War. It was reintroduced by the Scottish Region of British Railways in 1949. Running between Glasgow Queen Street and the golfing capital of St Andrews, the train was normally hauled by a 'B1' 4-6-0 and for some years passengers were treated to a ride in a set of articulated luxury coaches that had once seen service on the pre-war 'Silver Jubilee' (see pages 106–108). The train was diverted to Glasgow Buchanan Street in 1957 and lost its title on 5 September 1959. Despite this, steam-hauled passenger trains continued to run along this route during the summer months until 6 September 1965 when the Fife coastal line closed between St Andrews and Leven.

BELOW: *'B1' Class 4-6-0 No 61402 is seen here hauling the 'Fife Coast Express' at Polmont on 14 September 1957. Note the articulated coaches that were formerly used on the pre-war 'Silver Jubilee'.*

The Grampian

Glasgow Buchanan Street/Queen Street to Aberdeen

The Caledonian Railway introduced this service in the early 20th century and it was continued by the London Midland & Scottish Railway from 1923 (see page 76). Like many trains, 'The Grampian' was suspended on the outbreak of the Second World War. This named train was reintroduced by the Scottish Region of BR in 1962 and applied to the 8.25 a.m. departure from Glasgow which took exactly 3 hours to reach Aberdeen. With more intermediate stops the return service left Aberdeen at 1.30 p.m. and arrived back at Glasgow at 5.30 p.m. – both trains included a miniature buffet car. As with the other Glasgow to Aberdeen 3-hour expresses 'The Grampian' saw Gresley's 'A4' Pacifics perform their swansong between 1962 and 3 September 1966 when diesel haulage took over. In Glasgow, Buchanan Street was closed later that year and the train was diverted to run to and from

Queen Street station. Trains such as 'The Grampian' ceased to operate along this route on 4 September 1967 when the former Caledonian Railway's mainline between Stanley Junction and Kinnaber Junction via Forfar was closed. They were then diverted via Perth, Dundee and Montrose but with slower timings. 'The Grampian' lost its name in 1968.

I was very lucky to travel from Aberdeen to Glasgow on this train on 31 July 1964. Haulage was behind 'A4' Class 4-6-2 No 60019 *Bittern* of Ferryhill shed (61B) and I recorded maximum speeds of 72 mph between Aberdeen and Stonehaven, 73 mph between Forfar and Coupar Angus, 73 mph between Coupar Angus and Perth and a stirring 78 mph between Dunblane and Stirling and then the same between Stirling and Larbert. What a great way to travel! *Bittern* was withdrawn in September 1966 but has fortunately since been preserved.

BELOW: *Fitted with German-type smoke deflectors, 'A3' Class 4-6-2 No 60042* Singapore *makes a fine sight while hauling 'The Grampian' express near Dunblane in May 1964.*

The Granite City

Glasgow Buchanan Street/Queen Street to Aberdeen

Introduced by the Caledonian Railway in 1906 (see pages 11–12) and operated by the London Midland & Scottish Railway from 1933 (see page 76) until the outbreak of the Second World War, 'The Granite City' restaurant car train was reintroduced by the Scottish Region of British Railways in 1949, this time with a 10 a.m. departure from Glasgow Buchanan Street and a 5.15 p.m. departure for the return working from Aberdeen. Both trains carried a restaurant car but the down service took 3 hrs 41 min while the up journey was achieved in 3 hours. As with other Glasgow to Aberdeen 3-hour expresses 'The Granite City' was one of these trains hauled by Gresley's 'A4' Pacifics between 1962 and 1966. Diesel haulage then took over but the train was rerouted to run from Glasgow Queen Street via Perth, Dundee and Montrose following the closure of the Forfar line in 1967. 'The Granite City' express lost its title in 1968.

BELOW: *Made up of 'blood-and-custard' Gresley coaches, 'The Granite City' prepares to leave Aberdeen behind BR Standard Class 5 4-6-0 No 73007 in April 1954.*

The Saint Mungo

Glasgow Buchanan Street/Queen Street to Aberdeen

Having been introduced in 1937 by the London Midland & Scottish Railway (see page 86), 'The Saint Mungo' express between Aberdeen and Glasgow Buchanan Street was discontinued on the outbreak of the Second World War. It was reintroduced by the Scottish Region of British Railways in 1949 usually with 'Jubilee' Class or BR Standard Class 5MT 4-6-0 haulage until 1962 when Gresley 'A4' Pacifics relocated from their East Coast Main Line duties after the introduction of 'Deltic' diesels on that route. These superb locomotives performed their swansong on the Glasgow to Aberdeen 3-hour expresses until 3 September 1966 when diesels took over.

With the 'A4s' in charge of this restaurant car train, the summer timetable of 1964 shows the up 'The Saint Mungo' leaving Aberdeen at 9.30 a.m. (Monday–Friday), making 14 intermediate stops and arriving at Buchanan Street at 1.30 p.m. The down service was a true 3-hour train leaving Glasgow at 5.30 p.m. and, after stops at Stirling, Perth, Forfar and Stonehaven, arrived at Aberdeen at 8.30 p.m. Steam gave way to diesel haulage in September 1966 and Glasgow Buchanan Street station closed in November of that year, after which trains were then diverted to and from Queen Street station. Trains such as 'The Saint Mungo' ceased to operate along this route via Forfar on 4 September 1967 when the former Caledonian Railway's mainline between Stanley Junction and Kinnaber Junction via Forfar was closed. They were then diverted via Perth, Dundee and Montrose but with slower timings. The train lost its name in 1968.

'The Saint Mungo' express prepares to leave Perth for Glasgow Buchanan Street behind BR Standard Class 5 4-6-0 No 73008 on 13 March 1953.

Southern Region

Formed on the Nationalization of Britain's railways on 1 January 1948, the new Southern Region of British Railways (BR) took over the rail network of the former Southern Railway (see page 110). With its busy third-rail electrified commuter routes radiating out of London to Kent, Surrey, Sussex and Hampshire the region was the largest operator of passenger services out of the six regions of BR. Stretching from North Cornwall and North Devon in the west, to Weymouth, Bournemouth, Southampton and Portsmouth in the south and to Eastbourne, Brighton and Dover in the southeast, the rest of the network was served by steam-hauled expresses until the onset of further electrification and dieselisation in the late 1950s and the 1960s.

The Southern Region's termini in London were at Cannon Street, Charing Cross, Holborn Viaduct, London Bridge, Victoria and Waterloo. Suspended for the duration of the Second World War, third-rail electrification resumed in the 1950s with routes to the Kent Coast completed in 1961 and to Southampton and Bournemouth in 1967 – the latter finally brought an end to steam haulage in the region. In that year the remaining route on the Isle of Wight was electrified and vintage steam trains replaced by vintage London Underground

stock. Third-rail electrification also reached Hastings via Tonbridge in 1986, East Grinstead and Oxted in 1987 and Weymouth in 1988.

New steam locomotives continued to be built at Eastleigh Works until 1950 and it was then kept fully occupied until 1961 rebuilding over 90 of the Bulleid Pacifics. Brighton Works continued to build steam locomotives until 1957, including 41 LMS Fairburn 2-6-4Ts and 130 BR Standard Class 4 2-6-4Ts. Other construction work carried out at Brighton included the ill-fated experimental 'Leader' Class steam locomotive, prototype 1Co-Co1 diesel-electric locomotive No 10203 and prototype Co-Co electric locomotive No 20003.

The region operated one sleeper train jointly with SNCF, the 'Night Ferry' between Victoria and Paris Gare du Nord, which ran until 1980. Ocean liner boat trains operated between Waterloo and Southampton Docks. Channel Island boat trains between Waterloo and Southampton Docks continued to operate until 1960 when they were transferred to Weymouth Quay. Other boat

BELOW: *Bulleid's ill-fated 'Leader' Class steam locomotive No 36001 is romantically portrayed in this painting by Leslie Carr.*

trains that connected with Cross-Channel ferries also operated between Victoria, Dover and Folkestone.

The region suffered a huge loss in 1963 when all its routes west of Salisbury were transferred to the Western Region. The former Southern Railway line to Exeter was soon singled in many places and effectively downgraded to a secondary route with trains being hauled by worn-out diesels. Through trains such as the 'Atlantic Coast Express' ended and all of the remaining routes of the 'Withered Arm' west of Exeter, except to Barnstaple, were subsequently closed. Dr Beeching's 'axe' was wielded heavily on West Country railways but elsewhere on the Southern Region the effects of closures were not so keenly felt – the longest casualty was the Guildford to Shoreham via Christ's Hospital line which had closed by 1966.

Seen as a first step towards privatization, the Southern Region was abolished in 1991 and passenger services were then operated by Network SouthEast and InterCity until privatization in 1994.

Happy days at Basingstoke station! The date was 22 August 1964 and I was on a trainspotting trip from Gloucester. In the space of about 5 hours I recorded no less than 23 'Battle of Britain'/'West Country' Class Pacifics and 15 'Merchant Navy' Pacifics. Of the latter No 35023 *Holland-Afrika Line* was hauling the up 'Pines Express', No 35029 *Ellerman Lines* on the up and down 'Bournemouth Belle' and No 35013 *Blue Funnel* on a Waterloo to Plymouth express. Witnessing these steam trains roaring through Basingstoke has left me with many happy memories over 50 years later.

BELOW: *1Co-Co1 diesel-electric locomotive No 10202 hauls the down 'Bournemouth Belle' near Winchfield in 1952. Built at Ashford Works in 1950, this loco and two others were transferred to the London Midland Region in 1955.*

Atlantic Coast Express

Waterloo to Torrington, Ilfracombe, Bude, Padstow and Plymouth

The multi-portioned 'Atlantic Coast Express' ('ACE') was introduced in 1926 (see pages 111–112), was suspended during the Second World War, and resumed operating after the war. From 1948 it was continued by the newly-formed Southern Region of British Railways. By then the new Bulleid 'Merchant Navy' Pacifics were at the head of the train and journey times soon returned to their pre-war schedules. In 1952 the train was speeded-up with a mile-a-minute schedule between Waterloo and Salisbury and almost that between Salisbury and Exeter. At Exeter the train divided with the Plymouth, Bude and Padstow portions and the Torrington and Ilfracombe portions continuing their separate onward journey behind Bulleid Light Pacifics. On summer Saturdays the 'ACE' had become so popular with holidaymakers that the train departed from Waterloo as two separate trains. During its peak in the late 1950s extra relief trains, all headed by the rebuilt 'Merchant Navy' locos, were also added on summer Saturdays to cope with the amount of traffic.

Timings were continually improved until 1961 when the 171¾-mile journey from Waterloo to Exeter Central was scheduled to take a record 2 hrs 56 min – this included stops at Salisbury and Sidmouth Junction – and all this was achieved by 'Merchant Navy' Pacifics along what was the

BELOW: *Unrebuilt 'Merchant Navy' Class 4-6-2 No 35005* Canadian Pacific *makes a stirring sight as it hauls the down 'Atlantic Coast Express' at Battledown Flyover, to the west of Basingstoke, in 1949.*

very demanding roller-coaster route west of Salisbury. In the opposite direction the train was equally fast with the journey only taking an extra 2 minutes. Even as late as the summer of 1963 there were five departures from Waterloo: 10.15 a.m. with through coaches to Torrington and Ilfracombe; 10.35 a.m. with through coaches to to Padstow and Bude; 10.45 a.m. to Seaton with through coaches to Lyme Regis; 11.00 a.m. with through coaches to Torrington and Ilfracombe; 11.15 a.m. with through coaches to Plymouth, Padstow and Bude.

Although increased car ownership in the early 1960s can partly be blamed on the downfall of the 'ACE', the other contributing factor came in 1963 when all lines west of Salisbury came under Western Region control. Anxious to stamp its authority on their erstwhile competitors, the end was swift and painful. The last 'ACE' ran on 5 September 1964 and soon downgraded 'Warship' diesel-hydraulics took over services on what was to become a secondary route – much of the line west of Salisbury was singled and the branch lines to seaside resorts in Devon and North Cornwall were all closed over the next few years.

'West Country' Class 4-6-2 No 34016 Bodmin heads the Ilfracombe portion of the 'Atlantic Coast Express' over the River Taw towards Barnstaple Town station, summer 1953.

Bournemouth Belle

Waterloo to Bournemouth West

Introduced by the Southern Railway in 1931 (see page113), the 'Bournemouth Belle' Pullman train was reinstated after the Second World War and continued to be operated by the Southern Region of British Railway from 1948 with Bulleid's new 'Merchant Navy' Pacifics at its head. By 1963 the 79¼ miles between Waterloo and Southampton Central were being covered in 1 hr 21 min with arrival at Bournemouth Central exactly 2 hours after departure from London – a leisurely average speed of 54 mph for the 108-mile journey. Bournemouth West station closed on 6 September 1965 after which the 'Bournemouth Belle' started or terminated its journey at Bournemouth Central. Steam clung on to life on this route until the summer of 1967 providing the 'Merchant Navy' locos with their swan song. The 'Belle', for the last few months diesel-hauled, last ran on 9 July when third-rail electrification was switched on between Waterloo and Bournemouth.

BELOW: *Illustration for a BR poster of 1953 by 'Barber' of the 'Bournemouth Belle' Pullman train at speed in the southwestern suburbs of London.*

OVERLEAF TOP: *A foreign invader – ex-LNER 'V2' Class 2-6-2 No 60893 heads the 'Bournemouth Belle' in May 1953. This and other 'foreign' locomotives were temporarily lent to the Southern Region following a major crank axle failure on one of Bulleid's 'Merchant Navy' Class locomotives, after which the whole class was temporarily withdrawn.*

OVERLEAF BOTTOM: *A stylish leaflet issued by British Railways in 1951 for the 'Bournemouth Belle' Pullman train.*

Brighton Belle

Victoria to Brighton

In 1934 the Southern Railway (see page 116), introduced the all-Pullman electric 'Brighton Belle'. After suspension during the Second World War, it was reinstated and continued to be operated by the Southern Region of British Railways upon Nationalization in 1948, providing a journey time of 1 hour between London and Brighton. On Sundays during the 1950s the spare five-car set was used for a service between Victoria and Eastbourne known as the 'Eastbourne Pullman' but this was discontinued in 1957. Initially the 'Brighton Belle' operated three return journeys between Victoria and Brighton each weekday and two on Sundays but by the 1960s its age was beginning to show. The service was improved in 1967 with four return journeys, each taking only 55 minutes. Although refurbished and repainted in the new BR Pullman livery of blue and grey, the ageing electric units were nearing the end of their life and despite patronage by the great and the good the service was withdrawn by British Railways on 30 April 1972. Passengers travelling on the train on this last day were presented with a souvenir brochure and menu – the bar tariff makes interesting reading just one year after the introduction of decimalization: ¼ bottle of

BOTTOM LEFT: *Poster produced in 1958 for BR to promote rail services between Victoria and Brighton on the all-Pullman electric 'Brighton Belle'.*

BELOW: *Bowing out with champagne – the final day of services on the 'Brighton Belle', 30 April 1972.*

champagne 75p; miniature Dubonnet 22p; miniature 'Royal Scot' whisky 37p; can of Guinness 15½p; can of Bulmer's Cider 12½p; small bottle ginger beer 8p.

Fortunately this wasn't the end for the 'Brighton Belle's' Pullman coaches as nearly all of them were saved – some of them ending up in pub gardens, two on the Keith & Dufftown Railway while others were lovingly restored for use on the Venice-Simplon Orient Express. Moves are now afoot to restore two of the driving cars and

reunite them with their coaches so that the 'Brighton Belle' can run once again.

BELOW: *Looking good in the winter sunshine, the 'Brighton Belle' passes through Preston Park, Brighton, on 8 December 1965.*

BOTTOM: *Leaflet and timetable for the 'Brighton Belle' issued by British Railways in the 1950s.*

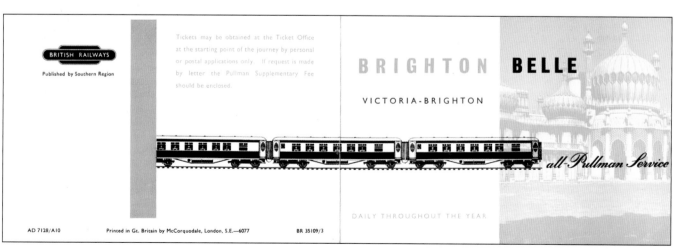

Channel Islands Boat Train

Waterloo to Southampton Docks/Weymouth Quay

A 'Channel Islands Boat Train' also ran from London Paddington via Frome and Yeovil Pen Mill to Weymouth Quay until 1960 (see page 245). In that year the Southern Region's 'Channel Islands Boat Train' between Waterloo and Southampton Docks ended, to be replaced by boat trains running on the Waterloo to Weymouth Quay route. During the days of steam haulage on this route Bulleid's Pacifics hauled the train between Waterloo and Weymouth Town – from here the boat train, loading at times to 12 or 13 coaches, was hauled along the street tramway section to Weymouth Quay by an ex-GWR 1366 Class 0-6-0PT (up to 1962) and then by diesel shunters until 1967. From July of that year the train was hauled by Class 73 electro-diesels between Waterloo and Bournemouth and then onwards to Weymouth Quay by Birmingham Railway Carriage & Wagon Company Class 33 diesels. It continued to operate in this form until 1987 when the service ceased.

BELOW: *A photograph full of period charm – ex-GWR '1366' Class 0-6-0PT No 1368 slowly departs from Weymouth Quay station on the town's street tramway with a Southern Region 'Channel Islands Boat Train' bound for Waterloo in the 1950s.*

The Devon Belle

Waterloo to Ilfracombe/Plymouth

Introduced by the Southern Railway in 1947 (see page 118), the summer-only all-Pullman 'The Devon Belle' continued to be operated from 1948 by the newly-formed Southern Region of British Railways during the summer months. However, patronage of the Plymouth portion was poor and this was discontinued in 1950 leaving the 'Belle' as a Waterloo-Ilfracombe service (Fridays, Saturdays and Sundays for the down train and Saturdays, Sundays and Mondays for the up train). Hauled by one of Bulleid's 'Merchant Navy' Class air-smoothed Pacifics, the down train, complete with rear end observation car, left Waterloo at 12 noon and arrived

at Ilfracombe at 5.27 p.m. Here the observation car was turned and the up train left Ilfracombe on the next day at 12 noon, arriving back at Waterloo at 5.20 p.m. In both directions there was a locomotive change at Exeter Central where the 'Merchant Navy' was replaced by one of Bulleid's light Pacifics (and vice versa). 'The Devon Belle' continued to operate on this route until September 1954 when it was withdrawn.

The two observation cars later saw service on the Inverness to Kyle of Lochalsh and the Glasgow to Oban routes into the 1960s. Fortunately both of them have survived and can be seen in action on the Paignton & Dartmouth Railway and the Swanage Railway respectively.

LEFT: *Unrebuilt 'Merchant Navy' Class 4-6-2 No 35021 New Zealand Line hauls the short-lived 'The Devon Belle' all-Pullman train between Woking and Basingstoke in the summer of 1952.*

RIGHT: *Heading for the West Country in style – American tourists being served drinks on 'The Devon Belle' in June 1953.*

BELOW: *The summer 1953 timetable for 'The Devon Belle'.*

To travel by the Devon Belle is to experience the utmost in comfort and complete relaxation. The excellent meal and courteous attention while the countryside glides past your window is half the fun of travelling all-Pullman.

An atmosphere of spacious luxury is preserved by limiting the number of passengers to the seats available ensuring that you arrive at your destination with a feeling of well-being and a determination to travel again by the Devon Belle.

Other all-Pullman trains are the Brighton Belle, the Bournemouth Belle and the Kentish Belle—your obvious choice when the occasion arises.

Tickets may be obtained at the Ticket Office at the starting point of the journey by personal or postal applications only. If request is made by letter the Pullman Supplementary Fee should be enclosed.

BRITISH RAILWAYS

12TH JUNE TO 19TH SEPTEMBER 1953

Fris, Sats. & Suns.*		Sats. Suns. & Mons.
12.0 noon *dep.*	WATERLOO	arr. 5.20 p.m.
3A.43 p.m. *arr.*	SIDMOUTH	dep. 1A.35 p.m.
3.35 p.m. *arr.*	EXETER (CENTRAL)	dep. 1.42 p.m.
3.46 p.m. *arr.*	EXETER (ST. DAVID'S)	dep. 1.33 p.m.
4.43 p.m. *arr.*	BARNSTAPLE JCT.	dep. 12.37 p.m.
4.59 p.m. *arr.*	BRAUNTON	dep. 12.23 p.m.
5.18 p.m. *arr.*	MORTEHOE & WOOLACOMBE	dep. 12.12 p.m.
5.27 p.m. *arr.*	ILFRACOMBE	dep. 12. 0 noon
5B.18† p.m. *arr.*	BIDEFORD	dep. 12B. 4 p.m.
5B.29† p.m. *arr.*	TORRINGTON	dep. 11B.55 a.m.

* Sunday service until 13th September only   †Arrive 10 minutes earlier Sundays

A—Change at Sidmouth Jct.   Pullman train available between
B—Change at Barnstaple Jct.   Waterloo and Sidmouth Jct.
                              or Barnstaple Jct. only

PULLMAN CAR SUPPLEMENTARY FEES

	1st Class	3rd Class
WATERLOO - EXETER CENTRAL SIDMOUTH JCT. BARNSTAPLE JCT.	7/-	4/-
and intermediate stations to ILFRACOMBE	8/6	5/-

Golden Arrow

Victoria to Paris Gare du Nord

The evocatively-titled 'Golden Arrow' all-Pullman service operated from Victoria to Dover from 1929 (see page 119). From Dover passengers crossed the English Channel by ferry to Calais – on the French side of the Channel the corresponding train between Calais and Paris was called 'Flèche d'Or'. By 1948 the train on the English side was being hauled by Oliver Bulleid's new air-smoothed 'Merchant Navy' and light Pacific locomotives based at Stewarts Lane shed. In 1951 the service was augmented by the introduction of new Pullman cars and was also temporarily renamed the 'Festival of Britain Golden Arrow'. Locomotives hauling the train were grandly adorned with a long golden arrow on each side and on the smokebox door. The Union Jack and French Tricolour fluttered from the buffer beam. Two of the first batch of brand new BR Standard 'Britannia' Class 7 locos, No 70004 *William Shakespeare* and No. 70014 *Iron Duke*, were specifically allocated to Stewarts Lane in 1951 to haul the upgraded 'Golden Arrow', a job they continued to do until they were transferred to Longsight, Manchester, in 1958.

During the 1950s the popularity and speed of air travel between London and Paris soon spelt the end for this luxury train which was now made up of 1st Class Pullman cars and standard 2nd Class stock. Electric haulage by BR-built (Class 71) Bo-Bo locos (E5000–E5023) was introduced in June 1961 and continued until September 1972 when this famous train ceased to run.

BOTTOM LEFT: *'West Country' Class 4-6-2 No 34039* Boscastle *arrives at Dover Marine with the 'Golden Arrow' Pullman train from Victoria, 2 October 1948. Built at Brighton in 1946, this loco has since been preserved.*

BELOW: *1950s' BR poster promoting the 'Golden Arrow' Pullman service to Paris.*

All dressed up and ready to go – BR Standard Class 7 4-6-2 No 70004 William Shakespeare is seen here at Stewarts Lane engine shed in the mid-1950s prior to hauling the 'Golden Arrow' to Dover.

Kentish Belle/Thanet Belle

Victoria to Ramsgate/Canterbury

The South Eastern & Chatham Railway introduced this service in 1921 and it was continued by the Southern Railway (see page 123) until the outbreak of the Second World War. The all-Pullman 'Thanet Belle' was then reintroduced by the Southern Region of British Railways for the summer seasons of 1948–50. The train ran non-stop from London Victoria to Whitstable and then called at Margate before terminating at Ramsgate Harbour. Festival of Britain year (1951) saw the train renamed as the 'Kentish Belle' with through coaches to and from Canterbury East being detached or attached at Faversham during the week – at weekends this portion was not included and the Faversham stop omitted. The Canterbury portion was not successful and had been dropped altogether by 1953 when two return services were provided on Saturdays and Sundays. A selection of motive power was used for this train, ranging from Bulleid's Light Pacifics to 'N15' ('King Arthur') Class 4-6-0s and 'V' ('Schools') Class 4-4-0s. The train was withdrawn at the end of the 1958 summer season to be replaced by characterless electric multiple units when Phase 1 of the Kent Coast electrification scheme was completed in June 1959.

Unrebuilt 'Battle of Britain' Class 4-6-2 No 34077 603 Squadron heads the all-Pullman 'Kentish Belle' out of Broadstairs, c.1955.

The Man of Kent

Charing Cross to Ramsgate

Introduced in 1953, 'The Man of Kent' was the only named train to operate out of Charing Cross during the British Railways' era. It was named after the Association of Men of Kent and Kentish Men, which was founded by 10 benevolent Kentish businessmen in 1897. Normally hauled by 'Schools' Class 4-4-0s or Bulleid Light Pacifics, the down train left Charing Cross at 4.15 p.m., briefly calling at Waterloo East, and arrived at Folkestone at 5.35 p.m. before ending its journey, via Dover and Deal, at Ramsgate. Starting its journey at Sandwich at 10.14 a.m., the up working left Folkestone at 11.10 a.m. and with a brief stop at Waterloo East arrived at Charing Cross at 12.30 p.m. The Kent Coast electrification soon put paid to this train which was withdrawn in 1961.

BELOW: *Unrebuilt 'Battle of Britain' Class 4-6-2 No 34084 253 Squadron speeds through Chelsfield with 'The Man of Kent' on 5 September 1957.*

Night Ferry

Victoria to Paris Gare du Nord/Brussels-Zuid

This sleeping car service between London and Paris/ Brussels began in 1936. The 'Night Ferry was reinstated by the Southern Railway in 1947 and continued by the newly-formed Southern Region of British Railways from 1948. After the war the long and heavy train was hauled by Bulleid's new 'Merchant Navy' Pacifics but even these needed a pilot in the form of an 'L1' 4-4-0 on occasions until electrification of the London to Dover route in June 1959. From then until 1976 the train was in the capable hands of Class 71 Bo-Bo electric locomotives and with their demise Class 73 electro-diesels took over.

In the 1960s departure from Victoria was at 10.00 p.m. and at Dover the blue-liveried Wagon-Lits sleeping cars and a couple of French luggage vans were shunted carefully on to a train ferry before the Channel crossing to Dunkerque. Arrival in Paris Gare du Nord was at 8.40 a.m. In the opposite direction the train left Gare du Nord at 10 p.m. and arrived, having attached British restaurant cars and coaches at Dover in the early morning, at Victoria at 9.10 a.m. Both trains also included through coaches either to or from Brussels. In a losing battle with airline travel the train ran in its latter years in a much-reduced form until its withdrawal on 1 November 1980.

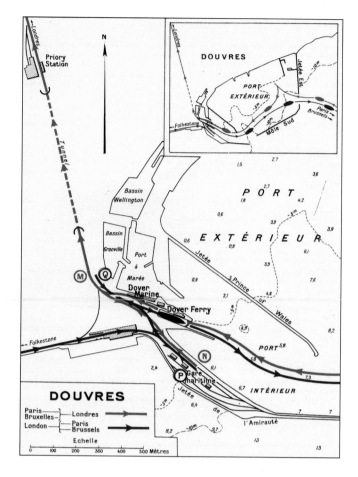

ABOVE: *Map in French showing the two routes used by the 'Night Ferry' at Dover Marine. Issued by the International Sleeping Car Company on 1 January 1958.*

RIGHT: *1950s' poster produced by BR in Flemish for Belgian customers to promote the Brussels to London portion of the 'Night Ferry'.*

BELOW: *The long and heavy 'Night Ferry' train required the double-heading of locomotives. It is seen here approaching London near Crystal Palace in the mid-1950s behind 'L1' Class 4-4-0 No 31788 and an unidentified Bulleid Light Pacific.*

Ocean Liner Expresses
Waterloo to Southampton Docks

Boat trains between London Waterloo and Southampton Docks were run for many years by the London & South Western Railway (see page 39) and the Southern Railway (see page 122). They were discontinued on the outbreak of war in 1939 but reintroduced in 1946 and continued to be operated by the Southern Region of British Railways from 1948. At Southampton Docks the trains connected with ocean liners from around the world. Collectively known as 'Ocean Liner Expresses'. Many of them ran under different names depending on the shipping line that was being met at Southampton.

In 1952 some of these trains were given names with headboards carried on the front of the locomotive. The all-Pullman 'The Cunarder', for instance, was introduced on 2 July of that year to connect with the New York service of *RMS Queen Mary* and *RMS Queen Elizabeth* – the first of these trains was appropriately hauled by 'Merchant Navy' Class Pacific No 35004 *Cunard White Star*. In the earlier years of British Railways the 'Ocean Liner Expresses' were usually hauled by 'N15' Class ('King Arthur') Class or 'LN' Class ('Lord Nelsons') 4-6-0s but their withdrawal between 1953 and 1962 saw the increasing use of Bulleid's 'Merchant Navy' Class locomotives, named after merchant shipping lines, until the end of steam in 1967. From then the trains were hauled by Birmingham Railway Carriage & Wagon Company Class 33s but by the 1970s most of this sea-going traffic had been lost to air travel and the rail terminals at Southampton Docks were closed and later demolished.

From 1952 the following named trains ran when required between Waterloo and Southampton Docks:

- 'The Cunarder' connected with *RMS Queen Mary* and *RMS Queen Elizabeth* for the Atlantic crossing to and from New York. This boat train consisted of both Pullman cars and 1st Class coaches.
- 'The Statesman', also conveying some Pullman cars, connected with the *SS United States* for the New York service.
- The 'Union-Castle Express' connected with Union-Castle Line sailings to and from South Africa.
- 'The Holland-American' connected with Holland-America Line sailings to and from New York.

- 'The South American' connected with Royal Mail line sailings to and from South America.
- 'The Greek Line' for Greek Line sailings to and from New York.
- 'The Sitmar Line' for Sitmar Line sailings to and from Australia.
- 'The Oriana' and 'The Canberra' for P&O sailings to and from Australia.

LEFT: *Welcome to the UK – the stylish 1950s' menu headers and wine list used in the restaurant cars of the various 'Ocean Liner Expresses'.*

RIGHT: *'Battle of Britain' Class 4-6-2 No 34081 92 Squadron gets away from Southampton Ocean Terminal with an 'Ocean Liner Express' bound for Waterloo, 1959.*

BELOW: *Dwarfed by the recently arrived RMS Queen Mary, rebuilt 'Battle of Britain' Class 4-6-2 No 34090 Sir Eustace Missenden, Southern Railway leaves Southampton Ocean Terminal with the up 'The Cunarder' in 1967, just before the end of steam haulage on the Southern Region.*

Royal Wessex

Waterloo to Bournemouth Central, Bournemouth West, Swanage and Weymouth

Yet another train that received its new name during the Festival of Britain year of 1951, 'The Royal Wessex' was the successor to the Southern Railway's pre-war 'Bournemouth Limited' express (see page 114) which had been withdrawn on the outbreak of the Second World War. The new train was hauled by one of Oliver Bulleid's new air-smoothed Pacifics and with a heavy load of up to 13 coaches (including portions to and from Swanage and Weymouth) travelled up to London in the morning and returned to Dorset in the afternoon. Such was the demand in the summer months that the Swanage portion was replaced by a separate through train between the resort and Waterloo, taking the Bournemouth-avoiding line via Wimborne. By the summer Saturdays of 1963 the main up train left Weymouth at 7.37 a.m. and after attaching coaches from Bournemouth West at Central station arrived at Waterloo at 10.51 a.m. The down train left Waterloo at 4.35 p.m. and arrived at Weymouth at 7.59 p.m. The 'Royal Wessex' was withdrawn following completion of the electrification of the Waterloo to Bournemouth route in July 1967.

BELOW: *The down 'The Royal Wessex' has just passed Eastleigh station behind 'Merchant Navy' Class 4-6-2 No 35008 Orient Line on 4 August 1962.*

Western Region

The Western Region (WR) of British Railways (BR) took over all of the former GWR (see page 64) network on 1 January 1948. The new region continued to operate express trains between Paddington, Bristol, South West England, South and West Wales and Birmingham and the West Midlands. More than any region of BR the WR retained much of its autonomy, acting as if Nationalization hadn't happened – between 1956 and 1962 it even painted its express passenger coaches in the traditional brown and cream of the GWR.

At Swindon Works the WR continued to build the highly successful 'Castle' Class 4-6-0s until August 1950 as well as more of the versatile 'Modified Hall' Class 4-6-0s

until November 1950. The region did have a short love affair with Crewe-built BR Standard Class 7 'Britannias' when 12 members of this class were allocated to Cardiff Canton shed in the late 1950s – they were regular performers on the 'Capitals United' and 'The Red Dragon' expresses for several years until being relocated to the London Midland Region.

Construction of steam locomotives at Swindon ceased in March 1960 with the completion of the last of 53 '9F'

BELOW: *Terence Cuneo's famous painting of a 'Castle' Class 4-6-0 crossing the Royal Albert Bridge was used for a poster to promote the centenary of Brunel's engineering masterpiece.*

1859 *Centenary* 1959
ROYAL ALBERT BRIDGE, SALTASH
WESTERN REGION DESIGNED AND BUILT BY ISAMBARD KINGDOM BRUNEL WESTERN REGION

Class 2-10-0s, No 92220 Evening Star – the last steam locomotive to be built by BR. At the end of 1965 the region became the first in Britain to eliminate steam traction. By the late 1950s the region had also controversially chosen to use diesel-hydraulic locomotives to haul its express passenger trains, instead of the diesel-electric types that were being introduced on all of the other regions. While many examples were bought from the North British Locomotive Works and Beyer Peacock, Swindon Works went on to build 38 'Warship' Class until October 1961 and 30 'Western' Class diesel-hydraulics until April 1964. The WR's experiment with diesel-hydraulics was somewhat of a failure and all had been withdrawn by 1979, replaced by more reliable diesel-electric types such as the Brush Type 4. The high-point of passenger travel on the WR was the introduction of InterCity 125 high-speed trains on their routes between London, South West England and South Wales in 1976 – journey times were slashed and such is their success that many are still in operation over 40 years later.

The WR operated sleeper trains between Paddington and Plymouth, Penzance, Carmarthen and Birkenhead and between Plymouth and Manchester. The region only operated one boat train service, between Paddington and Weymouth (for the Channel Islands), but this was withdrawn in 1960.

Boundary changes in 1958 saw the transfer of the former Somerset & Dorset Joint Railway (S&DJR) route between Bath and Templecombe from Southern Region to Western Region management – Swindon soon put an end to this much-loved railway which closed on 7 March 1966. Apart from the S&DJR route, steam traction ended on the WR on 31 December 1965, becoming the first region of BR to do so. A 1963 boundary change saw the same happen to former Southern Region routes west of Salisbury when Western Region management got their own back on this late 19th century back door incursion into the West Country – downgrading to a secondary route status and wholesale closures soon followed. In fact the Western Region had lost well over 700 route miles of railway by 1965, most of them victims of Dr Beeching's 'axe'. Also in 1963 the region lost its routes west of Birmingham (to Shrewsbury and West Wales) when they were transferred to the London Midland Region. The remaining Paddington to Birmingham mainline was then reduced to a secondary status in 1966 once the West Coast Main Line had been electrified between Euston and Birmingham. The Western Region ceased to exist as an operating unit of BR after 6 April 1992. Privatization of the railways was soon to follow.

On a trainspotting trip to London on 14 April 1962 I recorded the following named express trains and their locomotives at Paddington station in the late afternoon: 'Castle' Class 4-6-0 No 5014 *Goodrich Castle* on the 'Capitals United'; 'Warship' Class diesel-hydraulic D809 *Champion* on 'The Bristolian'; 'Warship' Class diesel-hydraulic D830 Majestic on 'The Mayflower'; 'Castle' Class 4-6-0 No 7035 *Ogmore Castle* on the 'Cheltenham Spa Express'; 'King' Class 4-6-0 No 6026 *King John* on the 'Cambrian Coast Express'; Castle' Class 4-6-0 No 7007 *Great Western* on the 'Cathedrals Express'; 'Warship' Class D601 *Ark Royal* on the 'Cornish Riviera Express'; Hymek diesel-hydraulic D7028 on the 'Red Dragon' – I wish I had a time machine to transport me back to those good old days!

One of my many visits to Swindon Works was on 24 November 1963. Despite the fact that steam traction was due to end on the WR in just over two years' time there was, surprisingly, still plenty of steam action to be seen. The bad news first! Locos on the scrap line included my all-time hero, 'Castle' Class 4-6-0 No 5017 *The Gloucestershire Regiment 28th, 61st* (awaiting removal to Cashmore's scrapyard in Newport), 'County' Class 4-6-0s Nos 1006 and 1027 and 'Hall' Class 4-6-0s 4924, 4996 and 5943. 'King' Class 4-6-0s Nos 6010, 6011, 6025 were also awaiting scrapping. In the shed (82C) there were no less than six 'County' Class 4-6-0s with only a few months of life left – Nos 1010, 1012, 1013, 1014, 1024, 1028. Now the good news! In the works being overhauled were five 'Grange' Class 4-6-0s (6813, 6831, 6858, 6861, 6866), two 'Manor' Class 4-6-0s (7808, 7820) and three 'Modified Hall' Class 4-6-0s (6976, 6980, 6998). Nos 4161, 6864, 6947 and 6980 were also seen in gleaming ex-works condition. Another great day at Swindon – nearly 60 years later, gone but definitely not forgotten.

Blue Pullmans

Paddington to Bristol | Paddington to Birmingham Snow Hill and Wolverhampton Low Level
Paddington to Cardiff and Swansea | Paddington to Oxford

Apart from the steam-hauled 'South Wales Pullman' (see pages 264–265) which was introduced in 1955, there were no other Pullman car trains on the Western Region of British Railways until 1960 when new streamlined diesel-electric Pullman trains were introduced between Paddington and Bristol and Paddington, Birmingham Snow Hill and Wolverhampton Low Level.

Back in 1954 the British Transport Commission had become the proud owners of the British Pullman Car Company and a year later the British Railways *Modernisation Programme* was published – one of its main objectives was the replacement of steam by diesel power. A committee was soon set up to look into the introduction of diesel-hauled express passenger trains and in 1957 it was announced that the Metropolitan-Cammell Carriage & Wagon Company of Birmingham would build five high-speed diesel multiple-unit sets to

be introduced in 1958 on the London Midland Region between London St Pancras and Manchester Central and on the Western Region between Paddington and Bristol and Birmingham.

At that time the design of these luxurious trains was fairly ground-breaking – the classic Pullman livery of brown and cream was replaced by blue (known as Nanking blue) and white with a grey roof, the passenger coaches were fitted with double glazing, air conditioning and sumptuous seating and passengers were served at their tables by staff dressed in matching blue uniforms. Sporting the Pullman Car Company's crest on the nose, the two streamlined power cars at each end of the train were each

BELOW: *The down Paddington to Wolverhampton Low Level 'Blue Pullman' speeds through the Oxfordshire countryside near the site of the closed Blackthorn station in August 1965.*

fitted with a 1,000 hp NBL/MAN diesel engine driving electric transmission with a top speed of 90 mph. The two LMR sets were six-car formation (this included the two non-accommodating power cars) providing 132 1st Class seats and the three WR sets were eight-car formation providing 108 1st Class and 120 2nd Class seats.

Following delays caused by extended trials and modifications, the first Blue Pullmans entered revenue-earning service on the LMR between St Pancras and Manchester on 4 July 1960 (see 'Midland Pullman', pages 190–191). Blue Pullman services on the Western Region between Paddington and Bristol and Paddington and Wolverhampton Low Level commenced on 12 September 1960. The Bristol service comprised two return journeys each day between the two cities but it was disappointingly slower than the steam-hauled 'The Bristolian' (see page 239). Sandwiched in between the up and down Wolverhampton service, this 'Blue Pullman' set provided an additional run to and from Birmingham Snow Hill in the middle of the day.

An additional service was introduced between Paddington, Cardiff and Swansea in the summer of 1961 with a record-breaking time for the whole journey. Three years later the South Wales 'Blue Pullman' set started to make an additional run between Paddington and Cardiff in the middle of the day. A steam-hauled (and later diesel-hauled) set of traditional brown and cream Pullman cars was always kept in reserve at Old Oak Common. Following the completion of electrification between Euston and Manchester Piccadilly the two LMR sets were transferred to the Western Region in March 1967, which allowed the introduction of additional services to Bristol, South Wales and a new service to Oxford. At the same time the 'Blue Pullman' service to Birmingham and Wolverhampton was withdrawn. The 'Blue Pullman' services ended in 1973 with the last train, an enthusiasts' special, running on 5 May.

BELOW: *Looking rather scruffy and down-at-heel, a 'Blue Pullman' service leaves Paddington on the last day of scheduled services, 4 May 1973.*

The Bristolian

Paddington to Bristol Temple Meads

Introduced in 1935 (see page 66), 'The Bristolian' was suspended on the outbreak of the Second World War. The non-stop service was reinstated by the Western Region of British Railways in 1954 with an 8.45 a.m. departure from Paddington and a 4.30 p.m. return from Bristol, thus giving businessmen more time for their meetings in Bristol. By now the eight-coach train was normally 'King'-hauled with timings of 105 minutes each way, identical to pre-war days. However, modification of some 'Castle' Class 4-6-0 locomotives at Swindon Works soon brought some electrifying performances.

Built in 1949, 'Castle' Class No. 7018 *Drysllwyn Castle* was the first of its class to be fitted with a double chimney and four-row superheater. Emerging from Swindon Works with its modifications in May 1956, the Bristol Bath Road-allocated loco was soon putting up electrifying 100 mph performances on 'The Bristolian'. Soon other 'Castles' were similarly modified and the train occasionally completed the up journey via Badminton in under 94 minutes at an average speed of 75 mph. The introduction of Swindon-built 'Warship' Class diesels in 1959 soon put an end to this steam spectacular – the last up steam-hauled train being hauled by No 5085 *Evesham Abbey* on 12 June of that year. The 'Warship' and later 'Western' Class diesel hydraulics carried on hauling this train until it lost its name in June 1965.

However, this famous train was not forgotten and in 2010 restored ex-GWR 'Castle' Class 4-6-0 No 5043 *Earl of Mount Edgcumbe* hauled a commemorative 'The Bristolian' to mark the 175th Anniversary of the GWR. Its return journey from Bristol to Paddington was completed in just under 1 hr 50 min, only 5 minutes slower than the 1950s' schedule, arriving at its destination 45 minutes early – an amazing feat for a 74-year-old steam locomotive which had spent the last 10 years of its previous life rusting away at Woodhams Brothers scrapyard in Barry.

BELOW: *'King' Class 4-6-0 No 6028* King George VI *speeds through Twyford with 'The Bristolian' on 27 May 1959. 'Warship' Class diesel-hydraulics took over haulage of this train two weeks later.*

Cambrian Coast Express

Paddington to Aberystwyth and Pwllheli

Operated by the Great Western Railway from 1927 onwards, the 'Cambrian Coast Express' ('CCE') was withdrawn during the Second World War (see page 66). It was reinstated initially as a Saturdays-only service in 1951. Hauled from Paddington by a 'King' or 'Castle' class locomotive, the train took 2 hours to reach Birmingham before continuing on to Shrewsbury station where the locomotive came off, replaced by a 'Manor' Class 4-6-0 when it reversed direction to West Wales. In 1954 the 'CCE' became a full weekday restaurant car service (Monday–Saturday) with the Aberystwyth and Pwllheli portions splitting or joining at Dovey Junction. By 1958 the train was leaving Paddington at 10.10 a.m. and arriving at Aberystwyth at 4.05 p.m. and at Pwllheli at 6.10 p.m. – some journey for the steam enthusiast!

Diesel traction in the shape of Brush Type 4s took over the Paddington to Shrewsbury leg in 1963 although 'Manor' Class locos continued to haul the train over the steeply graded Cambrian Line until 1965 when BR Standard Class 4 4-6-0s took over. The last steam-hauled 'CCE' over this section ran on 11 February 1967 and the train was withdrawn less than a month later.

I was trainspotting at Shrewsbury station on 18 April 1964 and recorded the down 'Cambrian Coast Express' which arrived from Paddington behind Brush Type 4 diesel D1683. This loco came off the train and was replaced by immaculately clean ex-GWR 'Manor' Class 4-6-0 No 7803 Barcote Manor which set off on time for the journey to Aberystwyth. Built at Swindon in 1938, this fine locomotive was withdrawn exactly a year later and scrapped at Bird's in Bridgend.

RIGHT: 'Manor' Class 4-6-0 No 7803 Barcote Manor *being prepared at Aberystwyth depot before hauling the up 'Cambrian Coast Express' to Shrewsbury on 18 February 1961.*

BELOW: 'King' Class 4-6-0 No 6027 King Richard I *is seen here passing High Wycombe at speed with the up 'Cambrian Coast Express' on 8 April 1961.*

Capitals United Express

Paddington to Cardiff

The 'Capitals United Express' was inaugurated early in 1956, just six weeks after Cardiff had officially become the capital of Wales. It provided a non-stop restaurant car service to London for Welsh businessmen, departing from Cardiff at 8 a.m., and arriving at Paddington at 10.50 a.m. The return service left Paddington at 3.55 p.m. and arrived back in Cardiff at 6.53 p.m. (winter 1958/59 timetable). It also conveyed through coaches to and from Swansea, Carmarthen and Fishguard Harbour. Engines were changed at Cardiff with a Cardiff Canton 'Britannia' 4-6-2, 'King' or 'Castle' 4-6-0 normally in charge for the non-stop run to and from Paddington. Steam haulage was replaced by diesel-hydraulics in the early 1960s and the train lost its name in the summer of 1965.

RIGHT: *A gleaming 'Castle' Class 4-6-0 receives the headboard of the newly-introduced 'Capitals United Express' at Cardiff Canton depot in 1956.*

BELOW: *Cardiff Canton shed's BR Standard Class 7 'Britannia' No 70029 Shooting Star enters Sonning Cutting at speed with the up 'Capitals United' express in the late 1950s.*

Cathedrals Express

Paddington to Oxford, Worcester/Kidderminster and Hereford

ntroduced by the Western Region of British Railways in 1957, the 'Cathedrals Express' carried an attractive locomotive headboard featuring a bishop's mitre atop of the train name which was picked out in white on a blue background in what can only be described as an 'Olde English' typeface. Running between Paddington and Hereford this restaurant car express left Hereford at 7.45 a.m. and arrived at Paddington at 11.30 a.m., returning at 4.45 p.m. and reaching Hereford at 8.30 p.m. (winter 1958/59 schedule). Despite a fast non-stop run between London and Oxford the train also stopped at Moreton-in-Marsh and Evesham – at Worcester Shrub Hill the

Kidderminster coaches were attached or detached before the train effectively became a stopping service to and from Hereford. The 'Cathedrals Express' became the last steam-hauled named train to operate out of Paddington with Worcester shed's usually immaculate 'Castle' Class locomotives being replaced by Brush Type 4 diesels in 1965 when the train's name was dropped.

BELOW: *Lit by the low winter sun, 'Castle' Class 4-6-0 No 5037* Monmouth Castle *speeds through Twyford with the 'Cathedrals Express' on 27 January 1959.*

Channel Islands Boat Train

Paddington to Weymouth Quay

Connecting with railway-owned ferries to and from the Channel Islands at Weymouth Quay, the Western Region's 'Channel Islands Boat Train' (also called the 'Channel Islands Boat Express') to and from Paddington was reintroduced in 1946 (see page 66) and continued to be operated by the Western Region of British Railways from 1948.

During the early BR era the down Western Region restaurant car service left Paddington at 8.20 a.m. (weekdays, winter 1958/59 timetable) and called at Reading, Trowbridge, Westbury and Yeovil Pen Mill before arriving at Weymouth Quay at 12.17 p.m. – the last mile of this journey was through the streets of Weymouth along the Harbour Tramway with the train being preceded by a railwayman with a red flag – cars parked in the way of the train were bounced away from the tracks. Trains along this section of the street tramway were hauled between Weymouth Town station and Weymouth Quay by

ex-GWR 1366 Class 0-6-0PTs. The up train normally left Weymouth Quay at 3.40 p.m. with stops at Yeovil Pen Mill and Frome before arriving back at Paddington at 6.46 p.m.

The Western Region's 'Channel Islands Boat Train' was discontinued in 1960. The service was then concentrated on the Southern Region's Waterloo to Weymouth Quay route (see page 223), steam-hauled until July 1967 before continuing to operate diesel-hauled in some form or other until September 1987. An enthusiasts' special was the last train to use the Weymouth street tramway in 1999 but since then, with the rails still embedded in Weymouth's streets, it has amazingly survived, although its future is now in some doubt.

BELOW: *Ex-GWR Glass '1366' 0-6-0PT No 1368 gingerly heads along the street tramway section at Weymouth with a Western Region 'Channel Islands Boat Train' on 4 July 1959.*

A sight regularly seen by the author: 1950 Swindon-built 'Castle' Class 4-6-0 No 7035 Ogmore Castle at its home shed of Gloucester Horton Road after arrival from Paddington with the 'Cheltenham Spa Express' in August 1960.

Cheltenham Spa Express

Paddington to Gloucester and Cheltenham Spa

The 'Cheltenham Spa Express' was introduced in 1923 and during the pre-war years received the nickname of the 'Cheltenham Flyer' (see pages 67–68), becoming for a short time in the 1930s the fastest train in the world. This high-speed service was brought to an end on the outbreak of war in 1939 never to return. However, the 'Cheltenham Spa Express' was revived in 1956 when the Western Region of British Railways gave the name to the 8 a.m. departure from Cheltenham St James' and the 4.55 p.m. return service from Paddington. Unusually the eight-coach restaurant car train was hauled between Cheltenham St James' and Gloucester Central by a tank engine – these were normally '5101' Class 2-6-2Ts but on occasions even '9400' Class 0-6-0PTs could be seen manfully struggling with the load. The up train reversed direction at Gloucester Central with a Horton Road (85B) 'Castle' in charge for the 8.19 a.m. departure to Paddington. Locos such as No. 5017 *The Gloucestershire Regiment 28th, 61st*, No 5042 *Winchester Castle* and No 5071 *Spitfire* were regular performers – the immaculately groomed 'Castle'

and the eight brown and cream coaches made a stirring sight for the author on his way to school each morning. The up train arrived at Paddington at 10.35 a.m. while the down train departed at 4.55 p.m. and arrived back at Cheltenham St James' at 7.35 p.m. On both up and down trains a Swindon stop was avoided with the train running non-stop between Kemble and Paddington.

By 1964 'Western' Class diesel-hydraulics were in charge, the loco headboard had disappeared and the reversal at Gloucester Central became a thing of the past when a new connection was laid in at Standish Junction. This allowed trains to run via the ex-Midland Railway station of Gloucester Eastgate and to continue to Cheltenham Spa Lansdown without reversing direction. The name was dropped in 1973 and Gloucester Eastgate was closed on 1 December 1975.

BELOW: *One of Gloucester Horton Road shed's well groomed 'Castle' Class 4-6-0s is seen at speed near Reading while hauling the up 'Cheltenham Spa Express' in the late 1950s.*

Cornish Riviera Express

Paddington to Penzance

Originally introduced by the Great Western Railway in 1904, the 'Cornish Riviera Limited' (see pages 28 and 69–70) continued to be operated by the Western Region of the new British Railways from 1948. This premier train between Paddington and Penzance was soon renamed the 'Cornish Riviera Express'. By the late 1950s the pre-war schedules were being achieved once more, although the slip coaches were a thing of the past, with the weekday (Monday–Saturday) down train departing from Paddington at 10.30 a.m. followed by a non-stop run to Plymouth behind a 'King' Class 4-6-0 – an unscheduled stop was made at Newton Abbot to attach a pilot engine to assist the train over the fearsome South Devon gradients. The train arrived at Plymouth at 2.30 p.m. where the 'King' was replaced by a 'Castle' Class 4-6-0 for the remainder of the journey to Penzance, stopping at Par, Truro, Gwinear Road and St Erth en route. Arrival at Penzance was at 4.55 p.m. The up train left Penzance at 10 a.m. and with the same stops arrived at Paddington at 4.40 p.m. On Sundays the train made more stops and was consequently much slower.

Steam haulage was ousted in the late 1950s with the introduction of 'Warship' Class diesel-hydraulics followed in the 1960s by the more powerful 'Western' Class locos. By the end of the decade the journey time to Penzance had come down to 5 hrs 35 min and more was in the pipeline – following haulage for some years by Class 47 and Class 50 diesel-electrics the 'Cornish Riviera' (as it was then known) became an HST 125 working in 1979, when locomotive haulage ended, and by 1983 Plymouth was being reached in 3 hrs 13 min and Penzance in 4 hrs 55 min. The train still runs but somehow the glamour of the past has completely disappeared.

BELOW: *Map showing the routes taken by the 'Cornish Riviera Express': 1904-1906 via Bristol; 1906 onwards via Westbury.*

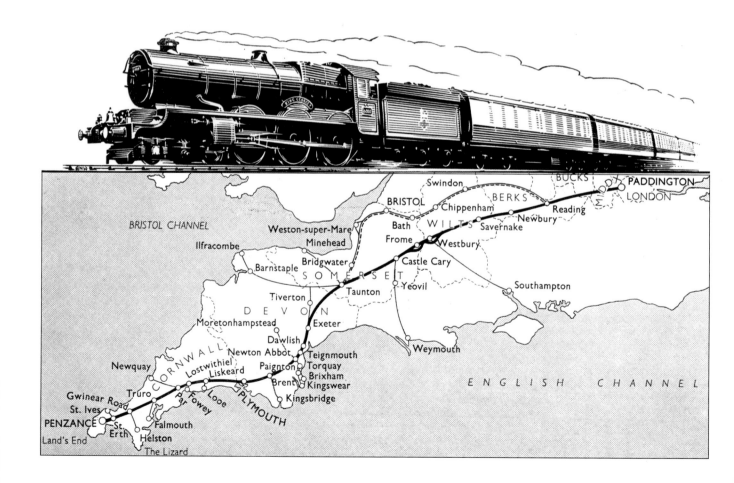

ABOVE: 'King' Class 4-6-0 No 6008 King James II *heads the 'Cornish Riviera Express' through Twyford on 3 May 1958.*

RIGHT: *With stylish artwork by 'Michie', this 'Cornish Riviera Express' restaurant car tariff dates from July 1958.*

BELOW : *The diesel invasion starts – built by the North British Locomotive Company of Glasgow, new 'Warship' Class A1A-A1A diesel-hydraulic D600 Active hauls the up 'Cornish Riviera Express' over the Royal Albert Bridge at Plymouth, 1958.*

The Cornishman

Wolverhampton Low Level to Penzance

The first 'The Cornishman' was the unofficial name given to the premier train operating from Paddington to Penzance via Bristol during the broad-gauge era (see page 28). Running non-stop between London and Exeter via the Bristol avoiding line it was at that time the longest such service in the world. By 1892 Brunel's broad-gauge had been replaced by standard-gauge and the train was discontinued in 1904 on the inauguration of the 'Cornish Riviera Limited' (see page 28).

Forty-eight years later, in 1952, the Western Region of British Railways revived the name which was given to a daily restaurant car service running between Wolverhampton Low Level and Penzance. An express it definitely was not as its route took it via Birmingham Snow Hill, Stratford-upon-Avon, Cheltenham Malvern

Road and Gloucester Eastgate before heading along the ex-Midland Railway route to Yate and then via Filton to Bristol Temple Meads where the Wolverhampton Stafford Road 'Castle' was taken off in favour of a Bristol Bath Road locomotive for the run down to Plymouth. Here the engine was changed once again for the run down to Penzance with a 'County', 'Hall' or 'Grange' normally in charge. Journey time for the down train was a leisurely 9 hrs 10 min (winter 1958/59) and for the up train 5 minutes longer. During the winter months the train also conveyed through carriages for Torquay and Kingswear which were attached or detached at Exeter. In the summer the Kingswear portion ran as a separate train.

The last steam-hauled 'The Cornishman' ran along its original route on 7 September 1962 with the final

northbound service being hauled between Bristol and Wolverhampton by 'Castle' Class 4-6-0 No 7001 *Sir James Milne*. Type 4 'Peak' diesels without headboards were then introduced with the train now originating or ending its journey at Sheffield Midland and running via the ex-Midland Railway line through Birmingham New Street to Bristol. In 1965 Bradford became the northern terminus until the train finally lost its name in 1975.

The route of 'The Cornishman' until September 1962, the former GWR mainline between Stratford-upon-Avon and Cheltenham, was closed in 1976 although the section from Broadway to Cheltenham Racecourse has since been reopened by the Gloucestershire-Warwickshire Railway.

LEFT: *The southbound 'The Cornishman' is seen here near Hatton South Junction in Warwickshire behind Wolverhampton Stafford Road's 'Castle' Class 4-6-0 No 7026* Tenby Castle, *c.1959.*

RIGHT: *Featuring artwork by 'Hundleby', this tariff graced the tables in the restaurant car of 'The Cornishman' in the late 1950s.*

BELOW: *An unidentified double-chimney 'Castle' Class 4-6-0 heads into Cornwall with 'The Cornishman' after crossing the Royal Albert Bridge at Saltash, 16 August 1959.*

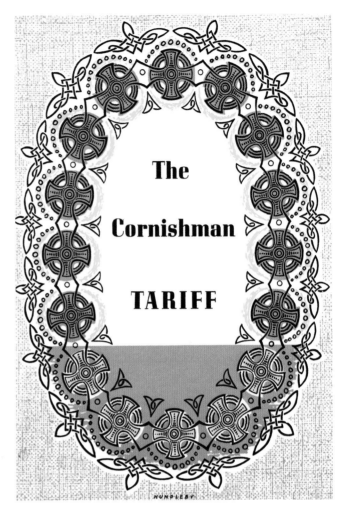

Golden Hind

Paddington to Plymouth

This much-needed early morning express taking businessmen from Plymouth up to London with a late afternoon return from Paddington was introduced on 15 June 1964. Hauled by new 'Western' Class diesel hydraulics the lightweight restaurant car train of seven coaches (later increased to eight) set the fastest ever scheduled time between Plymouth and London of 3 hrs 50 min – the return service was 5 minutes longer. With intermediate stops at Newton Abbot, Exeter and Taunton the last leg of the up journey took only 2 hrs 7 min. New Mk2 coaches introduced in 1970 accompanied an even faster schedule and in 1972 the service was extended to Penzance. Unusually for a named train the last coach had a nameboard attached to its rear end. The train was later hauled by Class 50 and Class 47 diesel locomotives but this all ended when HST 125s took over the train in 1979.

RIGHT: *The restaurant car menu issued for the inaugural run of the 'Golden Hind' on 15 June 1964.*

BELOW: *'Western' (Class 52) diesel-hydraulic D1020* Western Hero *waits for the signal to proceed after calling at Newton Abbot station while hauling the up 'Golden Hind' on 27 March 1966.*

GOLDEN HIND

MENU

INAUGURAL RUN 15 JUNE 1964

The Inter-City

Paddington to Birmingham Snow Hill and Wolverhampton Low Level

Introduced by the Western Region of British Railways in 1950, 'The Inter-City' restaurant car express between Paddington, Birmingham Snow Hill and Wolverhampton Low Level provided a fast service for businessmen visiting the West Midlands. Until the introduction of diesels in the early 1960s, the train was hauled by a 'Castle' or 'King' Class 4-6-0 and, in 1954, the schedule was speeded up so that Snow Hill was reached exactly 2 hours after leaving Paddington. In 1958 the down train left Paddington at 9 a.m. and, after calling at High Wycombe, reached Birmingham Snow Hill at 11 a.m. – Wolverhampton Low Level was reached a leisurely 25 minutes later. The up train took an extra 10 minutes, calling at Leamington Spa and High Wycombe before reaching Paddington at 7.10 p.m. New 'Western' Class diesel hydraulics started to take over haulage of the train in 1962 and a year later the route became the primary mover for traffic between London and the West Midlands when electrification work started on the LMR line out of Euston. The 'Inter-City' lost its name three years later and in 1967 the Paddington to Birmingham Snow Hill route lost its importance on the completion of electrification between Euston and Birmingham New Street.

Losing its definite article, 'Inter-City' was then used very successfully by British Railways as a brand name and was even licensed for use by the German and Irish state railways.

BOTTOM RIGHT: *A 1950s BR leaflet giving details of the route of 'The Inter-City' express.*

BELOW: *A 'King' Class 4-6-0 at the head of 'The Inter-City' is seen here at speed near Gerrards Cross, Buckinghamshire, 1951.*

The Mayflower

Paddington to Kingswear/Plymouth

'The Mayflower' was named after the ship that carried the Pilgrim Fathers from Plymouth to New England in 1620. Introduced by the Western Region in the summer of 1955, it left Plymouth at 8.30 a.m. and after stops at Newton Abbot (to attach through coaches from Kingswear), Exeter, Taunton, Westbury and Reading arrived at Paddington at 1.25 p.m. In steam days the restaurant car train was normally worked by a 'King' Class 4-6-0 with the down service leaving Paddington at 5.30 p.m. and, after calling at Taunton and Exeter (to detach the Kingswear coaches), arrived back at Plymouth at 10 p.m. By 1960 steam had given way to diesel haulage with 'Warship' and later 'Western' Class diesel-hydraulics taking over until 1965 when the train lost its name.

FAR RIGHT: *'King' Class 4-6-0 No 6016* King Edward V *at speed in Sonning Cutting with 'The Mayflower', late 1950s.*

RIGHT: *Designed by Eric Fraser, this restaurant car tariff from 'The Mayflower', c.1958, features the ship of the same name that carried the Pilgrim Fathers to New England in 1620.*

BELOW : *'Warship' diesel-hydraulic D839* Relentless *roars along the seafront at Dawlish with the up 'The Mayflower' in 1961.*

The Merchant Venturer

Paddington to Bristol and Weston-super-Mare

Receiving its name in 1950, 'The Merchant Venturer' provided a restaurant car service between Paddington, Bath, Bristol and Weston-super-Mare – it was named after a charitable organization of Bristol merchants that was founded in the 13th century. Strangely the down service was much faster than the up service with fewer stops and left Paddington at 11.15 a.m. (winter 1958/59 timetable), stopping only at Bath before arriving at Bristol Temple Meads at 1.22 p.m. Here engines were changed – in steam days normally a 'King' or 'Castle' Class 4-6-0 as far as Bristol with a 'Hall' 4-6-0 for the remainder of the journey – before the train ran non-stop to Weston-super-Mare arriving at 1.56 p.m. (2.04 p.m. on Saturdays). The up train was much slower with stops at Yatton, Nailsea & Blackwell, Bristol (engine change), Bath, Chippenham, Swindon and Reading with the entire journey taking a leisurely 3½ hours. It is recorded that the experimental gas turbine locomotive, No 18100, hauled 'The Merchant Venturer' in 1952 and ex-LMS 'Coronation' Class 4-6-2 No 46237 *City of Bristol* made a guest appearance at the head of the train during locomotive trials in May 1955. Diesel-hydraulic 'Warships' and 'Westerns' replaced steam in the early 1960s and the train lost its name in 1965.

RIGHT: *The attractive restaurant car tariff from 'The Merchant Venturer', c.1955.*

BELOW: *Old Oak Common's 'Castle' Class 4-6-0 No 5044* Earl of Dunraven *has just taken over the 'The Merchant Venturer' from a 'Hall' Class 4-6-0 at Bristol Temple Meads for the rest of the journey to Paddington, late 1950s.*

The Merchant Venturer

TARIFF

Pembroke Coast Express

Paddington to Pembroke Dock

Introduced by the Western Region in 1953 this train was a new restaurant car express linking London with South Wales and the seaside resorts of Pembrokeshire. Normally hauled for the first leg of its journey between Paddington by a 'Castle' Class locomotive, the down train left Paddington at 10.55 a.m. and ran the 133 miles to Newport non-stop in a blistering 131 minutes – the first ever mile-a-minute run on this route. Thereafter the train called at Cardiff, Swansea (where there was an engine change), Llanelly and Carmarthen arriving here at 3.40 p.m. Here there was another engine change and the train reversed direction usually behind a 'Manor' Class 4-6-0 for the all stations journey to Pembroke Dock, arriving at 5.26 p.m. (all times courtesy of the Western Region 1958 summer timetable). In the reverse direction Pembroke Dock was left at 1.05 p.m. and with the same stops and engine changes reached Newport at 5.20 p.m. From there to Paddington the train took 145 minutes, arriving in the capital at 7.45 p.m. Steam power was replaced by Hymek diesel-hydraulics in 1962 and the train lost its name in 1963.

RIGHT: *The attractive restaurant car tariff for the 'Pembroke Coast Express', c.1955.*

BELOW: *'Castle' Class 4-6-0 No 5039* Rhuddlan Castle *speeds through Sonning Cutting with the 'Pembroke Coast Express' on 19 April 1958.*

ABOVE: *'Castle' Class 4-6-0 No 5082* Swordfish *waits to depart from Cardiff General with the up 'Pembroke Coast Express', c.1959.*

BELOW: *Goodwick shed's 'Hall' Class 4-6-0 No 4962* Ragley Hall *waits to depart from Carmarthen with the final leg of the journey of the 'Pembroke Coast Express' to Pembroke Dock, 25 May 1963.*

The Red Dragon
Paddington to Carmarthen

Compared to the mile-a-minute down 'Pembroke Coast Express' (see pages 258–259) 'The Red Dragon' took a more leisurely journey between London and South Wales. Introduced in 1950 the restaurant car train was soon in the hands of Cardiff Canton's new BR Standard 'Britannia' Pacifics for the journey between Cardiff and London until these were transferred away to the London Midland Region in 1960. They were replaced by 'Castle' and 'King' Class 4-6-0s until the introduction of Hymek and 'Western' diesel hydraulics in the early 1960s. The summer 1958 timetable shows the up train leaving Carmarthen at 7.30 a.m. and arriving at Paddington at 1 p.m. while the down service, with more stops, left Paddington at 5.55 p.m. and arrived in Carmarthen at 11.48 p.m. – engines were changed at Cardiff while the Carmarthen coaches were attached or detached at Swansea. Strangely only the down train stopped at Swindon and Badminton while the up train ran non-stop from Newport to Paddington. It was a very long day for a Carmarthen-based businessman visiting London for a meeting but very enjoyable all the same during the days of steam haulage. The train lost its name in 1965.

LEFT: *The restaurant car tariff for 'The Red Dragon', c.1955.*

BOTTOM LEFT: *Cardiff Canton shed's BR Standard Class 7 'Britannia' No 70019 Lightning has arrived from South Wales at Paddington Platform 8 with the up 'The Red Dragon' on 10 September 1960.*

BELOW: *Cardiff Canton 'Castle' Class 4-6-0 No 5099 Compton Castle gets ready to depart from Paddington with 'The Red Dragon' express to South Wales, late 1950s.*

The Royal Duchy

Paddington to Kingswear/Penzance

The name 'The Royal Duchy' was given to the 1.30 p.m. Paddington to Penzance restaurant car train by the Western Region in 1955. The headboard carried on the locomotive included the coat of arms of the Duchy of Cornwall, requiring royal consent for its use. The return working left Penzance at 11 a.m. – both up and down trains conveyed through coaches from or to Kingswear (attached or detached at Newton Abbot). Until the advent of diesel-hydraulic 'Warship' diesels in the late 1950s the train was usually hauled between London and Plymouth by a 'Castle' class 4-6-0 – a pilot engine was added for the journey over the South Devon Banks between Newton Abbot and Plymouth. A 'County', 'Hall' or 'Grange' Class 4-6-0 usually hauled the train between Plymouth and Penzance.

An express it definitely was not as the summer 1958 timetable clearly shows: the down train left Paddington at 1.30 p.m. and after making 18 intermediate stops arrived at Penzance at 9.20 p.m. The up service left Penzance at 11 a.m. and after making 19 stops arrived in the capital at 7.15 p.m. Steam haulage was replaced by 'Warship' diesel-hydraulics as early as 1959 and the train lost its name in 1965.

RIGHT: *The stylish restaurant car tariff and afternoon tea menu (dated 8 April 1959) for 'The Royal Duchy'.*

BELOW: *NBL-built A1A-A1A 'Warship' Class D601 Ark Royal about to depart from Paddington on 8 May 1959 with the down 'The Royal Duchy'.*

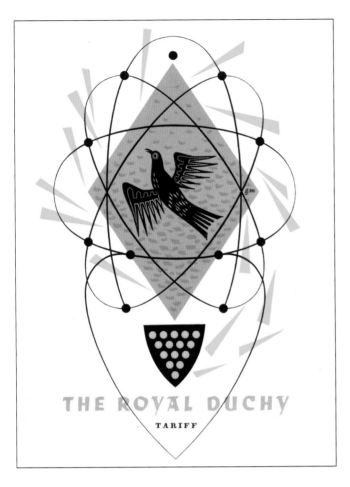

THE ROYAL DUCHY

TARIFF

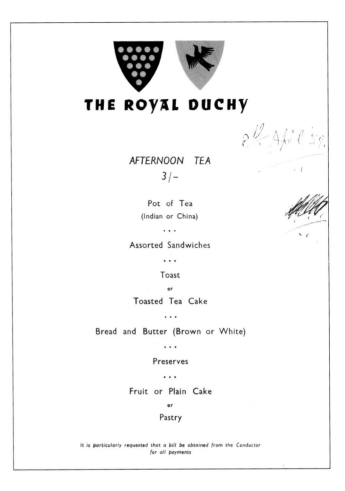

THE ROYAL DUCHY

AFTERNOON TEA
3/–

Pot of Tea
(Indian or China)

• • •

Assorted Sandwiches

• • •

Toast
or
Toasted Tea Cake

• • •

Bread and Butter (Brown or White)

• • •

Preserves

• • •

Fruit or Plain Cake
or
Pastry

It is particularly requested that a bill be obtained from the Conductor
for all payments

'Castle' Class 4-6-0 No 5072 Hurricane calls at Exeter St David's
on 21 May 1957 with the down 'The Royal Duchy'
destined for Penzance. It was a slow journey!

The South Wales Pullman

Paddington to Swansea High Street

Pullman car trains were a very rare sight on the Great Western Railway although one such Pullman train, the 'Torquay Pullman', was operated by the company from 1929–30 (see page 65). Its nationalized successor, the Western Region of British Railways, redressed this balance by introducing 'The South Wales Pullman' in 1955. Catering for business travel, the eight-coach set was hauled by a 'Castle' Class 4-6-0 for the 191-mile journey between Paddington and Swansea. The down train left Paddington at 8.50 a.m. and ran non-stop to Newport followed by stops at Cardiff, Bridgend, Port Talbot and Neath before arriving at Swansea at 1.10 p.m. The up service left Swansea at 4.30 p.m. and with the same stops arrived back in the capital at 8.45 p.m. (summer 1958 timetable). The train was replaced in September 1961 by the new diesel 'Blue Pullman' train (see pages 237–238) but the original set of locomotive-hauled Pullman coaches was kept on standby at Old Oak Common in case of failure of these new trains (and this sometimes happened as the author can testify when train-spotting at Swindon station in the early 1960s!).

RIGHT: *Stylish poster with timetable and fares for the inaugural 'The South Wales Pullman', 13 June 1955. Note the reference to the 'Attractive "Daffodil" Bar'.*

BELOW: *Below: Llanelly shed's 'Castle' Class 4-6-0 No 7009 Athelney Castle is seen here at the head of 'The South Wales Pullman', Platform 5, Swansea High Street station, c.1959.*

The SOUTH WALES PULLMAN

Commencing 13th June 1955, a Pullman Car Train will run between **LONDON** (Paddington) and South Wales; Mondays to Fridays (inclusive) as follows:—

Paddington	dep.	9.55 a.m.	Swansea (High Street) dep.	4.35 p.m.
Newport	arr.	12.21 p.m.	Port Talbot (General) ,,	4.57 p.m.
Cardiff (General)	,,	12.41 p.m.	Cardiff (General) ,,	6. 0 p.m.
Port Talbot (General)	,,	1.35 p.m.	Newport ,,	6.19 p.m.
Swansea (High Street)	,,	2. 0 p.m.	Paddington arr.	8.45 p.m.

PULLMAN SUPPLEMENTARY CHARGES
(for each single journey)
Children under 14 years of age half price

	Newport		Cardiff		Port Talbot		Swansea	
	1st	3rd	1st	3rd	1st	3rd	1st	3rd
Paddington	7/-	4/-	8/-	4/6	10/-	5/-	10/-	5/-
Newport	—	—	1/-	1/-	3/-	1/6	3/-	1/6
Cardiff	1/-	1/-	—	—	2/-	1/-	2/-	1/-
Port Talbot	3/-	1/6	2/-	1/-	—	—	1/-	1/-
Swansea	3/-	1/6	2/-	1/-	1/-	1/-	—	—

All seats are reservable in advance and reservations, which are limited to the total seating capacity, will be made on payment of the supplementary charge. This is additional to the appropriate first and third class fares.

Meals and refreshments are served at every seat

ATTRACTIVE "DAFFODIL" BAR

Folder giving full details obtainable at Stations, Offices and Agencies

WESTERN  REGION

STAFFORD & CO. LTD., NETHERFIELD, NOTTINGHAM.

Torbay Express

Paddington to Kingswear

ntroduced by the Great Western Railway in 1923 (see page 72), the 'Torbay Express' continued to operate through the Second World War. For a short period during the war it was combined with the 'Cornish Riviera Express' (see pages 69–70) and rerouted to run via Bristol but the train proved to be too heavy and the two trains soon resumed their separate existences.

From 1948 the 'Torbay Express' was operated by the newly-formed Western Region of British Railways and, hauled by a 'King' or 'Castle 4-6-0, by 1958 the regular 12 noon departure from Paddington was covering the 173½ miles to Exeter St David's in 172 minutes. After stops at Torquay, Paignton and Churston the train arrived at Kingswear at 4.10 p.m. The last part of the journey, from Goodrington Sands to Kingswear, was made along a steeply-graded 6-mile single-line section of track, the only place in the Western Region where a 'King' or 'Castle' locomotive was regularly performing such duties.

BELOW: *A throng of young trainspotters meet the down 'Torbay Express' at Reading station in September 1962. The locomotive is 'Warship' Class D862* Viking *of Plymouth (Laira) shed.*

The locos were turned for their return journey on a turntable at Kingswear station set alongside the scenic Dart Estuary. From the station passengers were conveyed by ferry across the River Dart to Dartmouth where there was a railway booking office on the quay, but no railway! It had been opened by the Dartmouth & Torbay Railway in 1864 and closed in 1972.

Back in 1958, the up 'Torbay Express' left Kingswear at 11.25 a.m. and with the same stops as the outward journey took 175 minutes from Exeter to Paddington where it arrived at 3.35 p.m. However, by the late 1950s new 'Warship' diesel-hydraulics had begun to replace steam haulage but over the following years extra stops were introduced leading to a longer journey time. The train lost its name in 1968.

BELOW: *'Castle' Class 4-6-0 No 5011* Tintagel Castle *makes a stirring sight at the head of the up 'Torbay Express' soon after leaving Greenway Tunnel on the single-line section from Kingswear to Paignton, c.1957.*

Index

Acknowledgements

t = top; b = bottom; l = left; r = right; m = middle
NRM = National Railway Museum

Photo credits:
Henry Casserley: 84
C. R. L. Coles: 180 bl
Colour-Rail: 104 b; 105; 131 (D. C. Ovenden); 132 (D. Hepburne-Scott);
    134 (M. J. Reade); 135; 143 m (Trevor Owen); 144 b (D. Preston);
    150 (P. Hughes); 152 b (D. C. Ovenden); 156 (M. J. Reade);
    167 bl (D. C. Ovenden); 174 (A. Gray); 176 t; 179 (Trevor Owen);
    181 (M. J. Reade); 185 (M. J. Reade); 186 b (P. Hughes);
    192 (D. C. Ovenden); 195 (B. J. Harding); 197 b; 198 b (A. Drake);
    199 bl (D. L. Dott); 204 (M. J. Reade); 207 (P. Moffat); 208 (Tony Cooke);
    210 (A. E. R. Cope); 211 (M. J. Reade); 212 (A. E. R. Cope); 213 (J. McCann);
    214 (Trevor Owen); 221 br; 222 m (R. Patterson); 229 (D. C. Ovenden);
    232 tr; 232 b (G. Parry Collection); 238; 239 (Trevor Owen); 244 (Trevor Owen);
    245 (Trevor Owen); 249 tl (Trevor Owen); 250 (P. Hughes); 251 (Trevor Owen);
    252 b (John E. Henderson); 254 (M. Chapman); 256; 258 b (Trevor Owen);
    259 b (R. Patterson); 260 b (D. C. Ovenden); 262; 263 (R. Green); 264 (P. Hughes)
Stanley Creer: 202
Gordon Edgar: 161 b; 266
Mike Esau: 227; 261
Mike Esau/John Ashman: 242; 247; 255
Mike Esau/Antony Linaker: 230 b
Mike Esau/Colin Hogg: 203; 220 t
Getty Images: 58 (De Agostini/G. Nimatallah); 74 (Hulton-Deutsch);
    87 (Science & Society Picture Library)
John Gilks: 237
John Goss: 171; 196; 240; 241; 246
G. F. Heiron: 8 b
Julian Holland Collection: back cover; 3; 54; 67 tr; 69 tr; 69 b; 78; 92 ml; 93 tl; 93 tr;
    97 tl; 99 mr; 104 bl; 106 t; 107 t; 107 b; 112 tr; 112 b; 116; 119 ml; 126; 127;
    129 tr; 130 br; 136; 137 bl; 138 tr; 139 bl; 143 b; 151 ml; 152 ml; 153 br; 157 m;
    157 b; 159 t; 161 tr; 163 tr; 165 tl; 165 tr; 167 b; 168 b; 170; 176 b; 177 tr; 180 br;
    181 br; 182; 187 tr; 197 tr; 198 mr; 199 br; 220 b; 222 b; 225 b; 230 tr; 232 tr;
    232 mr; 232 br; 248 b; 249 tr; 251 tr; 252 tr; 253 br; 254 tr; 257; 258 tr; 260 tr;
    263 tl; 263 tr
Alan Jarvis: 259 t
Locomotive & General Railway Photographs: 76
Milepost 92½: 68; 146; 177 b; 228
Gavin Morrison: 6/7; 140 bl; 142; 145; 159 b; 166 b; 175; 178; 184; 200/201; 205;
    223; 234
Science & Society Picture Library: front cover (NRM/Pictorial Collection);
    back cover PLC: Bridlington (NRM); 6 (NRM/Pictorial Collection);
    7 (NRM/Pictorial Collection); 8 (NRM); 9 (NRM); 10 (NRM); 11 (NRM);
    12 (NRM); 13 (NRM); 14 (NRM); 15 (NRM); 16 tr (NRM); 16 b (NRM);
    17 (NRM); 18 (NRM); 19 (NRM); 20 (NRM); 21 (NRM/Pictorial Collection);
    22 (NRM/Pictorial Collection); 23 (NRM); 24 (NRM); 25 (NRM); 26 (NRM);
    28 (NRM/Pictorial Collection); 29 (NRM); 30 (NRM); 31 bl (NRM); 31 br (NRM);
    32 (NRM/Pictorial Collection); 33 (NRM); 35 (NRM/Pictorial Collection);
    36 (NRM); 37 (NRM); 38 (NRM); 39 (NRM); 40 (NRM);
    42 (NRM/Pictorial Collection); 43 bl (NRM); 43 br (NRM/Pictorial Collection);
    44 (NRM); 45 (NRM); 47 (NRM); 48 (NRM); 49 (NRM/Pictorial Collection);
    50 (NRM/Pictorial Collection); 51 (NRM); 52 bl (NRM);
    52 br (NRM/Pictorial Collection); 53 bl (NRM/Pictorial Collection); 53 br (NRM);
    55 (NRM); 57 (NRM); 59 (NRM); 60/61 (NRM); 62 (NRM); 63 (NRM); 64 (NRM);
    65 (NRM); 67 b (NRM); 70 (NRM); 71 tr (NRM/Pictorial Collection); 71 b (NRM);
    72 (NRM); 75 (NRM); 77 (NRM/Pictorial Collection); 79 (NRM); 80 (NRM);
    81 (NRM); 82 (NRM); 83 (NRM); 85 (NRM/Pictorial Collection); 86 (NRM);
    88 (NRM/Pictorial Collection); 89 (MRM); 90 (NRM); 91 (NRM); 92 mr;
    92 b (NRM); 93 b (Daily Herald Archive/National Science & Media Museum);
    94 (NRM); 95 (NRM); 96 (NRM); 97 (NRM); 98 (NRM); 99 (NRM); 100 (NRM);
    101 (NRM/Pictorial Collection); 102 (NRM/Pictorial Collection); 103 (NRM);
    104 t (NRM); 106 b (Daily Herald Archive/National Science & Media Museum;
    108 (NRM); 109 (NRM/Pictorial Collection); 110 t (NRM); 110 b (NRM);
    111 (NRM/Pictorial Collection); 113 tr (NRM/Pictorial Collection); 113 b (NRM);
    114 (NRM); 115 (NRM/Pictorial Collection); 117 (NRM/Pictorial Collection);
    118 (NRM); 119 b (NRM); 120 (NRM); 121 (NRM);
    122 (NRM/Pictorial Collection); 123 (NRM/Pictorial Collection); 125 (NRM);
    130 bl (NRM); 133 bl (NRM); 133 br (NRM); 137 br (NRM); 138 b (NRM);
    139 bl (NRM); 140 br (NRM/Pictorial Collection); 141 (NRM); 144 tr (NRM);
    147 (NRM/Pictorial Collection); 148 (NRM); 149 (NRM); 151 b (NRM);
    153 b (NRM); 154 (NRM); 155 (NRM); 158 (NRM); 160 (NRM); 162/163 (NRM);
    164/165 (NRM); 166 tr (NRM/Pictorial Collection); 169 (NRM);
    172 (NRM/Pictorial Collection); 183 (Museum of Science & Industry);
    186 tr (NRM); 187 b (NRM); 188 (NRM); 189 (NRM);
    190 (NRM/Pictorial Collection); 191 tr (NRM);
    191 b (Museum of Science & Industry); 193 (Museum of Science & Industry);
    194 (NRM); 206 (NRM); 209 (NRM); 215 (NRM/Pictorial Collection); 216 (NRM);
    217 (NRM); 218 (NRM); 219 (NRM/Pictorial Collection);
    221 bl (NRM/Pictorial Collection); 224 (NRM);
    225 tr (British Transport Films/NRM); 226 bl (NRM);
    226 br (NRM/Pictorial Collection); 231 (NRM); 235 (NRM/Pictorial Collection);
    243 (National Science & Media Museum); 249 b (NRM); 253 bl (NRM);
    265 (NRM/Pictorial Collection); 267 (NRM)
The Street Railway Journal: 34

With thanks for research assistance and advice to:
Gordon Edgar

Front cover:
'Royal Scot' Class 4-6-0 No 6110 *Grenadier Guardsman* is seen here at speed while hauling the 'Royal Scot' express in 1937. This image formed part of a poster painted by Bryan de Grineau, famous for his artwork for Hornby and Meccano catalogues of the 1930s.

Back cover:
This early BR luggage label celebrates the centenary of the world's oldest named train, 'The Irish Mail', 1848–1948.